FutureWealth

FutureWealth

INVESTING IN THE SECOND GREAT WAVE OF TECHNOLOGY

Francis McInerney
&
Sean White

TRUMAN TALLEY BOOKS
ST. MARTIN'S PRESS
NEW YORK

Library of Congress Cataloging-in-Publication Data

McInerney, Francis.
    Future Wealth : investing in the second great wave of technology / Francis McInerney and Sean White—1st ed.
        p. cm.
    Includes bibliographical references and index.
    ISBN 0-312-25320-6
    1. Stocks. 2. High-technology industries—Finance. 3. Investment analysis.
I. White, Sean. II. Title.

HG4661 .M379 2000
332.63'22—dc21   99-055954

First Edition: March 2000

10   9   8   7   6   5   4   3   2   1

To the memories of David Ricardo and Marshall McLuhan

Table of Contents

Contents

Contents

ix

Preface

This book is about wealth creation in the twenty-first century.

Our ideas are codified into a number of organizational rules discussed in detail in this book. Collectively they form a general theory of information and the political economy. We wish to do for today's "third wave" theorists what David Ricardo did for Adam Smith two hundred years ago: give their ideas some beef. Ricardo explained how value was created in his time, and we don't think it's been explained properly since then.

Our premise is based on the falling cost of information, which we believe has been a driving force in history. In modern times, this is represented by Moore's Law, which says that the price-performance of microprocessors will double every eighteen months.

Moore's Law induced a Big Bang in the information universe in 1995, when Sony, Nintendo, and others introduced new video games with unprecedented power. They sold these devices for one dollar per MIPS. This is a mere dollar to process one million instructions per second, the standard measure of computer horsepower.

Like the publication of Gutenburg's Bible, the Big Bang is a pivotal event in history. It led to the Internet. The Internet was a sleepy, academic e-mail system until the Big Bang made PCs cheap and powerful enough to make it useful and widely available.

In turn, the Internet created the Black Hole in Cyberspace. The Black Hole is the grim reaper of information inefficiency. Those who know how to capitalize on the falling cost of information have grown and prospered. Those who do not have fallen deep into the Black Hole, never to reappear. Fail to harness the forces unleashed by the falling cost of information and you slip over its Event Horizon and into oblivion.

Applying the power of Moore's Law to the Internet, we anticipate the Information Singularity. This is the intersection of television and the Internet that will dominate the years ahead, absorbing dozens of industries. To prepare for it, we created a new business accelerator in Silicon Valley with several partners: BCE, Canada's top telephone company; Matsushita, a consumer electronics powerhouse; Nortel Networks, a top telecommunications equipment supplier; Paul Allen's Vulcan Ventures, a cable television investor; and two of the finest telecommunications venture capital firms in the world, the Centennial Funds and Vanguard Venture Partners.

Like Steven Hawking and others in astrophysics, we seek a general theory to explain what is happening in the information universe. We use their language because we think these events have cosmic implications—at least for investors, employers, managers, workers, and consumers.

What you read here are not predictions but observations of trends already underway. To others they may appear as random data points, but through the filter of our general theory, they form cohesive patterns which can be extrapolated into the future.

The shift to an information economy has been apparent for a

generation or more. However, the computer revolution did not confer as many benefits as it might have because the falling information costs were not applied to communications. This changed with a vengeance in the 1990s, in a process that has only just started. What's driving wealth creation now and will drive it for the foreseeable future is the application of computer technology to communications.

The Internet has made the pace of change in our business—telecommunications—torrential. Until the 1990s, change in the telephone industry was measured in decades. Networks were programmed with soldering irons. Now we measure change in "Internet years," which, like dog years, rush by at a rate of seven to one. In this new environment, a lead of a month or two over a competitor is decisive.

Many of the ideas in this book are adapted from the monthly letter we publish for our clients. The mission of our firm, North River Ventures, is to create shareholder value in telecommunications. In our *Client Letter,** we have successfully given our readers a huge time advantage by applying the theories presented in this book.

Nearly five years ago, we told subscribers that the U.S. big eight phone companies (the seven Baby Bells plus GTE) would be down to three by the end of 1999. Adding the proposed merger of Qwest and US West to the other mergers now on the table, there are exactly three: Bell Atlantic, BellSouth, and SBC. Moreover, we said then, SBC would kick off the process—which, two years later, it did. Our reasoning in 1994 was simple: in a world where information costs are in a free fall, debt- and cost-laden

*North River Ventures Inc. *Client Letter*. See www.northriver.com for more information.

3

common carriers have limited options. Consolidation is one of the few options and therefore is inevitable. You will see our reasoning laid out here.

In July 1994, we predicted that the Internet would explode, creating vast consumer surpluses that would restructure dozens of industries and "redirect spending from existing channels into the network . . . in the billions." A year later the Internet caught fire. By early 1999, Amazon.com was the world's largest bookseller and the market cap of Charles Schwab was bigger than that of Merrill Lynch. Time advantage: over four years.

In February 1995, we said that Wal-Mart's ability to substitute information for other resources like labor, inventory, and transportation would fuel exceptional growth. In January 1999, Wall Street analysts pronounced themselves "amazed" that Wal-Mart could be a $139 billion company still growing at 20 percent year after year. Time advantage: four years.

In April 1995, we predicted the U.S. government's plan to auction cellular telephone markets would lead to a fiasco. In June 1997, the FCC began default proceedings on $10 billion. Time advantage: over two years.

In December 1996, we predicted disaster for the Iridium satellite communications project saying that "no one can sell $3.00 minutes in a 1¢ a minute world." By mid-1999, Iridium was bankrupt.[1] Time advantage: over two years.

In February 1998, we predicted that Compaq's acquisition of DEC would derail the company. We told *Client Letter* readers to expect a "Value meltdown." In April 1999, investors got exactly that. Compaq shares went through the floor and the CEO and CFO were fired. Time advantage: fourteen months.

In March 1993, we described our four organizational rules for profiting from the falling information-cost curve. By January 1999, Dell Computer, Charles Schwab, Wal-Mart, and Cisco Systems were using our rules exclusively, generating exceptional returns. Time advantage: nearly six years.

To get out ahead in what others see as a business full of surprises and risks, we must recognize that the mechanics of wealth creation are fundamentally different from those taught in economics since Ricardo's time. The underlying principle is that the cost of information is always falling. Those ahead of the curve harvest the consumer surpluses that result. Those that try to go back in time—whether they are countries, companies, or people—to a past point on the information-cost curve are certain to fail.

Compared to faulting the losers, picking winners is not so easy. At the peak of the 1990s financial hysteria, companies and consumers paid ridiculously high prices for first-generation Internet plays. It reminds us of the Japanese buying Pebble Beach and Rockefeller Center at the height of the 1980s real estate market. Sayonara shareholder value.

In this book we return again and again to four companies—Cisco Systems, Dell Computer, Charles Schwab, and Wal-Mart—because they have turned our rules to advantage.

We like these companies because they are big and still growing quickly. They are highly profitable, have long track records of superior financial performance, have minimal debt, use capital efficiently, and have strong brand equity. They are not technology plays, but they all use the Internet to optimize their performance and to serve their customers better.

They all sell commodities. Dell's PCs and Cisco's Internet routers are standard devices available from many sources. Schwab faces innumerable competitors selling financial services in general and stock brokerage in particular that are indistinguishable from one another. As for Wal-Mart, modern retailing was invented over three hundred years ago by Mitsui.

Clearly, we all need the right tools to pick the companies we will work for, run, or invest in. This book will place those tools at your disposal. If you understand the forces at work in our economy, you will be able to meet the future with confidence, successfully make investments, confidently choose a career, and aggressively exploit new opportunities.

By creating a climate well adapted to the falling cost of information, the United States performed brilliantly in the 1990s. Most of the other "big" countries seem to be in trouble: India, Canada, Russia, China. Information entrepôts like Hong Kong and Singapore prosper. Others will prosper only if they become super entrepôts, like the United States.

The biggest question facing mankind today is China. The falling cost of information shifts power inexorably to individuals and away from the state. Since one of four people in the world is Chinese, the impact on China of falling information costs will have enormous repercussions for us all. China's Communist regime is futilely resisting its impact. As others move down the information-cost curve during the next generation, China's frustrations will mount, with consequences we all must face sooner or later.

New York, August 1999
www.northriver.com

PART ONE

THE NEW AMERICAN ECONOMY

The American economy was turned upside down during the past decade in one of the most tumultuous revolutions in world history. The result: the United States put more distance between itself and its commercial rivals than any one had imagined possible. Annual growth in the U.S. economy reached the size of the economies of whole countries. The Dow Jones Industrial Average went through the roof, reaching unthinkable heights. Three-quarters of the world's top fifty companies were American. The nation saw a burst of exuberant growth that few would have expected during the collapse of confidence following the end of the war in Vietnam a generation ago.

This book is about the sources of this extraordinary prosperity and what it means for investors, managers, and employees in the future.

We first proposed the ideas contained in this book a decade and a half ago. What got us thinking seriously about these ideas was a visit from some Canadian government officials who walked into our New York office in the late eighties and asked for urgent help. Canada could not figure out why companies succeed or fail in the information economy, and had no idea what role it should, or should not, play to encourage success. The Canadian economy was in the tank and these officials needed good advice fast.

Then, in 1990, we were approached by one of Japan's largest companies and asked what to do about persistent collapses in market share and the global failure of so many of its new products.

We told our Japanese and Canadian clients one thing: *the cost of information is always falling.* Only companies designed from the ground up to substitute information for other resources, like labor and capital, at a rate faster than the cost of information falls, will get ahead and stay there. Everybody else falls behind and loses.

We added that the faster the cost of information falls, the greater the challenge and the more urgent the agenda for change. Companies not prepared to take tough measures fast were almost certainly doomed. We spelled out for our clients what they needed to do, an agenda that you will see developed in this book, with examples to match.

What we learned we put into our 1993 book, *Beating Japan,** which outlines what happens when an entire nation falls behind the cost curve. In *Beating Japan* we explained what few others even recognized: the implosion of the Japanese economy.

Sadly, our Japanese client did not take our advice and, after a decade of weaving and dodging, paid the price: not long ago its chairman and president were fired, as were thousands of its

---

*McInerney, Francis and White, Sean, *Beating Japan: How Hundreds of American Companies Are Beating Japan—and What Your Company Can Learn from Them* (NY: Dutton, 1993); see www.northriver.com for more information.

employees. Few others in Japan took our advice either, even though our book was widely read there in Japanese. Many great names in Japanese industry got in trouble, just as we predicted they would. Now when we go to Japan, we are listened to with great care!

Canada hasn't done much better. The economy is in a permanent stall: overregulated, overtaxed, and plagued with high unemployment.

During the same period in the U.S., by contrast, a wide range of companies were built, or rebuilt, to our exact specifications. These went from strength to strength. Several of them, notably Charles Schwab, Wal-Mart, Dell Computer, and Cisco Systems, conform precisely to the advice we gave the Japanese ten years ago. They are the models for this book.

Each of these companies is organized not just to keep ahead of falling information costs, but to keep ahead of a curve that is incredibly steep, driven by the constant improvement in information price-performance in everything from new microprocessors to ever better software and communications systems. These firms are designed to tolerate enormous speeds; their managements know that you don't fly through the sound barrier in a plane made of plywood and canvas.

The pace at which U.S. companies are engineering the substitution of information for other resources is breathtaking. The key agents of change were put in place a generation ago: a powerful set of industrial reforms unleashed by President Carter; the Employment Retirement Income Security Act (ERISA) signed into law by President Nixon in 1974; and the Internet, a Cold War innovation designed to protect the U.S. military data network in the event of nuclear attack.

In combination, these tools have changed the face of American industry as few could have foreseen when Carter won the election of 1976. The Carter reforms tore up the U.S. transportation business, allowing industry to completely restructure the movement of goods and services to customers. ERISA mandated fully funded pensions that created the enormous pools of capital needed to finance change. The Internet allowed companies as varied as Dell Computer and Wal-Mart to capitalize on the Carter reforms in new and inventive ways. Dell and Wal-Mart used both tools to revolutionize distribution and logistics, returning exceptional value to investors, as we shall see.

The results of this reinvention during the 1990s were exceptional growth, low unemployment, and inflation that was virtually nonexistent—in short, the best economy of our lifetimes and probably anyone's lifetime, ever. If this isn't the innovation of the ages, we don't know what is.

Why shouldn't any other place in the world offer similar advantages? With rare exceptions, industrial democracies are in an almost permanent funk of unemployment and underemployment.

Part of the answer is in the nature of information itself. As we have said, the cost of information is always falling. Like water seeking its lowest level, ever cheaper information seeks out the simplest environment in which to work. Even small advantages will soak up cheap information like a vacuum pump.

What happens next is critical. Every time information becomes less expensive, more of it is substituted for other inputs like labor, capital, and natural resources, making goods and services of all kinds cheaper than they were.

Cheaper goods leave consumers with more money to spend on other things. If consumer surpluses are large enough, they generate rapid increases in industrial development and wealth. For example, when information became cheap enough to be combined with a few grasses, we got wide-scale agriculture and the city-states of the ancient world. The printing press launched Europe's centuries of global domination. Today, cheap computers are driving a new wave of wealth creation.

By creating consumer surpluses, falling information costs shift market power from producers to consumers. Thus, large drops in the cost of information unleash powerful centrifugal forces on the economy and have a major impact on a nation's social and economic fabric.

Whichever political organization better harnesses these forces confers exceptional advantages on its citizens and displaces less efficient organizations, as Japan is being displaced today.

Any system designed to maintain the high cost of information by force, supporting producers to the exclusion of consumers, will come under immense stress, and will collapse. That is what happened to the Soviet Union.

Today, information costs are falling in accordance with Moore's Law. This is a formula developed several decades ago by Intel cofounder Gordon Moore, who predicted that computer power would double every eighteen months. Such exponential improvements mean that consumers are expropriating market power from producers at very high speed, placing immense pressures on the economy—indeed on all citizens.

At such fast rates of change, only slightly less liberal economies quickly fall far behind their competitors. France and Germany, for example, have both suffered prolonged stagnation and weak employment growth because they have been unable to deregulate and liberalize their economies fast enough to profit from the freefalling costs of information.

In effect, Karl Marx was right. All power does go to the workers. And, to use the instructive Soviet example again, if this power shift is fast enough and you are in its way, you will get a big surprise.

While lots of ink has been spent on the subject of why and how the Soviet Union collapsed, little thought has been given to why the United States, which was subject to the same information-cost pressures and more, did not also give way.

America changed. And given its legal and political structures, no matter how we may curse them from time to time, coupled with the expansionist attitude of its people, no matter how much we may curse that too, the U.S. is better able to substitute information for competing resources than are other nations.

This ability to substitute information rapidly accounted for much of the growth in stock market values during the great bull market run.

It has given us Wal-Mart and its ability to use telecommunications to put more choice on the shelves at the cost of less inventory than its competitors. Long past $100 billion in annual sales, Wal-Mart still grows at the rate of a high-tech start-up.

It has allowed Charles Schwab to substitute its Internet-accessible computers for the bricks and mortar of your local stock broker's office. Schwab pushed its market capitalization above that of Merrill Lynch.

It has allowed industrial powerhouse Cisco to sell 60 percent and more of all its products on line. Newcomer Cisco's market value topped that of its hundred-year-old competitor Lucent Technologies.

And, of course, it has allowed Dell Computer to dispense with retailers in the sales and support of the most complex product a person can buy: a computer.

If you ever wondered how the Dow reached such heights, look at the nature of American democracy. Whatever its faults, it allows its citizens to harness the falling cost of information better than the system of any other nation on the planet, generating exceptional wealth and opportunity. That's some piece of technology.

Since the birth of knowledge, the prime creator of wealth has been the falling cost of information. For most of our million-year history, information costs have fallen slowly or not at all, and little sustainable wealth has been created as a result. However, sudden shifts in information costs in recent millennia have punctuated these long periods of slow change, creating vast amounts of wealth very quickly.

Each time this happens, there are winners and losers. Some investors make fortunes; others lose them.

We are now in the middle of another global upheaval as information costs have entered free fall, radically altering how wealth is created and magnifying enormously the risks for investors, managers, employees, and entrepreneurs.

Those who fail to learn how to make the falling cost of information work will be marginalized just like the long-gone computer giants of the fifties and sixties. Investors will squander their savings. New ventures will be stillborn. Careers will stall. Workers will lose good jobs.

Those who take the lessons of this book to heart will prosper. The reforms our book outlines have been underway in the U.S. for a generation already, giving U.S. investments exceptional advantages over those in other countries that have just begun the painful adjustments called for in these pages.

Europe may look prosperous enough to the tourist. But beneath the surface, its markets are fractured and highly regulated, and there are few home-grown Dells or Wal-Marts. The results are stagnation and unemployment that just won't go away. Even Canada, so close to the United States, has been unable to capitalize on the lessons of this book. Unemployment in Canada lingers at between two and three times U.S. levels. Canadians, with every advantage, just can't seem to do any better.

Asian countries are staggering under the twin burdens of political and corporate ineptitude, and they desperately need to reform both. The countries slowest to respond to both challenges at once, like China and Japan, entered prolonged contractions in the 1990s. Singapore, for all its political immaturity, at least has the rule of law which allows business to respond sensibly to market forces. In South Korea and Taiwan, by contrast, political maturity outstrips corporate maturity. All three countries, however, responded better than China and Japan, which can handle neither political nor corporate reform.

All the while, the information economy is sorting nations into a new pecking order through its relentless pressure on cycle times. Those markets that make it easy for companies to outsource production and use the Internet to reach customers directly move straight to the head of the line. Those that do not, quickly lose all the advantages they gained from traditional production methods and begin to decline, as happened in Japan.

Such declines are not irreversible, of course, but there is no question that the markets that favor rapid information substitution outstrip their commercial rivals. Their citizens will reap the rewards well into the new century as worker productivity and real wages go up.

In this book, we examine how wealth will be created in the years ahead, and how our readers can profit from this change. We explain how to identify the best investment opportunities and how to avoid the dogs. We also consider the broader social, political, and economic implications of falling information costs which will change our lives in far-reaching ways that we haven't even begun to understand.

The point of this book then, is very simple: the information economy has its rules, just as all economies do. There is no mystery to them, but they do need to be understood. You can apply them to create wealth.

Clearly, some organizations, companies, and countries are up to the challenge. Others are not.

Our favorite example is the Catholic Church, just about the only organization we can think of that is actually growing and prospering after a couple of thousand years. The faithful, of course, attribute the Catholic Church's success to its message. No doubt, without a good message it would have failed long ago. However, what keeps this church going decade after decade and century after century when others have long since gone is organizational flexibility.

Simple testimony to the vigor of its organization is this: The pope—an old and ailing man who is the farthest thing possible from a movie star—is the only person alive today, or ever, who can pull crowds of a million or more people.

Investors need to think about how the Catholic Church does it. How does a company create such enduring value? How does an IBM or a General Motors withstand the pressures of cycles as dramatic as those the Catholic Church has met and overcome during the last two thousand years? How does a small company, a start-up, or a prospective IPO prepare itself to create value over the long haul?

Just like the Catholic Church, which weathered the Reformation, organizations today face a period when all the rules are changing. One of our arguments—which many executives will not like—is that the church did not survive in spite of having all its assets stripped away in the sixteenth century, but because of it.

Likewise, companies that embrace the modern-day Reformation will return far more to investors than those that try to fight it. We will give examples of both.

Our book is structured in three parts. In Part One, "The New American Economy," we look at the fundamentals of the information economy and how the falling cost of information works.

In Part Two, "How Money Will Be Made and Lost in the Twenty-first Century," we look at how the falling cost of information generates wealth, and at things like the Black Hole in Cyberspace which one of America's leading executives, Jim Crowe, CEO of Level 3, told *USA Today* and *Barron's* was his "epiphany." In Part Three, "How To Secure Your Piece of the Pie," we examine a range of industries—from computers, as you might expect in a book on the future of wealth creation, to agriculture and commercial real estate, which you might not.

We have built the book on the examples of four companies—Cisco Systems, Charles Schwab, Dell Computer, and Wal-Mart—because these firms cover a huge range of industries, from industrial high tech to disposable diapers. Not one of them offers anything out of the ordinary. Indeed, each of them sells things you can get from a whole host of other suppliers. This has the merit of making these firms easier to understand than a company that only the techno-elite could appreciate.

All four went through periods of struggle and upheaval. These periods came not when the companies were gleams in the eyes of venture capitalists, but after they had established real market value for their investors. Their battles to redo their operations were public ones where success could be measured on the stock market every day. This is something investors can grasp: real problems being solved with serious investor money in the balance.

That is the core of this book. Companies the world over must solve their problems now with investor cash at stake. The faster the cost of information falls, the more quickly these problems must be solved and, of course, the more tools there are to solve them. Investors need a guide to show them what works and what will not so they can make their moves quickly and get ahead.

We begin with a brief history of information.

1

A Brief History of Information

Throughout history, the falling cost of information has driven change by shifting the balance of market power from producers to consumers.

For most of written history, information costs have fallen imperceptibly. Long periods passed between major costs discontinuities. The evolution of information from the invention of writing to the printing press took many thousands of years. But once discontinuities such as movable type began, they occurred with increasing rapidity.

Knowing that a discontinuity is happening doesn't make picking winners easy. When large drops in the cost of information occurred, as with the development of the printing press, only certain types of organizations survived. The key, therefore, is having the right organization, something we will return to time and again.

Progress from the printing press to the Bill of Exchange and other commercial instruments took only hundreds of years. Moving from this Commercial Revolution to the Industrial Revolution took only a century; from the Industrial Revolution to the telegraph, only half a century; and from the commercial computer

THE FALLING INFORMATION-COST CURVE

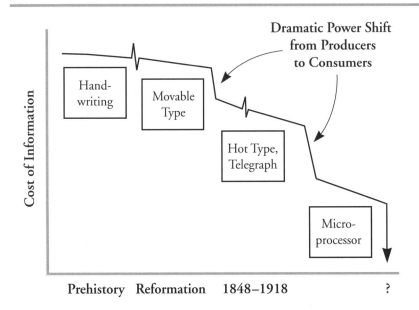

Dramatic Power Shift
from Producers
to Consumers

Cost of Information

Hand-writing

Movable Type

Hot Type, Telegraph

Micro-processor

Prehistory   Reformation   1848–1918   ?

to the personal computer, only twenty-five years. Now, seemingly daily, new products are announced which double the power of previous generations of microprocessors and associated hardware and software. Information costs are in a complete free fall.

Thus, our experience since the dawn of civilization has been one of increasingly compressed cycles of change. Each of these, like the Reformation, has been dramatic, and has had profound effects on all aspects of our lives. What we are living through today is every bit as tumultuous. To understand it we need to understand the nature of information.

Information was once so precious that it was considered sacred, far more scarce and valuable than labor, land, or other natural resources. Information on how to grow crops, when to plant them, and when the seasons were expected to change was painstakingly collected. Commonly, this information was held in temples and controlled by the religious elite with the full authority of the state.

Scarce and very expensive to acquire, information had great value to those who controlled it. From the earliest Mesopotamian king to Lenin and the leaders of the world's industrial giants, rulers have recognized that information is power. Controlling it has meant keeping power.

At the same time, high-cost information made early civilizations vulnerable. Nothing devastated these societies more than the sacking of their temples: with the loss of that building went the loss of all knowledge, from when to plant crops to how to rebuild the temple itself. A crude predator could eliminate thousands of years of carefully collected information with a stroke, and often did. Such "lost" civilizations are still being unearthed.

For millennia, information costs didn't fall by much. Information was expensive to collect, expensive to store, and without machinery, it was even expensive to use. Empires and city-states rose and fell, and knowledge increased, but the costs of acquiring, managing, and disseminating information stayed pretty much the same.

Large empires in China, India, and Italy used bureaucracy and administrative skills to bring down information costs and widen information dissemination, but these efforts had little lasting impact. With its 53,000 miles of roads, Rome eliminated traditional dependence on water transportation and built an empire that lasted nearly two thousand years, spreading imperial administration from the North Sea to the Red Sea and beyond. Couriers of the Imperial Post could cover one hundred and fifty miles per day over the well-engineered (and safe) roads of the empire, reaching London from Rome in less than a week.[1] This was a period of wealth creation on a scale that would not be seen again until railways were built across Europe and America, seventeen hundred years after the time of the Roman emperor Trajan.

Rome also divorced the management of knowledge from temples by creating large libraries for civil administration and learning. But information was still tied to geography. You had to go to the library; it didn't come to you. Information dissemination remained a problem until fairly recent times.

Christianity made important strides. The monastic system preserved information following the collapse of the western half of the Roman Empire. But it didn't do much to cut the costs of acquiring information or of increasing its dissemination. Indeed, for a time, monasticism may even have increased these costs. Illuminated texts were extremely laborious to reproduce.

The cost discontinuity in Christianity came with the invention of the portable temple. When a priest can say a Mass anywhere, the church goes to the people. Information, for the first time, was on the move, and Christianity became a portable, go-anywhere, cross-any-ocean phenomenon. This cut the cost of information dramatically. Islam benefited from the same process and quickly crossed the globe from the Atlantic to the Pacific through the Asian landmass.

This was also a major change in "software." Making temples portable and information mobile was a shift in thought, not technology. Today, software changes like this one are essential to firms trying to create innovative organizations that apply knowledge to production and customer service instead of money to natural resources, machinery, and labor.

The next major software change, the translation of the Bible into the vernacular, allowed people to have the temple to themselves. This too brought down costs. However, information still had to be collected manually and recorded by hand, a slow and expensive process. But the first hesitant steps in the secularization of information had been taken: information no longer had to reside in temples. It was losing its sacred character.

The effects of secularization were explosive. Gutenberg's fifteenth-century invention of movable type caused the most dramatic drop in the cost of information since the development of handwriting. It made books commonplace and universally available.

In the sixteenth century, information, and with it the immense power that resided in the church and state, moved suddenly into the hands of individuals. Everywhere that literacy moved, established institutions collapsed, often with frightening speed. Inexpensive books literally made the library at Alexandria available to anyone. Common people gained access not just to religious ideas, but to scientific knowledge and political ideas as well. Individuals for the first time appropriated the power to interpret information and to create it. They could print books. The power shift that followed was cataclysmic.

Just like the Information Revolution today, the Reformation spread across growth markets like wildfire. It especially flourished along major trade routes, following the business paper trail across northern Europe and into North America. Incumbent rulers naturally resisted this shift in control over information, and dueling books were soon followed by dueling nations.

But it was in combination with the discovery of the New World, perhaps the most important event in history, that the printing press had its most profound consequences. The existence of portable secular information in the hands of the newly empowered and "reformed" colonists created a force that tore into the Northern Hemisphere of the New World, consuming native lands and almost overwhelming the "unreformed" colonists to the south—though not, notably, their fellow reformed colonists to the north.

The reformed colonists saw their rights as "self-evident" and not bestowed on them by a church or state. Low-cost information enabled them to create a political process of their own and to assume, for the first time, an educated electorate. The secularization of information was complete. Low-cost information, in effect, created America.

Low-cost information also created the modern corporation. Unencumbered by churches or kings, the reformed had ideas of their own on how best to exploit their environment profitably. They found themselves for the first time in a position to organize, and they did, creating one of the most enduring and adaptable organizations on earth: the publicly traded company.

By substituting information for craftsmanship, the Industrial Revolution made literacy a mass phenomenon. In the nineteenth century, improvements in printing technology were made that, among other things, lowered the cost of newspapers and made mass circulation available on a daily basis. The upheavals of 1848 ripped through Europe, bringing down much of the reconstruction of the post-Napoleonic world.

With the invention of the telegraph, information became available everywhere instantly, rapidly "democratizing" stock markets, for example, and increasing their access to savings. Unprecedented social upheaval followed. While revolutions swept Europe and new nations like Germany emerged there, the United States was engulfed in a civil war whose gruesomeness exceeded that of even the Napoleonic Wars. With the telegraph, the golden age of the great Rothschild banking house, with its secure private courier system, passed into history.

By the mid-twentieth century, the burgeoning volume of information needed management. The computer age began. Computers cut information costs further than ever. Soon we had microprocessors, and the opening shots of the personal-computer revolution were fired.

What makes PCs different from any other information tool is

that people aren't only on the receiving end anymore. They can buy information, sell information, and most important, create information. Personal computers are the ultimate information-generation machine. The PC completes the shift in power from producers to consumers. The personal computer is a social force of unprecedented magnitude.

In many businesses over the last two decades, restructuring around the falling cost of information meant moving knowledge out of headquarters and into the field. Cheap and plentiful information has displaced labor, land, natural resources, and capital. Personal computers have empowered line workers. Post-PC devices are doing the same for families and children.

From the holy to the banal, the falling cost of information has driven the growing empowerment of consumers at the expense of producers. Cheap information makes it easier for customers to voice—indeed to force—their preferences on producers.

The Internet has given consumers with PCs the power to exercise market control as never before, unleashing the centrifugal forces of disintermediation on just about anything that moves, from stock markets to retail stores and even our democratic institutions. On electronic networks of every kind, from television to the Internet, consumers exercise the new power they hold. Consumer reaction is instant be it through the Internet, at the polling booth, or most important, at the cash register.

It is no coincidence, therefore, that the companies that have managed to profit most from the information revolution are the ones that devote the most energy to maximizing customer responsiveness.

It is also no coincidence that, just as the Reformation unleashed powerful new organizations such as modern corporations, the Information Revolution is driving completely new concepts in organization and management. As corporations allowed us to successfully exploit the North American continent, perhaps the biggest wealth-generating phenomenon of all time, the new organizational models described in this book will allow us to exploit the Information Universe, possibly an even bigger wealth-generating phenomenon.

Having understood the nature of information, we next have to understand what it does for us.

Every time the cost of information falls, it can more easily be substituted for something else, be it labor, capital, or natural resources, than before. As we saw earlier, information and grasses combined to make agriculture, and agriculture creates a sustainable consumer surplus. When this is done on a wide enough scale we get profound changes in our society. Agriculture gave us early civilizations and a whole new way of living. But, though it wasn't clear at the time, these early drops in the cost of information began the slow, inexorable shift of market power away from producers and into the hands of those with the consumer surpluses.

Today we would say of this process; the customer is always right. Why? Because the customer has the money! But we all know that the customer didn't always have the money and that the consumer economy is a new phenomenon in history.

And the fact is that this slow, ever quickening movement of market power into the hands of consumers has been accompanied by large shifts in political power as well. If the customers are always right, they are as right in their legislatures as they are in their stores.

By shifting power from producers to consumers, the falling cost of information destabilizes any political regime that stands in its way. No government can propagandize and control a people that has ready access to cheap satellite dishes.

Moreover, since these shifts in market power are directly proportionate to the speed at which the cost of information falls, in a time like ours when the cost of information is in a complete free fall, we should expect political shifts the world over that will be spectacular, and profoundly disruptive. The collapse of the Soviet Union is only one case.

Thus, the falling cost of information has huge foreign-policy implications. China is at the brink. It cannot take advantage of the falling cost of information without letting so much power flow into the hands of its people that the regime dissolves.

Moreover, China is trying to compete with low-cost labor. This drives its political, military, and economic policies alike. A military built on low-cost manpower can never compete with one built on the low cost of information, as the war in Kosovo so conclusively proved. China's massed military might, even its nuclear arsenal, will be no match for a nation farther down the information-cost curve than China. Kosovo showed that a mass military like Serbia's may be forced to leave the field without ever having engaged an enemy, with consequences that can be enormously destabilizing at home. Kosovo also demonstrated to China that the straits of Taiwan might as well be six thousand miles wide.

We can predict with some certainty that by 2010 China will have been transformed into a fully functioning and powerful democracy, or into a mess. Either outcome will make China's relations with other countries highly complex. However complex, though, the process is easy to understand: China can adapt to falling information costs or drop behind. Either way, the events that happen there will dominate world events for years to come.

Next, the Iron Laws of Information. These are the patterns that information follows in its never ending empowerment of consumers and creation of wealth.

2

Iron Laws of Information

In advising the Canadian government during the late eighties, we developed the Iron Laws of Information to explain the consequences of the falling cost of information. Fail to observe them, we told the Canadians, and you are toast. Respect them, and you will create enormous wealth-generating opportunities for your country where there were none.

The Iron Laws are as follows:

1. Cheap information *always* chases out expensive information.
2. Disorder *always* increases.
3. Profit *always* flows to the least regulated company or market.
4. The first three laws *always* operate simultaneously on *any* organization.

The **First Iron Law** says that Gresham's Law—cheap money always chases out expensive money—applies as well to information as it does to economics. With a phone and a cheap computer, for example, anyone can get around high-cost phone calls in one country by getting someone with a phone in a country with cheaper phone rates to call them back, thereby draining money from one market into another and killing investors who backed the wrong horse.

The First Iron Law says, in effect, that *cheap information allows customers to move the effective point of sale to ground favorable to themselves, not producers.* Companies not designed to accommodate this shift are sinkholes for value. We see this with companies that use technology to let their customers order from them in the comfort of their homes or offices. Companies that don't accommodate the First Law lose share even if their products are clearly superior to those that do.

This First Iron Law quickly separates countries into leaders and followers. There are plenty of governments around the world that could never accept its implications and that would do anything to flout the First Law, with consequences that are completely predictable.

Thus the First Iron Law also says that a manager's spending priority should be whatever closes the gap between the company and its customers. Spending mainly to increase capacity or add customers is a big mistake and will not improve competitiveness.

But this is the very mistake many of the world's largest—and highest-cost—media companies are making. TV networks, cable companies, and telephone companies around the world have spent hundreds of billions on acquisitions in recent years in an endless string of what are always labeled "the biggest deal in history." The First Iron Law says that spending this way compounds, rather than reduces, their vulnerability.

The **Second Iron Law** says that the Second Law of Thermodynamics applies to information: disorder always increases. When the cost of information falls, computer power moves rapidly away from the big machines—and big companies—that seemed ready to run the world a few decades ago to the billions of little ones that fit in the palm of your hand.

In 1995 Nintendo, Sega, and others introduced toys so powerful that you could trace a telephone connection from one toy clear around the world to another without *ever* encountering a computer as powerful. Each of these toys is a wormhole into another world of computers, usually strung together by kids at home, of unknown size and number of dimensions.

What IBM could manage a few short decades ago—all the world's computer owners—couldn't be managed today by any firm no matter how big. There are just too many devices owned by too many people and organizations around the world over which to keep track.

Companies can grow and profit *only* if they can harness these centrifugal forces. This means whole new organizations and new ways of thinking which we will profile in *Future Wealth*.

The **Third Iron Law** says that value added always flows to the least regulated. The simplest way to understand how the Third Iron Law works is to look at dial-a-porn services. Since no one regulates who can call whom in a free society, or the computers and software they use to do it, dial-a-porn operators can and do sell services across borders into countries where these services may be illegal. With fully interactive video—and the Second Iron Law hard at work—it is not difficult to see where this will go.

For centrist governments like those in France or China, the Third Iron Law undermines the very pillars of their social and economic policies. As a democracy, France has enough give to adapt, though not to take the lead. China does not, and the consequences will be dire.

The **Fourth Iron Law** says that the first three Iron Laws operate simultaneously. They will not drive your business or investments selectively or in sequence. You must plan on them working on all aspects of all operations at once.

Fast-growing companies like our models Cisco, Dell, Schwab, and Wal-Mart observe these laws scrupulously in *everything* they do. They design their organizations around the Iron Laws to ensure that nothing they do risks stumbling over these unforgiving sentinels of value creation.

This tells investors several things:

1. Always expect better price-performance and don't invest in companies that can't deliver it and keep delivering it.
2. Assume that information economies are messy places without order or structure—like the Internet—and that this messiness will only increase. So don't invest in companies offering one-size-fits-all answers. Future markets will all be chaotic.[1]
3. Think of government regulation as one giant Maginot Line around which cheap information always finds a way. Don't invest in countries that are highly regulated—as investors discovered in Asia in the late nineties—or in companies that work under government control, even if that regulation seems to spell guaranteed rates of return. Sooner than most people imagine, the falling cost of information will kick in and those returns will vanish, leaving investors holding the bag.
4. Watch out for companies that expect change to happen one event at a time. The Iron Laws apply all at once and management has to be ready for this. Many traditional brand leaders are learning this lesson the hard way as they try to defend their businesses in the face of proliferating alternatives.[2]

Next: how to profit from the Iron Laws.

3

Profiting from the Iron Laws

Investors want to find the next Cisco, Microsoft, or Intel. They don't want to wind up with the next Wall Street dog.

The Iron Laws change the way investors look at opportunities but they don't eliminate investment fundamentals. Irrespective of the impact of the laws, there is no substitute for companies with balanced finances, effective brand management, the right technology, and strong leadership. The key is knowing how the Iron Laws affect a company's ability to deliver on these core capabilities that every firm must have.

Finances: we look for companies with little or no debt that have the resources to respond to unpredictable change.

Brand Power Redefined: with the Internet, consumers talk back in real time, undermining old-fashioned brand promises. We look for companies that know how to use information technology to build a new "brand envelope" of deep and enduring service relationships.

Technology: we look for companies with technology that stays on the right side of Moore's Law, which says that microchip price-performance doubles every eighteen months.

Management: the most difficult part of the equation. A woman once asked Napoleon which troops are best. His reply: "Those which are victorious, Madame." We look for companies with the management style to survive and prosper, long after their founders are gone.

There's a lot of wishful thinking going on among investors and corporate managers. Many hope today's industry leaders will just muddle through somehow, lowering prices a bit here, tweaking their products there, and still hang on to their markets. Incumbents have an advantage for sure, but this is not how competition will play out during the decades ahead.

We believe that the Iron Laws require a new organizational model, which we discuss in the next chapter. We also believe that this new model gives managers shorter "interior lines" than their competitors. Some companies we look at in *FutureWealth* have such short interior lines that they are almost hollow inside. These firms have taken the lead in replacing large parts of their organizations with Internet-based tools that allow information on customers, or on their own human resource and finance operations, to whiz around at super speed, eliminating the need for paper shufflers. Some companies are incredibly fast.

New model companies travel less from one point on the competitive map to another. Thus they respond more quickly than the incumbent leaders who have to travel the "exterior lines" to get to the same place.

How do interior lines work? Most Americans will remember from high-school history the example of Robert E. Lee, who for so long held off Union attempts to conquer the South during the Civil War. General Lee's forces were arrayed in a large semicircle around the Confederate capital in Richmond. When his forces had to move inside the semicircle from one end to the other, they had a much shorter distance to follow than Union forces, which had to march all the way around the outside of the semicircle. This way, Lee used "interior lines" to outmaneuver Union forces slogging farther to get to the same point.

Similarly, for every step a Cisco or Wal-Mart takes, their competitors may have to take three. Put another way around, every step the competitor takes against one of these companies puts it two steps *behind*. The only way to make up for this shortfall is to use the one thing laggards don't have: speed.

We will see in our chapter "The Four Keys to Value Creation" that there are key essentials to ensuring that you have the advantage of interior lines. Investors need to benchmark the companies into which they put their hard-earned dollars against these keys.

New model companies designed around the Iron Laws of Information can force market leaders to defend themselves with their weakest hands: lack of speed.

Time and again, new model companies force lumbering competitors to move their entire operations forward at speeds slow enough to make them easy pickings. Time and again, companies that aggressively substitute information for other resources get the advantage of interior lines, destroying much larger and better-established competitors.

This explains why some of the biggest names in business seem to disappear so fast. And it also explains why companies like Charles Schwab can achieve valuations so much higher than incumbents in their markets. It's not that Schwab is overpriced. It is that Schwab faces brick-and-mortar incumbents whose value the market has failed to discount properly.

The simplest way for an outsider to measure a company's relative interior line advantage is to look at its "velocity of capital." This is operating income divided by total capital, something that anyone with an annual report can calculate in a few seconds. Companies with high velocities of capital, like Dell, have relatively few assets holding them back. This enables them to move more quickly than their competition. Low velocities of capital indicate a lack of vigor that may well be terminal.

In the next chapter we will look at the biggest constraint on competing while the cost of information is falling: how the speed of falling information costs warps time itself. We call this "Moore Time" after the cofounder of Intel, Gordon Moore.

4

Competing in Moore Time

Dr. Gordon Moore, cofounder of Intel, effectively predicted the speed at which the cost of information is falling thirty years ago when he said that microprocessor price-performance would continue to double every eighteen months.

To compete in a world where price-performance changes so dramatically, decisions have to be made at warp speed. Otherwise products are obsolete long before they can be brought to market. We have come up with the term "Moore Time" to distinguish time that is compressed by the constraints of this kind of decision making from time in the normal, or calendrical sense.

Moore's foresight didn't mean much to people in the sixties, since even the cheapest computers were far beyond the reach of the average company, let alone the average person.

Today, however, computer price-performance hits everyone. There are cheap and powerful computers in homes, cars, and televisions. And, as it has since the invention of the transistor over half a century ago, price-performance continues to double every eighteen months.

Because the Moore Curve is exponential, companies that fall behind in Moore Time see their markets move away from them at exponential speeds. Market value usually follows.

When markets move in Moore Time, a two-year product plan can turn what was a competitive advantage of months, even years, into a disadvantage of decades. A disadvantage this big usually means value meltdown and market exit.

For investors, this explains the shareholder panic that has ripped through the computer business over and over again during the last half-century. These companies fell out of Moore Time. With each succeeding generation, companies have risen, fallen behind the Moore Curve, and collapsed. One day Wang Labs dominated the word processor market; then its expensive systems were replaced by a couple of hundred dollars' worth of software. IBM stumbled, lost huge amounts of shareholder value almost overnight, and had to be rebuilt from scratch.

Investors in computer stocks have had five decades to get used to this. Now it is the turn of everybody else.

As computers "infect" more businesses and reach deeper into our daily lives, these problems have spread far beyond the computer business into everything from agriculture to real estate. No investment is safe. In recent years, companies far removed from Gordon Moore's computer chips have had the same problems generating value as DEC and IBM, and have had to make far-reaching changes.

The most obvious example of a market moving in Moore Time is, of course, the Internet. The number of industries the Internet touches is simply staggering: with so many companies now forced by the Internet to compete in Moore Time, shareholders everywhere are vulnerable.

Our rule is that companies that do not constantly substitute information for all other resources lose their competitive advantage, quickly fall behind the Moore Curve, and see their value evaporate.

Like all revolutions, the Moore Time revolution eats its own children. Microsoft, of all companies, was caught flat-footed by the public's speedy acceptance of an Internet unleased by Microsoft's own operating systems. If Microsoft proves unable to compete in Moore Time it will become the next Wang, a one-product, one-generation company with no future. Bill Gates understands this better than anyone else.

Competing in Moore Time is like flying through the sound barrier. As we noted, it can be done, but not with a plane made of plywood and canvas. It means completely rethinking how a company should be put together, from the airframe to the engines, and how it should be flown. Everyone has to be retrained and reorganized, from the pilots to the ground crew. The process is never ending. There is no such thing as stability in Moore Time. If IBM can be surprised by the popularity of its own personal computers and if Microsoft can be surprised by the Internet, no company is immune.

The good news is that there are solutions to the Moore Time problem. Most of the rest of Part One is about the specifics of what companies have to do to get ahead and stay ahead in Moore Time. We then discuss these, company by company, in Part Three. We will show that, with the right information strategy, companies can deliver levels of customer service unknown in the past, gain unprecedented holds on their markets, and offer excellent value to investors as a result.

Investors must find those companies that know how to turn falling costs to advantage. The key is understanding the rules for the information-cost curve and identifying the companies that play by them. That's what this book will do.

Our remedy for competing in Moore Time is to ensure that information moves from customers to decision makers and back in ever increasing speeds. Survival means making the internal mechanisms of a firm small enough and simple enough that customer information does not get refracted into oblivion by a company's internal processes.

Competing successfully in Moore Time, therefore, means making lines of communication completely transparent to customers. An organization that is even *slightly* opaque to customers risks falling behind the Moore Curve and becoming a sinkhole for investor dollars.

Most companies have well-defined planning, engineering, marketing, and sales departments. The interstitial costs between these functions, as much as the inefficiencies of an aged plant, make competitors high-cost suppliers. Reorganization is difficult, but companies with high interstitial costs will not grow again without fundamental redesign.

Few organizations make this transition. For those that do, the going is extremely hard. IBM and AT&T laid off hundreds of thousands of employees. After a decade and a half, IBM is a growth company once again; AT&T is only just beginning to be one.

In fact, we must look to history for guidance. Like the microprocessor, the printing press unleashed a sudden fall in the cost of information. The resulting Reformation had a devastating impact on the Catholic Church. The church suffered several decades of revenue and market-share losses, particularly in the high-growth regions of northern Europe. Finally, the church responded with the Counter-Reformation. Reinvigorated, it went on to reclaim large parts of Europe and to stake out much of the New World. Little remained of the old church, other than the real estate that hadn't been nationalized. *Five hundred years later,* the church remains the largest organization in the world. Its management hierarchy is remarkably lean. That's value creation!

Newcomers have a big advantage. They can achieve high velocities of capital right from the start, avoiding the baggage that weighs down incumbents. Wal-Mart, the world's largest retailer, looks nothing like the companies it displaced. Wal-Mart achieved a velocity of capital double that of Sears and Kmart. This made Wal-Mart easier to finance. It's also easier to run and needs fewer people. Assets are baggage, and baggage requires baggage handlers. Wal-Mart's sales per dollar invested and per employee are well ahead of Sears and Kmart's, which spent a decade reorganizing, downsizing, and refocusing. Wal-Mart's is a wealth creation engine that runs on less fuel—capital—than any of its rivals.

Organized around a powerful Intranet, Wal-Mart revolutionized the distribution of atoms. Sam Walton rethought the purpose of the enterprise, and used information technology first available in the 1970s to create a seamless, low-cost process for distributing merchandise. In twenty years, Wal-Mart became the fourth largest company by sales in the world.[1]

In retailing, capital intensity went down. Building a brand, however, costs real money, and may benefit from scale. Wal-Mart combined scale and low costs to displace its far bigger rivals. Wal-Mart grew organically, not through acquisition. Acquiring Kmart, a company with a velocity of capital so slow it stalled, would have doomed Wal-Mart. Wal-Mart created a powerful brand, with a no-questions-asked guarantee policy, great selection, and low prices. One reason Wal-Mart works is that frontline employees have decision-making power that allows them to deal directly with customer requests. Less time is spent dealing with their own organization simply because there's less of it.

Next, we look at how the Internet is restructuring business.

5

The Internet Model

What makes the Internet so potent is its ability to take advantage of the marginal cost of communications. It does so by breaking down messages into small pieces that can use all the momentary silences in the network, which cost virtually nothing to use, and reassembling the messages at their destination. Phone companies base their bills on much higher average costs in which we pay for the whole communication, silences included. Consumers use the Internet to reprice these average cost-based services to what they are really worth, which is basically nothing.

Thus the Internet is by far the least expensive of all media, and a natural marketplace. There is no cheaper way for people to communicate, and no cheaper place for them to do business. Much business has already migrated to the Internet. Soon, the rest will follow.

What holds the Internet back from achieving its potential is the limited bandwidth available to consumers. Most companies now providing connections to homes—telephone companies, wireless companies, and cable television operators—offer limited capabilities and high prices. These limitations force consumers to substitute cheaper computing power for bandwidth, driving a new generation of consumer electronics that will move faster than most people expect, and much, much faster than today's networks can support. Eventually, however, cheap, fast Internet access will make each home a node on the Internet, unleashing powerful secondary effects on dozens of other businesses.

Until very recently, companies the world over, especially those in information technology, talked long and hard about "convergence." They foresaw a world in which computing, communications, and consumer electronics converged on one another. Under this assumption, they looked for ways to neutralize the risk of clashes, often by acquiring interests in each other.

This process, which began in the mid- to late seventies, proceeded uninterrupted for nearly twenty years. For example, IBM bought ROLM, Siemens bought Nixdorf, and AT&T bought NCR. Every one of these acquisitions failed. Similar efforts by horizontally integrated companies like NEC to launch combined "computer and communications" programs also suffered major reverses. None achieved the synergy that was sought.

What has happened is something quite different. Ever since the Internet's marginal cost-based pricing allowed it to explode onto the scene, it has begun to subsume these industries one by one. The Internet is pulling consumer electronics companies and software suppliers into its powerful gravitational field.

Where the Internet creates real investor value, however, is in its powerful secondary effects. It implodes underlying industries like publishing, banking, and entertainment, releasing vast consumer surpluses and creating huge amounts of new wealth. One of the big lessons in this book is that the real way to make money in the

Internet, therefore, is not by buying so-called "dot com" companies, but by buying companies that absorb other businesses such as finance and real estate.

Next, the Hubble Effect: what happens when a company ignores the Internet?

6

The Hubble Effect

Edwin Hubble was one of the twentieth century's greatest astronomers, after whom the NASA space telescope was named. Hubble postulated that galaxies move away from ours faster the further they are away from us.

The information economy has similar properties: the more layers of distribution between a producer and a consumer—wholesalers, retailers, and so on—the faster the consumer moves away from the producer. This is what all those computer manufacturers found out when Dell started selling direct to customers over the Internet.

Our first book, *Beating Japan,* was about one gigantic Hubble Effect: an entire nation so removed from its overseas customers by layers of management and distribution that its customers were racing away from it at high speed.

In our view, the deep crisis in which Japan found itself during the nineties was driven primarily by the inability of Japanese companies to close up the gap between themselves and their customers. There are deep institutional reasons for this, as there usually are in any organization slow to respond to changing market forces. But the sight of an entire nation so marooned is startling.

In *Beating Japan* we identified core flaws that make a company victim to the Hubble Effect.

First, there are firms that are highly integrated vertically and horizontally. These firms have to move too many divisions to get the job done in a timely fashion. Take a firm that makes a computerized system of some type and also owns an upstream maker of computer chips used in that system. We have worked with a company like this; it couldn't add a new feature that customers were begging for because the chip division judged the opportunity a poor one and refused to supply the needed part. An internal coordinating committee created additional problems. Since the tail can't wag the dog, customers went elsewhere. Mistakes like this in Moore Time are devastating. This company experienced a permanent market share collapse, and had to withdraw from a business in which it had operated for nearly a century and had a legitimate claim to global leadership.

Second, there are firms with management that is too highly centralized. These outfits focus inward on themselves, making decisions that benefit departments or individuals over customers. Centralization may look as if it speeds up decision making, but it usually does the opposite, tying decisions up in internal issues of no material benefit to the people paying the bills.

Third, many firms have too many layers of management. We worked with one Japanese firm that had parallel management structures in the U.S. and Japan. No one knew who to report to, and customers were, as a result, put on hold until they simply got fed up and went elsewhere. The organization was so complex that no one inside or outside the company could understand it, let alone make it work.

Finally, companies often convince themselves that their excellent technologies should be enough to please customers. But, as the examples on which we built this book show, the most successful firms deliver customer service, not products, because this cannot be bought elsewhere.

Many in Japan see what we think of as serious flaws in their business structures as something of which to be proud. Overly complex organizations give everyone a well-defined place and balance complex internal needs in the most socially appropriate manner. The American way of defining all these functions out of existence by substituting information for them is anathema in Japan because it defines millions of hard-working people out of a job without providing valuable alternatives to which they could move.

What emerged in Japan was a kind of stasis. Executives knew what had to be done but dared not do it. All the while the Hubble Effect bit deeper as customers moved away at ever faster speeds and the competitive situation became less and less recoverable.

When we wrote our first book, we said that Japan's recovery would be easy to spot. The country would begin the process of reordering business to eliminate the four "fatal" flaws just described. Unfortunately, this didn't happen.

What happened instead is that unemployment rose as cost pressures destroyed industry. Few real changes were made in how companies are run. Supply-chain management outside the car industry remained almost unknown. To pay for this, Japan was squandering one hundred fifty years of post-Meiji wealth. The streets were full of well-dressed people and fine cars, but asset values fell hard, credit was nonexistent for small companies, and banks were plagued with monstrous volumes of bad debt.

The price of miscalculating the Hubble Effect can, as Japan shows, be devastating. Ironically, the one person who long ago understood the consequences was Konosuke Matsushita, the Japanese founder of the Matsushita empire. Next, his golden rule.

7

Konosuke Matsushita's Golden Rule

Our understanding of how to profit from the falling cost of information was inspired by the late Japanese industrialist Konosuke Matsushita, founder of the Matsushita family of companies and the Panasonic brand. No manager should be without a well-worn copy of *The Matsushita Perspective: a Business Philosophy Handbook*.[1]

What made Matsushita so exceptional is that he started his company just after the turn of the century with only a hundred yen. From that tiny investment he built the greatest engine of shareholder value in history.[2]

Matsushita operated on one very simple principle from which he never deviated: our customer is God. Matsushita used whatever tools were available to place himself and his firm closer to customers than his competition. Matsushita was blunt: to survive, a company must benefit society. A certain sign that a company is of no benefit to society is that it makes no money. Matsushita taught that the only way to benefit society is to be closer to your customers than anyone else.

Very early in his career, therefore, he discovered the advantage of having the shortest possible interior lines. He understood how to deal with the Hubble Effect.

In Matsushita's day, a well-orchestrated system of branded distributors accomplished this goal. He nurtured these distributors assiduously, paying careful attention to them. He exploited to the limit the channels to market available to him at the time. More than once, Matsushita stripped entire layers of distribution out of his business when he found that fewer middlemen made his company more responsive to customer needs and more profitable to boot.

But Matsushita's day is long gone. Distributors, no matter how well branded, keep producers and customers apart. In writing this book, we asked ourselves: what would Matsushita do today if he was the new kid on the block in Silicon Alley?

This is the central lesson of our book: information costs are falling so fast that, like Matsushita in his prime, everyone has to rethink how to get close enough to customers to harness the forces unleashed. Those who don't rethink their fundamental business processes get crushed. Matsushita regularly rethought his business and built incomparable amounts of shareholder value.

Matsushita was not a staid, conservative businessman like the contemporary Japanese "salaryman" commonly profiled in the press today. Out on the street at the age of nine, barely literate, he lived by his wits, which were formidable.

He was a revolutionary. He constantly reminded his employees of the three great Shoguns who built the Japanese nation-state in the late sixteenth century. Oda Nobunaga, Toyotomi Hideyoshi, and Tokugawa Ieyasu. The Japanese know from years of schooling that these men were exceptionally tough and decisive leaders. They did not do things by halves, except perhaps in the way large numbers of their opponents were dispatched! Still less did they let themselves be distracted by Japanese tradition. They went against nearly a thousand years of history to create a unified country. The average business today faces a challenge no less daunting.

Matsushita devoted so much time and energy to the beginning of the Tokugawa era for a very good reason: he wanted management to understand that it was building a great enterprise for which it would have to take great risks.

This book is about the companies that do what Matsushita would do—tear up the plan and start over again—and those that do not, either because of fear or ineptitude.

Next, the future of nations in the world of falling information costs.

8

The Future: The Information Entrepôt

When countries keep the price of information artificially high, others can use the Iron Laws to siphon off their business. With this strategy, the United Kingdom is becoming the information entrepôt of Europe, capitalizing on the tightly regulated high-cost regimes in France and Germany.

Britain is now the place where data heads to be collected, managed, and then redistributed at marked-up prices to the other members of the European Union. The consequences of the United Kingdom's policy for the continentals is incalculable. Riding its low-cost information strategy, Britain is emerging as the dominant force in services in the European Union. It could easily wind up controlling EU banking, advertising, accounting, and insurance markets by early in the next century. A new age of British knowledge-imperialism will have begun. Britain's information costs are lower and its overseas connections are wider and deeper, giving it significant economies. Using the Iron Laws, Britain keeps itself less regulated than its neighbors and is thus better adapted to exploiting the markets of the twenty-first century. Ireland's transformation in only a decade from European also-ran to its front ranks has been even more remarkable.

Singapore and China show what happens when governments get this backwards. In these countries, political managers are trying to "control" the Internet. By doing so they are stunting the tools essential to the full integration of distribution into manufacturing. The result: politicians are placing a ceiling on growth. Opportunities will go elsewhere in Moore Time.

No other countries have committed themselves to development with the single-minded purpose shown by Singapore and Hong Kong. Already, the people of these two small city-states enjoy a standard of living approaching that of Europe. For their policy makers, the challenge is to maintain economic momentum in the face of competition from other Third World up-and-comers, particularly China.

Singapore

It is easy to forget what Singapore was until a generation ago: an impoverished, crime- and disease-ridden British colonial backwater virtually destroyed during the Second World War. Today Singapore attracts the high-wage, high-tech jobs that once were the exclusive domain of the U.S., Europe, and Japan, even turning away investment that does not match its profile of future opportunities.

What got Singapore from there to here in such a short time was the resolve of its government. Such single-minded purpose is rare among nations. And, when combined with the equally purposeful desire to ensure the profitability of its industry—something lacking in Europe and the U.S., where governments often act irrespective of impact on profitability—Singapore's firm and un-swerving approach is unique.

If business moves elsewhere, the island state doesn't have another large geographic region to attract opportunity and soak up jobs, the way the booming southeast of the U.S. took up the slack for the Northeast. Singapore has to keep employment high while managing the same changes that are roiling industry else-where. Moreover, the government knows that its stranglehold on power is based on its extraordinary ability to manage the econ-omy. If it fails, its tight grip on the country will slip.

The government has attacked on two axes: build a new infor-mation economy, and use information technology to reposition existing industry on a more competitive basis. Doing this is not simple. Selling high-tech products means facing price pressures from others. During the Asian economic crisis of the late nineties, Singapore lost share of the U.S. market for high-tech goods to other Asian countries whose currencies fell, making their products relatively inexpensive.

Being a high-cost producer is nothing new. Singapore's tough environmental standards, for example, which on their face make business more expensive, do not cost Singapore jobs. On the con-trary, Singapore remains one of the most popular locations for multinationals in Asia. Even oil giants like Exxon favor Singapore for their regional refining and petrochemical investments, despite the city-state's rigorous environmental standards. The country has demonstrated an ability to handle its position dexterously.

With a deep but well-protected natural harbor, Singapore was settled by the British as a free port between China and India, and the city's current prosperity rests on trade. Singapore is first and foremost an entrepôt for goods, money, and information. Indeed, foreign trade is more than three times the size of the total econ-omy (compared to about 25 percent in the U.S., for example).

When founded by the British a century and a half ago, Singapore was not much more than a swamp ringed with a few fishing villages. Since independence in 1960, the city-state has rocketed into the ranks of industrialized nations. In the first decade after independence, per capita growth averaged nine percent annually, in the second decade, just over six percent annually. By the early 1990s, the city's per capita wealth already exceeded that of Spain and several other members of the European Union. It shows; there is no evidence of poverty in Singapore.

What got Singapore to the top of its game and kept it there is management. The entire country is run more like a company than a democracy. Its leading political light since independence has been Lee Qwan Yew, who constantly reminds anyone who listens—and many of those who don't—that his main goal is the shareholder value, as it were, of the average Singapore citizen. If this has come at the expense of undiluted democracy. Mr. Lee points to the outstanding success his country has had in building its standard of living.

Perhaps the smartest thing Singapore does is permit the easy flow of information. Singapore has, by some measures, the lowest telecommunications costs in the world. While other countries talk, Singapore is already wired. Furthermore, its people are educated to the highest world standards. In short, Singapore has created a climate in which business can profitably substitute knowledge for other resources.

However, the information economy challenges Lee's vision in ways that will be hard for him or his successors to overcome. As we have seen thus far in *FutureWealth,* falling information costs are the motive force in wealth generation. This much Singapore gets. The country has worked hard to turn itself into an Asian information entrepôt that will live off the information trade the same way it lived off shipping and oil refining in the past.

What it does not get is that falling information costs shift the balance of power to consumers. When costs fall as fast as they are doing today, that shift is absolute, as the Internet demonstrates with stunning clarity every single day.

For Singapore, therefore, becoming an information entrepôt means accepting the absolute power of its citizens, not its government—something that the current regime finds completely unacceptable.

So, we have a complex picture: a well-managed country with strong foreign reserves, low external debt, and well-funded banks; a highly attractive economy in a sea of Asian roller-coaster business cycles; but a nation headed for a major confrontation with the falling cost of information.

If Singapore cannot deal with the political and social issues thus raised, it will rob itself of its own future.

Singapore is fast becoming the test bed for dozens of economies around the world, countries where the future is information but the regime cannot let go of enough power to make this future come about. What happens here will be a bellwether for others. Moreover, regimes like China's have been influenced in the past by Singapore policies, largely because Communist Party leaders felt that Singapore's means of maintaining party discipline while boosting the standard of living could be used by China to keep the Party in power during a period of rapid economic growth.

Singapore's excellent management was rewarded when it quickly recovered from the Asian economic crisis of the late nineties. But dirigisme is everywhere. The government is trying to force local banks to merge in the belief that the country can sustain no more than two,[1] a policy that flies in the face of Web-based banking systems that have no country or physical location.

Clearly then, Singapore, which has gone to all the trouble to wire itself for the modern world, hasn't yet understood what that world will look like.

Hong Kong

Like Singapore, Hong Kong has British roots and, with little or no manufacturing after the Second World War, was just as poor. Immigrants from southern China are in the majority in both cities. And like Singapore, Hong Kong's prosperity was built on free trade with the world, developing its industrial base in textiles, electronics and, ultimately, services. Today, it's hard to believe that just thirty years ago these two cities were as poor as dozens of other Asian and African nations.

With free trade, Singapore and Hong Kong enjoyed the fastest rates of growth over the past generation among developing countries. The countries have similar levels of wealth. But where the government of Singapore masterminded every step of that country's path to growth, Hong Kong was strictly laissez faire.

However, for all its seeming health, Hong Kong faces serious problems. Immediately after its July 1, 1997 handover from Britain to China, Hong Kong's economy collapsed. Property prices fell 55 percent and the economy entered the most serious recession since data have been collected.

China bungled Hong Kong's much needed move to democracy, shackling the country with an unworkable political structure that is coming apart at the seams. At the very point where Hong Kong has to deal with the most serious threats to its economy ever, it has a legislature with no power and an executive who tries to rule by fiat—just the policy that four centuries ago cost so many European kings their heads.

On the economic front, Hong Kong faces hard questions. Traditionally, the city relied on manufacturing and trading. But those manufacturing jobs are moving to mainland China, and Hong Kong is being bypassed by Chinese ports that trade directly with the world; nearby Shenzhen alone has three ports. Hong Kong's re-exports from China grew an average of 25 percent a year from 1970 to 1995, a simply staggering rate of growth over so long a period. Not surprisingly, over the same period, output per worker grew more than two-and-a-half times, even faster than in Singapore. Now these re-exports are shrinking. Shenzhen shipped from 1.8 to 2 million containers in 1998, all out of Hong Kong's hide.[2]

Such structural shifts will make it very hard for Hong Kong to recover its former position.

On paper, there are great opportunities in finance. After all, Hong Kong is Asia's financial hub. But here again, the timing is all wrong, as we have seen: financial industries the world over are being disintermediated and Hong Kong is increasingly being forced to dance to the tune of some anonymous server located anywhere from Utah to Ireland. Charles Schwab can project itself as easily into a living room in Hong Kong as it can a living room in Peoria (it already has a Chinese language Web site). And, as Cisco and others are proving, even the most complex business services can be delivered over the Web to anywhere in the world. What advantage does this give Hong Kong? Little, if any.

Hong Kong hits this turbulence ill-positioned. In the past, it was a colony surrounded by an often hostile China. Its isolated position made labor and property scarce, driving up prices of both. The handover to China and the collapse of the Asian economy hit the country with a double whammy. Hong Kong is no longer isolated from China, forcing it to revalue its labor and property accordingly. This has been a painful adjustment.

Combined with the generalized collapse of the Asian economy, Hong Kong's reemergence as just another Chinese port makes the need to get ahead of information costs pressing. The city has been struggling. Its political classes have no voice; its executive is ineffective, and its administrators struggle nobly on, trying to hold the thing together.

Hong Kong has only been saved from the worst by its effective rule of law. The system, built by the British and left intact in the handover, works remarkably well. But as in every constitutional system in the world, when one branch of government fails, the others move in to fill the gap. In the case of Hong Kong, the emasculation of the legislature and the inability of the executive to manage by fiat without the consensus of the populace has pushed the judiciary into the forefront, where it would not normally be.

In the U.S. we are used to shifts like this. If the Congress and President don't agree on something that people want changed, the courts step in, as they did with racial integration a generation ago and may do again with gun control. But for China the ebbs and flows of constitutional democracy are unfathomable.

Thus, the shift in power to the Hong Kong courts has created conflict with the regime in Beijing, which is forcing the branch of government the least capable of managing the falling cost of information—the Communist party—to assume more day-to-day management of Hong Kong.

So, in this hotbed of capitalism, where government regulation is simply a nonstarter, all three branches of government are moving quickly away from one another, leaving a power vacuum that only China can fill.

While big companies drive Singapore's prosperity, and might be better adapted to Hong Kong's management-by-fiat environment, the entrepreneur is king in Hong Kong. Multinationals are comfortable with Singapore's rigorous regime; Hong Kong's small businessmen are much more jealous of their prerogatives.

Hong Kong wants to maintain its position as the leading Asian "dragon." The uncertainty that surrounds Britain's return of control over Hong Kong to China will continue to surround it for years to come. That giant sucking noise everyone hears in Hong Kong is the flow of jobs going across the border into southern China.

To offset this loss of jobs, Hong Kong must make a rapid transition from low-wage, low-tech, low-quality production to high-wage, high-tech, high-quality—but still low-cost—industry. The only way to make this shift is to boost the productivity of Hong Kong's workforce. Cheap information is integral to this improvement. The people of Hong Kong struggled to build middle-class lives. Will it now all slip away?

9

The Four Keys to Value Creation

When we first proposed that all wealth is generated by the falling cost of information, we faced an immediate challenge. What kind of organization could tolerate the stresses of freefalling costs and the resulting powerful shift of market power into the hands of customers?

This is no small question. When the Reformation hit Europe during that great information-cost discontinuity of the sixteenth century, not a single organization of any type survived intact. What we were looking at therefore was the complete rupturing of every organization on the planet.

It was essential to create the outlines of what kind of structure could survive these forces and how it would work. Hence our Four Keys. These are the tools that unlock value at the heart of any organization and carry it forward into the shearing forces of falling information costs.

We calculated that only organizations designed along specific lines would be capable of getting ahead of falling information costs, harnessing the curve's centrifugal forces, and generating large amounts of shareholder value.

We specified that these organizations would have to be:

1. Vertically and horizontally disintegrated
2. Decentralized
3. Flat, with no more than four layers
4. Designed to deliver customer service

The Four Keys work for the simple reason that they allow information to move quickly from customer to decision maker and back to customer with minimum interference. And they allow companies to scale and scale fast. They also happen to map precisely onto the major flaws we found in Japanese corporate organization and described in our first book, *Beating Japan*.

At that time, no single company met all four of our criteria, though many met one, and sometimes two of them. History has proven us spot on; today there are several companies—the models we discuss in this book—that meet all four criteria and have succeeded beyond all expectation.

The bull market rewarded these companies. By decade's end, Wal-Mart was the ninth most valuable company in the world and fourth in sales. Cisco, relatively small in terms of sales, was the nineteenth most valuable company in the world. Dell was twenty-eighth, far outranking Ford and GM, companies that outsell it many, many times.[1] Charles Schwab had a bigger market cap than brokerage titan Merrill Lynch.

The benefits of our principles of organization are truly extraordinary. Companies that follow them religiously outperform everybody else.

In 1997, Dell was 204 days of sales behind the number-two PC maker, IBM—more than half a year.[2] Dell ended 1998 less than two weeks of sales behind IBM. In only twenty-four months, Dell improved its relative position by an entire year. An astonishing achievement.

Hewlett-Packard has the right products to dominate the fast-growing post-PC market, but needs the organization to deliver them. We are privy to brand research that shows that among consumers with personal computers, Hewlett-Packard has the most recognized brand name, giving the firm exceptional brand equity and a powerful place from which to launch almost any consumer-electronics initiative.

In spite of this advantage, in only one year H-P fell from twenty-fourth most valuable company to fiftieth,[3] and this during one of the biggest growth opportunities in the company's history—it was the second-fastest growing PC supplier in 1998 after Dell; its printers dominated every office and many homes the world over. But H-P just couldn't turn these benefits into shareholder value because its organization didn't work well. While Dell was using information technology to integrate distribution into its manufacturing, H-P was still struggling with resellers for its printers. While Cisco sold highly engineered industrial equipment over the Internet, H-P still relied on channel management and OEMs. In response it was broken up into separate companies and has brought in a new president from outside the company.

Merger-crazy companies think that size will turn them into so many new Wal-Marts, shortening the connection between themselves and consumers. But by doing exactly the reverse of our Four Keys, these mergers do not take into account how the collapsing cost of information changes the way consumers and producers communicate. Thus, mergers all too often compound the problem rather than solve it: a formula for value meltdown.

What the merger-crazy fail to recognize is that Wal-Mart's business is distribution, not retail. Through its clever application of low-cost information, Wal-Mart has streamlined the movement of products from factories to customers in a way that has yet to be duplicated. Wal-Mart does a better job of logistics than many companies in the logistics business—companies like Ryder and Federal Express[4]—because Wal-Mart knows that its business is logistics. Wal-Mart has not expanded through acquisition—with the exception of a few outlets bought at fire sale prices, and strategic acquisitions to enter protected foreign markets like the U.K.—because this expertise could not be bought.

The effect on producers of Wal-Mart and the so-called "category killers"—like Home Depot in hardware, Staples in office supplies and Barnes & Noble in books—is devastating. Producers are rapidly becoming indentured servants to those with direct customer contact. "Brand equity" has shifted from producers to sellers. Value added is in the sales process, not in products.

Indeed, this misreading of the markets is "paving cow paths" at its worst. What is needed for success today is something like the upstart English bank, First Direct, which rapidly gained half a million customers without a branch bank system by doing all transactions over the telephone.[5]

While the worst casualties will be in the retail and wholesale sectors, there will be lots of "collateral damage" elsewhere. Manufacturers that rely on intermediaries may be put out of business. It's bad enough that they are kept on razor-thin margins by their retailers; what's worse is that they have no direct customer feedback on which to base their decisions.

Survivors will be those that can add value to products themselves, by going direct to consumers, at least for part of their sales. Merck & Co., the drug company, took this path when it bought Medco Containment Services, a direct-mail drugstore.

In a similar way, Ticketmaster wants to be America's travel agent. Over the past twenty years, Ticketmaster has revolutionized the market for buying tickets for sporting and other events with low-cost information. The company now has its sights set on airplane tickets, four-fifths of which are now sold by travel agents.[6]

Millions of jobs are at stake here. Retail employment ballooned over the past decade, and is set for a fall. There are 11,000 banks in America, for instance, in which 750,000 people work. The retail sector, like farming at the end of the nineteenth century, will be transformed over the next decade.

This transformation is not just happening in the U.S., but throughout the industrialized world. Even in Japan, one of the last bastions of multilevel distribution, change is afoot. Like Wal-Mart in the U.S., convenience store giant 7-Eleven has used cheap information to transform itself into a distribution company, and has thereby transformed its entire industry. The same process is underway throughout retailing in Japan, where 10 percent of the workforce is employed in retail and an additional 10 percent in wholesale.

The Four Keys to Value Creation emphasize one thing: *value is added in the sales process, not in products.* By their nature, the Four Keys allow companies to add value simply and effectively.

Making sales work when product cycles are increasingly compressed by Moore Time means building longer customer relationships. The longer these relationships, the less likely they are to be disrupted by a sudden shift in price-performance. If Schwab, for example, puts a virtual dealer's desk in your home or office, it locks you into a system you may feel is so good that you become impervious to sudden drops in price from Schwab's competition. In fact, Schwab charges a large premium for its on-line services. It uses information technology to keep customers during any number of Moore Time cycles.

Indeed, most companies are terrified of competing in Moore Time. Their intuition tells them that extending customer relationships will simply add a layer of cost to an already killing environment. Some things, we tell them, are counterintuitive—like revving an engine before down-shifting to slow a car—and longer service cycles are one of them. As the Schwab example shows, the idea is that longer service cycles actually remove cost.

All too often, however, companies react to compressed product cycles by shortening service cycles as well. Doing this makes collapse inevitable and is something investors, and managers, have to watch with care. Usually vendors that rely on chains of distributors—the Hubble Effect—make this mistake.

A sure sign that a manufacturer is a victim of the Hubble Effect and has not made the internal changes described here is to compare its gross and net margins to those of Dell. One of our clients has a gross margin much higher than Dell's, because it is a much better manufacturer, but a net margin that is almost nonexistent. This company is flaming off margin through giant stacks of operating inefficiencies. Product leaves the factory in great shape and runs smack into a killing wall of margin-absorbing management and distribution.

In the years since we published our Four Keys, we have elaborated on them somewhat, following our general principle that extending customer service is the key antidote to Moore Time.

We tell clients that using the Schwab formula, they should design into their products and services customer relationships that are in inverse proportion to collapsing product cycles; that is, they should be designed to stretch to infinity.

We needed a six-year-old laser printer repaired. We had bought the printer mail order and the manufacturer still had on record our name, address, and preferred credit card. A return authorization form was faxed through immediately, and when we didn't return the completed form within the hour the manufacturer called us back to see if there was a problem. That was after six years. This supplier knows how to lock onto a customer through endless product generations, garnering both after-market sales, upsells, and product replacement sales.

Ultimately, extending service cycles means integrating customers into operations the way Proctor and Gamble did for Wal-Mart.

Wal-Mart's problem is simple: how to keep seventy thousand products on its shelves and nothing in inventory. The solution is direct, real-time links between the cash registers in its stores and the factory computers of its suppliers. Products themselves are immaterial.

Procter and Gamble initially resisted this intrusion into its operations. But Wal-Mart prevailed. P&G learned, and soon led the industry in demand-pull order entry systems, shipping 40 percent of all its products this way. P&G gave Wal-Mart a *four to five year lead* over its competitors. Said Wal-Mart CEO David Glass, what P&G has done is "absolutely essential" to Wal-Mart.[7] How many suppliers can say that their customers call them "absolutely essential?"

In effect, extending service cycles and integrating customers into operations means using processes, rather than products, to add value and lock in profits and growth. Process, not product, is the center point on which companies will prosper in the twenty-first century.

Schwab's virtual trading desks are not a stock trade or even a discounted trade; they are a process its customers use every day that also happen to raise the costs to customers of changing brokerages. A win-win for Schwab and its customers, a lose-lose for everyone else.

Automobile manufacturing, one of the world's biggest businesses and most difficult to manage, is an excellent example of process on a gigantic scale. In 1998, four of the world's top ten industrial companies were car makers, accounting for 44 percent of the top ten's sales—some $562 billion.[8] These firms are plagued with cost and quality challenges that drive right through violent cycles in demand.

The pressure to strip down and get closer to customers has turned automobile producers on their heads. What used to be vertically integrated firms with highly centralized management and almost no customer contact of any kind have become increasingly disintegrated—outsourcing large parts of their operations—and more deeply integrated with their customers than ever. Perhaps the best example is the Chrysler minivan. To revitalize its big lead in this fast-growing segment, Chrysler followed up its original minivan success by restricting all redesigns to customer input. If customers didn't ask for it, Chrysler didn't do it. The result: a highly successful product and a market stranglehold.

But companies like Chrysler cannot respond quickly to customers if they have to spend all their time on upstream operations. The answer is to outsource everything from design to manufacturing. Chrysler outsourced coordination of its minivan interior to Textron.[9]

Outsourcing in turn places enormous pressures on parts suppliers. You cannot outsource entire car systems to, say, a brake or stereo manufacturer. The pressure is building on suppliers of these systems to do something more than ship parts in boxes. This pressure will drive down the number of major automobile parts makers from five thousand in the late nineties to two thousand in the next few years.[10]

One of the firms most successful in outsourcing to car manufacturers is Lear Corporation. Lear is the world's largest producer of car seats, selling to Fiat, Ford, Saab and Volvo.[11] Lear saw that it would have to do a lot more for its customers if it was to retain its position, let alone grow. It decided to become the world's first and largest producer of complete car interiors, a $40 billion-a-year market.[12]

Lear takes on all of its customers' design and engineering work and has the "lift" to integrate these right into its customers' manufacturing operations. Smaller suppliers find themselves selling to Lear instead of to Ford or Fiat. The benefit to Lear is tangible. In a decade, its content per vehicle in North America increased from $60 to $285 and in Europe from $7 to $111. Its stock price nearly quadrupled in five years, outperforming its industry by nearly two-and-a-half times.

Next, how to completely lose your bearings on the Internet.

10

Internet Madness

During the bull market, Internet investors stopped thinking. Granted, the Internet has transformed industry; its impact is difficult to overestimate. But the Internet is not self-financing. For the first twenty-five years of its existence, the U.S. government covered expenses. Then investors picked up the tab. Few seemed to know what they were buying or why.

Telecommunications has been growing as a share of the economy since the first telegraph message was sent. This process has continued almost unabated for the past seventy-five years. Consumers and business alike have diverted spending to communications from other activities, creating huge amounts of wealth in the process. The Internet accelerates this shift.

Economic recessions, moreover, may further boost Internet demand. During the 1930s, communications was an "inferior good," something that people substitute—like pasta for pork—when times are bad. While the economy collapsed during the Great Depression, telecommunications boomed, jumping as a percentage of gross domestic product. So in periods of recession, people will replace a personal or business trip with some form of Internet communications.

The fundamentals for Internet investing, therefore, are excellent. As this book says repeatedly, we are at the dawn of the "virtual economy," where information and communications will be substituted for real goods and transportation on a scale never seen before. Because virtual resources are nearly free, the opportunities are nearly limitless.

Whatever the real prospects for the virtual economy, however, Internet investments must generate a profit sooner or later. No matter how important, the Internet is nothing special as an investment. So far, investors have been remarkably patient, if not foolish.

America Online is the world's most successful Internet service provider, by far the leading player.[1] For a long time, AOL's profits were paper-thin and its road to profitability was pretty rocky. After years of losses, AOL turned a profit in the late nineties in a complicated transaction that treated a $380 million asset sale as current income, boosting performance. A couple of years previously, AOL washed out $385 million of deferred marketing expense.[2] With sales in the $5 billion range and profits nearing $400 million, AOL traded at around one hundred fifty years of earnings. A little rich.

At the same time, Yahoo!, the premier "portal" or gateway site to the Web, traded at over five hundred times profits.[3] Yahoo!'s revenue model is based on advertising. But no matter how strong Yahoo!'s brand, the market it relies on was in trouble. Internet ad rates were falling in a glut of unsold Internet banner capacity. Worse, Internet ads that in 1997 got a 2 percent "click through" rate—that is, people would click on them to see the underlying ad 2 percent of the time—got only a half percent click through a couple of years later.[4]

Yahoo!, AOL, and many others were banking on advertising to boost revenues and margins.[5] But even with rapid growth pushing expenditures into the billions, there just isn't enough advertising to go around. Internet viewers can use software to avoid advertising, something unavailable to TV audiences. If Web browsers incorporate this feature, returns for most Internet investors will recede even farther into the new millennium. Ad revenues alone won't give investors the kind of returns they ultimately expect.[6]

Some see electronic commerce as a panacea for persistent losses. Last year, on-line bookseller Amazon.com, a high-profile e-commerce play, had revenues of over $600 million. It also operated at a loss. Nevertheless, its market cap reached $22 billion,[7] equivalent to about half of all U.S. book publisher sales. On top of this, Amazon issued $325 million worth of junk bonds that have no coupon for the first five years.[8] We read in a book that bonds once paid interest, and equities paid dividends.

What made Amazon such a success is that it grabbed 80 percent of the on-line book market, and in spite of the fact that a basket of books actually costs more on Amazon than on lower-priced on-line sellers, it has the brand high ground.[9] Amazon's success has been mirrored by the collapse of the independent bookstore. These saw their market share drop from 33 percent to 17 percent in only two years.[10] So, Amazon's growth has meant profits neither for itself nor for the companies it has displaced.

Plenty of companies profit from e-commerce, but they are *not* Internet plays. Dell Computer sells billions of dollars of PCs on line,[11] and has the highest margins in the PC business to show for it. Charles Schwab, the largest on-line brokerage house, does more than 60 percent its trades on line.

In the short term, these companies may destroy more value than they create. By disintermediating rivals and alternative channels, they do an extraordinary amount of damage. Dell, for example, used the Net to eliminate a layer or two from PC distribution. It has forced competitors to shuffle from fire sale to fire sale as they try to burn off inventory in unsustainable distribution pipelines. Schwab is having the same effect on Wall Street. Of the ten largest on-line brokers, only one is a traditional Wall Street player.[12] But they all share one characteristic. They grow their businesses profitably, making them valuable investments.

This disintermediation is just the beginning. More people are employed in the retail and wholesale businesses than in any other; retailing dominates the urban and suburban landscape worldwide.[13] The future will look entirely different. Like cybertermites, e-commerce will eat away at the distribution edifice that evolved over the last century.

This cyberinfestation is working its way house to house. A Japanese client of ours told us how he orders his computer equipment in Japan from Cyberian Outpost, an on-line computer store based in Connecticut. He receives his orders within days by FedEx, and at prices far less than he would pay in Tokyo's famed Akihabara electronics district. Not surprisingly, Japan is now Cyberian's biggest foreign market.[14]

Thus, the disintermediating power of the Net can strike anywhere in the world, cutting deeply into long-established businesses. There is no better example of the Iron Laws at work than what Cyberian is doing to Japan's rickety distribution system from a server located on the other side of the world.

Disintermediation is even farther along in industrial markets. GE now solicits bids from all over the world on the Internet. GE's lighting division cut material costs by some 20 percent by casting a wider net. Bidding on-line was twice as fast as and took 60 percent fewer people than what it replaced.[15]

In the nineteenth century, more money was made building and using the railroads than running them. Nobody has profited from the Internet like Cisco Systems, which makes the Internet's rails. Cisco is also a user, generating most of its revenues on-line, a remarkable achievement for an industrial company that sells highly engineered products.[16] When Sprint named Cisco prime contractor for a new network to replace its obsolete phone lines, Cisco disintermediated telecom giants Lucent and Nortel Networks, a huge accomplishment for a newcomer.

Despite the lack of returns in pure Internet plays, investors keep on coming. Level 3 Communications, a new Internet carrier, raised $2 billion in 1998, $500 million more than originally planned because demand was so high, and at a near-record low premium over treasuries. L3 made no profit, and had virtually no communications sales, but has a great strategy and an all-star management team.[17] CEO Jim Crowe, who you will see quoted in this book several times, made billions for investors, selling MFS Communications to MCI WorldCom. It is essential to understand that MFS did not make a cent of profit in the telecommunications business itself, accumulating instead half a billion dollars in losses, which were cheerfully absorbed by MCI WorldCom shareholders.

MCI WorldCom, in turn, achieved very high multiples for its stock. According to some measures, MCI WorldCom accounted for more than 50 percent of all Internet backbone traffic in 1998, including that of AOL, one of its best customers.[18] Still, it is said that MCI WorldCom and the other so-called "Tier One" long-distance phone companies lose money on Internet circuits.[19]

So far, the market has rewarded those companies that take the most egregious risks. The reasoning is that the Internet is like the Oklahoma land rush. On April 22, 1889, the U.S. government opened up the Indian territory to American settlers. At noon, as the bugle sounded, tens of thousands raced across the boundary line. The rules were simple: stake your claim, then worry about growing something. On the Internet, this means creating brand and market presence, at all costs, before somebody else gets there.[20]

At work is a kind of Gresham's Law, which says, "cheap money

drives out good." Bad investments may be chasing out investments that service their debt and—imagine!—pay dividends to
shareholders.

Nobody knows what a profitable Internet company looks like.
Once Internet Winter settles in, we may find out. Investors must
ask themselves what will happen when access to capital is shut off
for all their Internet plays.

Expect two things. One: there will be casualties. Two: survivors
will know how to make money. There will be a period of mergers,
bankruptcies, and liquidations. Assets will be repriced to produce
a return. Buyers will have cash to spend, but they will not throw
their money away.

Price increases will not be part of the successful Internet formula. With the amount of extra capacity coming on-line in the
next couple of years, capacity will stay well ahead of demand. Barriers to entry will be easily crossed for *all* Internet activities.

Regulators could alter the pricing equation. Like the Internet,
railroad expansion was about selling securities first and foremost.
By the late 1880s, interest expense was crushing the railroads,
which were financed primarily with junk bonds. At the same time,
fierce competition was slashing margins. In response, the federal
government created the Interstate Commerce Commission to fix
rates. Regulation put an end to "predatory pricing." Freight rates
soon rose, and debt holders were made whole. Then, as now, governments sell this sort of thing as protecting the "little guy."

In the U.S., the FCC could easily stabilize prices and socialize
operating losses by levying fees on Internet calls. Most other countries already meter Internet calls. These charges would be found
money for the phone companies, of course, but would not do any-
body else any good. It is no coincidence that the Internet is largely
an American phenomenon. Elsewhere, fees for local calls depress
demand.

While a government bailout is always possible if Wall Street screams loudly enough, such a bet is hardly the stuff of serious investing. The time has come to look for value. It is not enough to pick the right industry. In his seminal work, *The Intelligent Investor*, Benjamin Graham noted that in the 1950s and 1960s losers outnumbered winners among airlines and mainframe computer companies.[21] Internet investors must find Graham's "margin of error."

Conservative finances are a prerequisite to value investing. Graham orthodoxy says that companies must have strong earnings and—that word again! —a dividend payment record.

To these measures, we add the importance of the velocity of capital that we discussed earlier. Sales should be a high multiple of plant, receivables, or inventory. High turns keep debt and other capital requirements low. Without interest to pay, a company can absorb unexpected shocks. Just as important, fewer assets means less baggage, or as Dell CEO Michael Dell put it, "There are fewer things to manage, fewer things to go wrong."[22]

The Internet has created powerful diseconomies of scale. Therefore, carefully question scale-driven investments. Companies should not own silicon assets with poor residual values. Moore's Law is the investor's residual-value Magna Carta.

Moore's Law does not apply, however, to digging trenches, building radio towers, or knocking on doors. Survivors will outsource everything that does not have a direct effect on customers. At the same time, while customer relations are key, direct sales organizations are enormously expensive. They can quickly be "stranded" by Dell-style Internet disintermediation. This leaves Internet sales and carefully structured distribution agreements with proven partners.

Most Internet investors are betting on the come. At this stage, we believe it is more important to do it right than to do it first. The most profitable PC companies—Intel, Microsoft, and Dell— were not the first to market. Neither was Standard Oil or Ford

Motor Company. Any company that expects to go back to the well for additional funds may be in for a nasty surprise.

The Internet is a key technology. But Internet players must deliver phone-grade reliability. That, and simplicity, are what consumers want.

Last, there is brand on the Internet.

In the past, a brand was a name and a promise. As we will see in Part Three of this book, it's become a process and its execution. Where Coke can promise refreshment and deliver, Schwab's virtual dealer terminals are an entire process that must be executed flawlessly twenty-four hours a day anywhere in the world in whatever environment the customer chooses, from a plush office to the seat of a backhoe on break from earth moving.

Brand today means trust well beyond advertising hype. An effective brand envelopes customers with service. It manages the way a customer experiences a product. Ideally, this should be the case on the Internet, where longer service intervals can offset ever faster product introductions and minimize price competition that we discussed earlier in "Competing in Moore Time."

As we said at the beginning of this chapter, the Internet started as a free service bankrolled by the U.S. government. Now investors are picking up the tab. Some businesses benefit enormously from e-commerce. Many more do well selling Internet-related equipment. Few, if any, profit from the direct provision of Internet services and infrastructure. Some on-line retailers are spending $26 on marketing and advertising for every $1 in orders they receive.[23]

The supply of "greater fools" willing to underwrite Internet losses will eventually evaporate. Beware.

Finally, let us look at how all this wraps into the larger picture of economic theory by revisiting the greatest economist of our century, John Maynard Keynes.

11

A New *General Theory*

In the 1930s, the economist John Maynard Keynes solved the riddle of the Great Depression with *The General Theory of Employment Interest and Money*. The book has been debated on and off for over sixty years, but Keynes—who earned his street cred by predicting that the Treaty of Versailles, which was supposed to end the First World War, would only provoke a second—remains the preeminent economic thinker of all time.

When he wrote *The General Theory*, Keynes was troubled by one thing; "the evidence indicates that full, or even approximately full employment is of rare and short lived occurrence."[1] He strove to explain how an economy could park itself at low rates of unemployment for years without wages dropping so far that all who wanted jobs got them. Endemic unemployment was the central experience of the interwar period, and he made solving the problem his life's goal.

At the turn of the millennium, we had the opposite experience. America, unleashed for the first time since August 1914 from the privations and limitations of hot wars, cold wars, reparations, and regional conflicts of every kind, returned high growth, low unemployment, and negligible inflation for the benefit of its citizens. People who should know better were amazed by the Dow's recent performance.

But even a casual look at the Dow over the half century since the end of the Second World War shows how much value Vietnam sucked out of the U.S. economy. The fact is, since the outbreak of war in 1914, the Dow has been knocked sideways several times by the forced misallocation of resources. As the century drew to a close, we saw what the economy can do, and should long since have done.

What we have to explain, therefore, is how a nation the size of the U.S. could grow like one gigantic Wal-Mart. The answer, as we said on the very first pages of this book, is that we have a new factor input to go with labor, capital, and natural resources: low-cost information.

Our ability to substitute information at will for every other resource is altering the economy in a fundamental way. The falling cost of information improves productivity, keeps inflation low, and drives sales. At its core, the falling cost of information allows us to maintain low unemployment for prolonged periods and see real growth into the bargain.

Some of the productivity benefits are hard to measure but have a huge impact on wealth creation. In our own case, the business we run today with four people would have taken a dozen people to manage ten years ago and twice that many twenty years ago. Some of the things we do now in a minute or two, like create color slides representing new business ideas, twenty years ago would have taken weeks and uncountable numbers of layout artists, editors, photographers, and photoprocessors. Cheap software has made the whole issue go away.

If videoconferencing were as easy as picking up a phone, we

could double our business without adding a single person. This is how the Moore Curve is eating inflation and driving productivity. Just like what we do, what Schwab, Cisco, Wal-Mart, and Dell do today was not doable under any circumstances only a generation ago.

What this calls for is a new General Theory, one that introduces the falling cost of information into Keynes's labor equilibrium equations. Without it, the economics we were taught just don't make any sense.

The flood of cheap information carried by cheap communications has not washed away economic cycles. However, it has eliminated inflation, the curse of post–World War II growth. We are in a period much like that between the Civil War and World War I, when falling transportation costs caused a surge tide of unprecedented expansion. This period was punctuated by mostly short, mostly sharp financial panics. Such a panic occurred in Asia in 1998, initiated by the collapse of several Asian currencies. We expect more to come.

PART TWO

HOW MONEY WILL BE MADE AND LOST IN THE TWENTY-FIRST CENTURY

In Part Two, we show the impact of falling information costs on business and what investors and managers need to know to harness these forces profitably.

Throughout history, as we have said, wealth has been generated by one fundamental force: the falling cost of information. Those who have known how to harness it have made fortunes. Those who have not have been destroyed.

If a CD, for example, can be delivered over the Internet for $5 rather than for $18 through a store, the customer gets $13 to spend on something else. That $13 generates new wealth. When this happens on a large enough scale, it creates the Cornelius Vanderbilts, Henry Fords, Konosuke Matsushitas, and Bill Gateses of the world.

Economists David Ricardo and Karl Marx long ago grappled with this question of wealth creation and its impact. Both believed that capital was the accumulation of generations of labor. For Ricardo, capital was to be managed carefully to generate profits (something he did for himself very nicely, leaving a substantial fortune on his death). Ricardo's theory of competitive advantage has its root in this labor theory of value.

For Marx, capital had a darker, more dramatic side. Sooner or later, he expected, workers would become sufficiently angry at being unable to benefit personally from the means of production—their own accumulated labor, as he and Ricardo believed—that they would take to the streets.

Marx foresaw what Ricardo did not: that there is something in the nature of humans that drives us towards these power shifts on a titanic scale. He also saw that the ultimate beneficiaries had to be the "masses," the bulk of the population. He correctly predicted that if power shifted to the masses, the social, economic, and political impact would be enormous beyond comprehension. Indeed, he was most often criticized during his life and afterwards not for the horror of his predictions, but for being unable to describe in any detail what society would look like once the revolution came to pass.

Living as he did in the age of the telegraph and before the telephone, Marx had no way of knowing that the *force motrice* of change is not worker alienation but the falling cost of information. Combined with near-universal literacy (in the developed world, at least), cheap information technology has broken the chains that bound labor to capital.

Even though communism has now come and gone, a revolution has occurred, just as Marx predicted. Workers do indeed own the means of production: cheap information is a tool useful only when there are literate workers to employ it. The cost of information has fallen far enough to empower Marx's "masses" with microprocessors—the means of information production—and we are living through exactly the period of dramatic upheaval he said would result. Consumer empowerment has restructured governments and companies the world over, as organizations as varied as the Soviet Union and IBM have found to their cost.

The cost of information is a function of *both* processing and communication costs. In recent decades, processing costs have fallen sharply, but Moore's Law has not been applied effectively to communications. Regulation and the common carrier debt has severely restricted telecommunications competition, artificially inflating prices. Consequently, communications costs have fallen less dramatically than they might otherwise have done. Anyone who has experienced the frustration of crawling through an Internet video with today's network speeds knows just how much productivity remains to be tapped.

That's why we believe that there is a pent-up burst of industrial efficiency waiting to be unleashed. Decades of investment by industry in computers have not produced the productivity benefits they should have.

Now we are entering a period when the full impact of falling information costs will be realized. Deregulation is ending the pricing power of today's communications monopolies and oligopolies. And the world over, carriers are looking at ways of monetizing their debt mountains to free up the cash to bring improvements to communications.

These changes will hit hard and fast in the near future as the world's information infrastructure is rapidly reordered. Companies that know how to take advantage of these shifts will grow very quickly. Those that do not will vanish in a twinkling.

12

The Big Bang

In the mid 1990s, microprocessors drove the cost of information low enough to affect consumer markets for the first time, *giving ordinary people* absolute *power over information production and dissemination.*

Consumers responded to this power shift not by taking to the streets as in revolutions past, but in an explosion of demand for new products and services. We call this event the Big Bang.

The Internet is the Big Bang's first shock wave. Many aftershocks will follow, and with each we will see the rise and fall of generations of Microsofts and Intels as the Big Bang tears into consumer-electronics and entertainment markets.

Since the Big Bang, matter has been moving outward from the center of the universe, expanding the periphery of space-time. Similarly, the Big Bang of information, which just occurred, is rapidly pushing intelligence out from the big computers of thirty years ago to the tiny devices of today, and rapidly expanding cyberspace by doing so. This Big Bang phenomenon will reorder industry and impact investors the world over.

THE BIG BANG

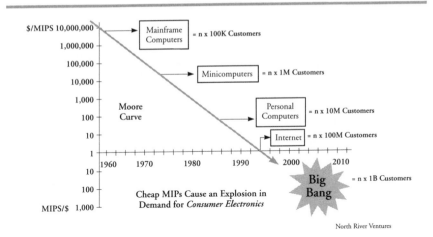

Cheap MIPs Cause an Explosion in Demand for *Consumer Electronics*

North River Ventures

The primal force behind the Big Bang—ever cheaper computers—has been with us for decades. But, while microprocessor price-performance improvement has been steadily doubling every eighteen months for nearly a half century, its effect, as we have seen, has been confined to the computer industry. Twenty years ago, a computer that could process a million instructions per second (called a MIP) cost a million collars.[1] Midway through 1995, however, this price crashed through the dollar-per-MIP barrier, making computer power widely accessible to consumers for the first time and unleashing the full force of the Big Bang.

The Big Bang hit hard as the Internet—a sleepy system used mostly by academics to communicate their findings to one another—suddenly exploded onto the market, ripping into industry after industry. By expanding cyberspace the Big Bang is generating stupendous opportunities well beyond the computer business.

No corner of the globe is insulated from the Big Bang. To understand how fast this change is occurring, we created the concept of Moore Time which we described in Part One.

What you will see in the next few years is cyberspace expanding in Moore Time. To grasp the impact of this, we'll do some simple arithmetic.

There are about 1.2 billion middle-class consumers in the world. Let's say there are four members to each family, so 1.2 billion people gives us 300 million homes. Personal computers might rapidly penetrate 50 percent of those homes, making a market for 150 million machines.

Thereafter PC growth will slow markedly. There might come a day when 70 percent of homes have PCs, but this is some time off. After 50 percent of homes are covered, we can safely say that the PC market won't grow much faster than the single-digit growth of the global middle class.

This tells us that there are distinct limits to the number of PCs, and that we are approaching those limits now.

Let's look at this while keeping in mind the Big Bang. As the price-performance of computer power improves, devices get even smaller, cheaper, and more powerful. As we will see when we look at Sony in Part Three, it is possible to think of all of those 1.2 billion consumers having many devices, from toys to phones, that are much more potent than today's PC. Instead of a PC market of hundreds of millions, therefore, the Big Bang heralds a post-PC market of many billions.

Replacement cycles, too, will be different. A PC maker can count on a certain percent of customers replacing their computers every three years or so. A post-PC maker can count on a high proportion of products being replaced in only a year. Many post-PCs will be disposable.

The question investors have to ask is who will make it in this business, and are any of the current players capable of making the transition to post-PCs in Moore Time. Remember, as we saw in Part One, Moore Years are measured in calendar months, but each calendar year is several Moore Decades. The loss of a single calendar year means death.

Like the universe itself, cyberspace is not infinite, but it has no boundary. The Big Bang will push power well beyond devices like PCs and PlayStations. Consumer-electronics giants like Matsushita, Sony, Philips, and Toshiba see enormous opportunities to revive their product lines by integrating network intelligence into them.[2] Games suppliers like Nintendo and Sega are already designing their products to become information hubs of every home in the consuming world.[3] Intel is making new kinds of chips that take the company far beyond the personal computer market that it dominates.[4] Microsoft is repositioning itself as a post-PC company. Progress like this will revolutionize lifestyles.

It is by no means certain that the dominant consumer-electronics companies of today will make the Big Bang transition easily. Most have only just begun to deal with the digitization that has coursed its way through computers and telecommunications for decades. All are used to markets, like TVs, where standards and price-performance change at a snail's pace. Most have no software experience to speak of. Their corporate cultures are maladapted to competing in Moore Time and are in need of major revision.[5] Nevertheless, as we shall see, these firms have launched major offensives across a broad front. It's do this, or die. Many will die.

As the force of the Big Bang tears into market after market, there will be excellent opportunities for newcomers, and investors should be looking for these now. The right ones will generate enormous amounts of Big Bang value in Moore Time—very, very fast.

Market Impact: consumer electronics, communications, entertainment, media, utilities, financial, health care, education.

13

Black Hole in Cyberspace

The Black Hole in Cyberspace is a point-of-information price-performance so powerful that it swallows underperforming companies whole.

The Black Hole is the grim reaper of the information age, inexorably destroying companies that are unable to keep ahead of information costs. By radically changing pricing power, the Internet is creating a Black Hole in Cyberspace that is destroying value on the one hand and creating powerful new opportunities on the other.

The Black Hole has been inhaling computer companies for decades. For the first time, the Black Hole is drawing in others, from consumer electronics to entertainment. At stake are millions of jobs and hundreds of billions in shareholder value. Investors need to understand Black Holes.

When Internet IPOs can generate billions in value in their first minutes of trading, investors need to know exactly how the Black Hole in Cyberspace creates and destroys value—or get sucked into it themselves.

Here is a painful example of the Black Hole at work. In mid-1995, a colleague of ours sent a ten-page fax to Germany, noted the elapsed time, computed the long-distance charge, and told us that this single ten-page fax would pay for five hours' use of America Online as it was then priced.

His alert prompted us to make the price comparison on page 86 for sending a forty-two-page business plan that we had to hand from our office in New York to three locations: within New York itself, to Los Angeles, and to Tokyo. We compared the cost of sending the document via six different channels, all of which we use. The results were startling. This chart is our original Black Hole in Cyberspace.

Jim Crowe, CEO of Level 3, told *USA Today* and *Barron's* that our Black Hole chart was his "epiphany." He said, "That's when I realized this was not driven by the cool people on the cover of *Newsweek*. It was driven by economics. When we figured it boiled down to bucks, all of us took notice."[1] Take note he did. He turned our chart into $14.4 billion, as we shall see.

With our Internet service, which then costs $25 per month for up to sixty hours of use, we could upload forty-two pages to anyone in the world with an e-mail address in two minutes. We could do the same via America Online, but the cost was much higher—though still trivial. Until this time we would have either sent it via FedEx or fax, two alternatives which are now distinctly unappealing.

There were ways to shop around within the table. While sending a forty-two-page document cost about the same to Tokyo via FedEx or fax, a twenty-pager would go for half as much by fax. But no matter what you did, the Internet was always cheaper than any alternative.

Customers know exactly what to do with pricing like this. We mentioned in the previous chapter that in November 1994, six

THE BLACK HOLE IN CYBERSPACE

COST OF DELIVERY FOR A 42-PAGE DOCUMENT IN 1995

New York to:	New York	Los Angeles	Tokyo	Comments
Internet [2]	1.4¢	1.4¢	1.4¢	2 minutes at 9600 baud
America Online[3]	6¢	6¢	6¢	2 minutes at 9600 baud
U.S. Mail[4]	$3.00	$3.00	$7.40	first class/air mail
Federal Express[5]	$15.50	$15.50	$26.25	overnight letter
AT&T (peak)[6]	NA	$9.86	$28.83	31 minute fax at 14.400 baud; CustomNet Service
AT&T[7] (off-peak)	NA	$6.88	$28.09	31 minute fax at 14.400 baud; CustomNet Service
NYNEX (peak)[8]	44¢	NA	NA	31 minute fax at 14.400 baud; day rates
NYNEX (off-peak)[9]	16¢	NA	NA	31 minute fax at 14.400 baud; night rates

months before computer price-performance passed the MIP barrier, there were only 21,000 commercial Internet addresses.[10] By April 1995 there were some 42,000—an accession rate of 4,200 domains a month. By July 1995, the point at which the MIP barrier was crossed, that number had jumped 48 percent to 62,000—an accession rate of nearly 6,700 domains a month and an increase in the rate of accession of 60 percent. This was the First Iron Law of Information at work: cheap bits chasing out expensive bits.

Today we routinely see a hundred thousand new domains a month, and that is without the impact of the next wave of Big Bang post-PC products.

The impact of this shift was devastating. Nothing, for example, did more for telephone companies than the fax eruption of the last decade. As fax machines became ubiquitous, demand for new lines for them exploded, too. Every one of these is like an annuity to the telephone company and its investors, generating revenue month in and month out as well as a huge increase in network use. By mid-decade, fully half of all telephone traffic in cities like Washington was fax.

But, as the example of the forty-two-page fax to Germany showed, the facsimile machine is the supernova stage of traditional communications. The force being discovered in the information universe was the Black Hole, a price point that can devour fax whole. That Black Hole was the Internet.

Look at all the communications companies below the Internet price line on the Black Hole chart. Since we first published the Black Hole, NYNEX has disappeared, AT&T has been split up and seen two CEOs fired, and AOL ran into pricing and capacity difficulties and sold off its network. Ironically, shippers—Fedex and the Post Office—have benefited from e-commerce.

How did Jim Crowe turn the Black Hole into $14.4 billion? He was at the time CEO of MFS, a supplier of high-speed communications services to business. He repositioned MFS to take advantage of Black Hole pricing and a year later attracted MCI WorldCom, which shelled out the big ones for his company, making him a very wealthy man.[11] Jim and his original investors have since started Level 3, which has roared into the market with a value of $22 billion, half a century's worth of sales! We will look more closely at Jim's strategy in Part Three.

The next frontier will be video. Since video depends on low-capacity telephone lines for the "last mile" to PC users, the Internet will look elsewhere for high-bandwidth video connections. DirecTV (now working with AOL), cable (with AT&T's acquisition of TCI and MediaOne and Paul Allen's acquisitions of cable properties), and a new generation of high-capacity wireless called MMDS, will have clear advantages. As these spread, many low-capacity phone companies will find themselves cut off from both ends of the market at once—cheap fax substitutes at one end and high-value video-on-demand services at the other.

This process will unleash another restructuring of the communications business bigger than the so-called "deals of the century" that ripped through that industry. Phone companies are heavily capitalized companies in nearly every market worldwide. An attack on so much of their business will force a restructuring that should free up lots of new investment vehicles. We expect, for example, that as Black Hole pricing forces its way into video, our local phone company will securitize its assets to free up the cash to fight back. A new generation of IPOs for these assets will hit the market, many of which will have huge capitalizations from day one, real assets, and enormous growth possibilities. There's gold in those copper wires.

That the Internet will divert much traffic from the old phone networks, and create much more new demand as well, is therefore a certainty. When the cost of anything drops to one thousandth of what it was or less,[12] opportunities for new demand are unpredictable, even unimaginable.

All of the foregoing explains the mania for Internet shares. These stocks gave the market its first real opportunity to exploit the forces of the Black Hole. That's why the feeding frenzy on the Street pushed an essentially salesless firm that sells Internet browsing software, Netscape, to a market valuation of $2.7 billion the first minute its shares opened.[13]

When Netscape hit the market in 1995, we predicted that it was only the first such opportunity, and that during the next eighteen to twenty-four months the market would be swamped by similar offerings designed to take advantage of Black Hole pricing. We were dead on: Netscape has since been bought by AOL, but the "dot com" mania persisted.

This process will be turbulent. After it rips through telecommunications, the integration of video into the Internet will rip into industries from real estate to automobiles.

Market Impact: communications, media, financial, transportation, energy, entertainment.

14

Event Horizon

The Event Horizon is the circumference of the Black Hole in Cyber-space. It is the place where companies teeter before they disappear. Some, like IBM, manage to pull themselves clear. Others, like DEC, do not. Viacom, Disney, Time Warner, and Kodak are approaching the Event Horizon.

Here's how the Event Horizon works. Viacom bought video-rental chain Blockbuster in 1994 for $8.4 billion just as DirecTV's satellite service took all the growth out of that business and right after Viacom spent another $9.6 billion for filmmaker Paramount. After years of trying to adapt Blockbuster's revenue model for a market where a satellite can deliver videos for a fraction of what a store can, Blockbuster was spun off. Its new value: about $3 billion.[1]

When Viacom bought Blockbuster, the Dow was trading at 4000. With a 10,000-plus Dow when it was sold, Viacom should have been able to price Blockbuster at $21 billion. Effectively, Viacom lost not the $5.4 million on the face of the Blockbuster transaction but the $18 million in potential shareholder value that it took to pull Viacom away from the Event Horizon.

In effect, the falling cost of information forced Viacom to defend itself with its weakest hand. Viacom had loaded up on $10 billion in debt[2] to manage its flurry of acquisitions and almost immediately began to see financial problems. Soon the company was moving to spin off its cable networks to TCI, sell Madison Square Garden, and close 10 percent of its Blockbuster outlets. Even after $3 billion in asset sales, net debt remained stubbornly stuck in the $10 billion range.[3] By early April 1997, Viacom's stock had slid 58 percent, closing in on half its pre-binge high.[4] Blockbuster management was tossed out and Viacom started talking about selling off the company. Not long after, Viacom was reduced to going cap in hand to Hollywood studios to ask them to reduce the prices they were charging Blockbuster.[5]

In the next few years, Viacom sold USA Network to Seagram, and the bulk of Simon & Schuster to Pearson. Having, in effect, broken up its media empire to unload debt, the company was able to beat Blockbuster into shape and float shares in the once troubled division.

While Viacom has come back from the Event Horizon, enormous amounts of value have been absorbed in the effort.

What went wrong? First, the Event Horizon is a magnet for debt-laden companies. The falling cost of information is a deflationary force that makes large amounts of debt a huge disadvantage. Second, the Internet disintermediates everything it touches, favoring economies of scope, not of scale. Viacom chose debt and scale, driving it to the brink of destruction.

Kodak faces similar challenges. In its case, the digital camera eliminates the need for film, film processing, and film-processing products like papers and chemicals. In other words, the core of

Kodak's revenue stream is about to evaporate into a stream of bits and bytes flowing from digital cameras to in-home printers, and over the Internet to relatives and friends.

Kodak has a second weakness. Whatever action Kodak takes to defend itself against the digital camera challenge, it has a large network of film processors, from mom-and-pop outfits to professional labs, which have been the engines of cash flow. It can either protect these or cut them off.

While it must deal with these strategic problems, it also has to fight off archcompetitor Fujifilm, which is also seeking to fend off digital incursions. Thus Kodak doesn't have the luxury of using assured cash flows from a declining film-processing market which it can redirect into some kind of digital strategy, or maybe out of film altogether. Fuji can be counted on as a spoiler.

To manage these very substantial risks, in 1993 Kodak brought in George Fisher, the highly successful CEO of Motorola, to be its new CEO. On the face of it, this made sense. Who better to engineer Kodak's transition into the digital age than someone who had masterminded it. Fisher wasted no time in selling assets and soon unloaded $8.7 billion worth of them, slashing debt by 80 percent. In three years, Kodak's stock price doubled.[6]

But the main challenge to Kokak wasn't in unloading assets or in developing digital alternatives to film. The challenge was to reform distribution, while reaping the remaining profits from film processing. Unfortunately, Fuji struck hard in 1997 with major price cuts that tore the growth and cash flow out of Kodak's core business.

One of Fisher's biggest disappointments was an early decision to use the Internet to support Kodak's dealers and processors by making it easier for consumers to work with them.[7] Shoring up its cumbersome distribution network was a costly defensive battle Kodak could never have won because it did not deal with the issue: film processing and the dealers that support it are simply too expensive. This strategy left Kodak to hope that cheap color-printer technology would not live up to its promise. But this technology was proven, dooming Kodak's distributor defense from the start. The result: 19,900 jobs were lost in late 1997.

Finally, Kodak recognized that the Internet disintermediates. Its AOL joint venture, You've Got Pictures, is a big step in the right direction.

Has Kodak retreated from the Event Horizon? Probably not. It has not solved the Fujifilm conundrum and won't—Fuji is just as desperate. Kodak seems no closer than it was a decade ago to solving the core question: what happens when photoprocessing disappears into the bitstream? But with AOL, Kodak is taking the high ground.

Under these circumstances, the accomplishments of Lou Gerstner at IBM are Herculean. Gerstner is the only person we know who has halted and then reversed his company's fall into the Black Hole in Cybersapce. IBM today is a growth company again.

Market Impact: telephone companies, consumer electronics, entertainment, photoprocessing.

15

The Dead Zone

There is a fast-growing gap between the power of computers and the speed of communications. While computer power improves at exponential rates, the home-to-home and business-to-home networks that connect computers are lagging farther and farther behind. *This is the Dead Zone, a place where wealth creation goes into a stall.*

Every kind of industry is affected by the Dead Zone: so long as computers cannot talk to each other at their full potential, camcorders cannot communicate, mail-order companies cannot offer the virtual shopping they are capable of, and Hollywood cannot bypass cinemas to deliver *Titanic* into living rooms. The Dead Zone slows car companies trying to build closer relations with car buyers. It cripples pharmaceutical companies trying to restructure distribution directly to customers' homes. It devastates entertainment companies trying to reverse years of declining TV viewing. It prevents doctors from "seeing" their patients. And it hurts schools trying to enhance learning and cap ever increasing costs to taxpayers.

At the miserable speeds your phone company now provides, why would you buy another computer more powerful than the one you have? Next question: what does it mean to shareholders in Microsoft, Intel, and all the other high-tech darlings if the Dead Zone kills off demand for more powerful personal computers and post-PC devices?

Microsoft and Intel don't grow on contracting markets for their products. And neither do their shareholders. But that is the prospect these companies face unless your local phone company can somehow extricate itself from the Dead Zone.

The Dead Zone has the power to drive the economy into a recession that will last as long as it takes to eliminate the Zone. At current levels of common carrier debt, and pure inertia, this recession could easily last a generation. It is the main reason why Bill Gates has invested in cable television: anything to force the pace.

As the Dead Zone grows, it exerts enormous centrifugal forces on communications companies, compelling them to deliver data at speeds they cannot handle and at prices they cannot afford. Many will not survive. Worldwide, these companies account for trillions' worth of shareholder value.[1] That's real money.

The Dead Zone is an opportunity for investors willing to bridge the technology gap between computers and communications, as the full power of the Internet, wireless, satellite, and other technologies is unleashed during the next decade.

Companies stuck in the Dead Zone will find themselves whipsawed yet again by market forces. Those free from its grip will grow rapidly, yielding higher than market returns.

To see the killing forces of the Dead Zone at work, take Bell Atlantic. The price-performance of personal computers connected to Bell Atlantic's network increased several thousand times in the eleven years following its divestiture from the Bell System. During the same period, the cost to Bell Atlantic of connecting an additional customer to the same old phone service with roughly the bandwidth of a hundred years ago fell only 3.2 percent a year.[2]

Like phone companies the world over, Bell Atlantic was caught in the Dead Zone. The Zone opened up in 1983, just about the time Bell Atlantic was divested by AT&T. What is truly frightening for investors, however, is that companies like this moved further into the Dead Zone at the rate at which microprocessor performances improves. That is to say, their rate of acceleration into the Black Hole in Cyberspace doubles every eighteen months!

Investments stuck in the Zone have a real problem. Customer demands grow with the power of customers' computer-driven devices. Yet phone company ability to deliver depends on network price-performance that has gone nowhere in decades. This has to be a major warning sign of trouble ahead. To get out of the Zone, phone companies must achieve much higher price-performance themselves.

For the moment, phone companies in the Zone are in an artificially strong position. So long as they do not—because of government sanction or lack of technology—pass on to their customers the benefits of microprocessor price-performance, they generate huge monopoly rents. The smart ones are raising cash to upgrade their networks.

To see how big and attractive these rents are, we asked ourselves a simple question that had the effect of applying the Moore Curve to phone service. The size of the monopoly windfall we got from this little bit of arithmetic was an eye-opener.

Assume for a moment that your cable company charges $30 a month for a two-way connection. We can safely say at this point that you would only be willing to pay a competing two-way carrier in proportion to the capacity it offered. So, if your two-way cable TV delivered thirty million bits of information a second for $30 a month, you would only pay someone who delivered thirty thousand bits something like 1¢ a month.

This tells us that the phone service for which the average American pays $20 a month is worth no more than 1¢ a month in the open market. It generates a monopoly rent of around $19.99 a month or about $240 a year. For a company with, say, 15 million phone lines in service, this amounts to $3.6 billion. In the U.S. alone, therefore, carriers are generating these rents at the rate of about $38 billion annually.[3] Global figures would at least double or even triple this figure.

This is not a new market either; it has already been budgeted and paid for by hundreds of millions of well-heeled middle-class consumers the world over. Predators look at this and see hundreds of billions in cash flow just waiting to be siphoned off.

Companies in a Dead Zone like this have few choices. The real value of their products and services are worth only a small fraction of what they are being sold for, making them exceptionally vulnerable to competition. Not unnaturally, they fight back with everything they've got. In the case of phone companies, that means raising every regulatory and administrative barrier possible to keep those monopoly rents coming.

For investors, the prospect that a company as heavily capitalized as a phone company is only really worth a cent a month per customer—basically nothing—should be truly frightening.

As the late advertising genius David Ogilvy liked to say, "The consumer is not a moron."[4] A pent-up price-performance factor of 3,000 for basic phone service will force people to seek alternatives. When they do, phone company shareholder value will evaporate.

The Internet has shown the way. It has allowed long-distance consumers to use the fast-growing power of their personal computers to "right-price" service well ahead of high-bandwidth availability.

How many industries are stuck in the Dead Zone? Dozens. High-speed TV-Internet combined with prepackaged engineering reports could eliminate the 5 percent commission of real estate agents, cutting closing costs on a home to a fixed price of a few hundred dollars. Large national real estate chains, worth lots as bricks and mortar, could be reduced to nothing overnight. Already something like 25 percent of all car buyers go to the Internet before buying a car. Some even buy their cars over the Net. With TV over the Internet, General Motors could get by with a few test-drive centers and delivery by Federal Express to support its Internet sales. All the efforts made by investors to build nationally branded car dealerships would wind up in the Dead Zone.

In the telephone business, the Dead Zone has precipitated a series of exits by the largest of players: NYNEX, Pacific Bell, GTE, US West, and Ameritech in the U.S., and Telecom Italia in Europe.

Fast two-way connections are coming quickly to close out the Zone in communications. In Europe, several years ago, DirectPC introduced for consumers a two-way VSAT (Very Small Aperture Terminal) satellite service from the Eutelsat II satellite, running at rates of between 6Mbbs and 12Mbps.[5] In the U.S. AOL and DirecTV are working on video Internet for DirecTV's 7.5 million satellite customers. AT&T has spent $120 billion on cable TV companies TCI and MediaOne. Sprint has bought some high-powered wireless licenses which, with the smart antenna technology now coming on stream, could bring two-way TV to neighborhoods quite inexpensively. Telephone companies around the world are investing in DSL (Digital Subscriber Line), to rejuvenate their copper plant.

The predators are gathering for this business, as they will gather for many others. Investors need to think through their portfolios carefully, asking which of their investments are stuck in the Dead Zone? Which have cash flows that could be quickly redirected elsewhere as the cost of information falls and an information-rich technology like the Internet sucks them up?

Eliminating the Zone will revolutionize consumer electronics and software. Companies serving these markets will gain spectacularly once the Internet and TV are combined, and they will have endless new sales opportunities (see Part Three). Zone-trapped carriers are already finding themselves arrayed against consumer-electronics and software powerhouses in whose interest it is to relieve them of their monopoly rents as quickly as possible.

Soon, every home will be a television station and every camcorder will be a network address. Whole ranks of industry will find themselves in the Dead Zone.

Market Impact: energy, transportation, communications, financial, health care, education, manufacturing, entertainment.

16

Market Physics

When Jim Crowe called our Black Hole in Cyberspace his "epiphany," he took the idea on the road, explaining it to MFS investors, and later to Level 3 investors, wherever he went. At one of these meetings, held at New York's Waldorf-Astoria hotel, he did us the great favor of saying that there was no mystery to our proposition; it was simple "market physics."

A look at the Moore Curve in the "Big Bang" chapter shows how Market Physics work.

The Curve shows that *each drop in information costs unleashes a new market in an order of magnitude larger than itself.* Thus, where there were only ten thousand big computers, called mainframes, several decades ago, at the next order of magnitude shift in price-performance, the market size jumped to hundreds of thousands of smaller, midsized computers. The next shift down unleashed millions of personal computers; and the next, tens of millions of home computers.

So each improvement in price-performance generates ever

larger markets. Cyberspace, while not infinite, as we have seen, has no boundaries.

The size of the opportunities unleashed attracts investment money and drives existing market dominators into a frenzy of denial or anticipation, and sometimes both. The denial comes when they don't want to believe that there is another market bigger than their own, and try to insist that the evil day will never come and that their position at the top of the heap is impregnable. This sort of hubris nearly killed IBM.

The anticipation occurs when they try to leap from the existing business, which they are good at, into the much larger new one, about which they probably know nothing and which they are not designed to handle. Microsoft, for example, wants very much to dominate the post-PC business because this market will be so much larger than PCs. Both denial and anticipation happen in companies unable to make up their minds: they see the way things are going but don't have the nerve to cannibalize their own business to get there.

The Moore Curve also reveals that *no player dominant at* any *point has ever been able to dominate the next market down the curve.*

In the sixties and seventies, an entire generation of mainframe suppliers—the so-called BUNCH: Burroughs, Univac, NCR, Control Data, and Honeywell—was crushed as the companies were unable to stay clear of the Event Horizon and slipped into a price-performance Black Hole.

In the eighties, information costs fell still farther, and this time it was the minicomputer makers—Wang, Datapoint, Data General, and DEC—that went to the Event Horizon.

Companies now approaching the Event Horizon include consumer electronics suppliers, common carriers, and, as we have seen, a wide range of other hitherto untouched companies.

Thus, what Microsoft is trying to do—move from dominance of hundreds of millions of desktops to dominance of billions of post-PCs—has never been done before and is unlikely to be done now. This is what sits at the center of Microsoft's battles with the U.S. Justice Department. If it cannot evolve its software from computers to consumer electronics, Microsoft will be unable to jump from the office market to the much larger post-PC market.

Putting this in raw terms, if a PC market of hundred of millions of machines made Microsoft worth more than half a trillion dollars, the post-PC market of billions of machines stands to make Microsoft worth many, many times that. Microsoft would have to be mad not to want to capture this market. Market Physics say this won't happen, however.

Market Physics say that you can use the Big Bang chart and our discussion of Moore Time to assess acquisitions. A smart company will always invest down the curve into the next biggest market. These markets also challenge existing organizational structures, as we have been at pains to point out.

But some companies do the unnatural: they buy back up the curve, as AT&T did when it bought NCR and Compaq did when it bought DEC. Not only are these firms buying the "past" —buying into price-performance points that have long since seen their day—but they are spending shareholder money to acquire decades of disadvantages in Moore Time. These acquisitions are easy to spot because they are all over the media when they happen, and they are easy to assess on our Big Bang chart. Companies that move back are buying a world of higher information costs and destroying value.

Those companies that have survived the transition from one part of the information-cost curve to another have done so as essentially different businesses.

Hewlett-Packard is a case in point. H-P was best known as a somewhat faceless maker of test equipment and minicomputers for the scientific and engineering markets. H-P reemerged as a consumer-electronics brand. If H-P becomes a post-PC market dominator, it will be because it has completely transformed itself from its past.

Market Impact: local telephone service, cable television, wireless, telecommunications equipment suppliers, investment banking.

17

Entropy and the Internet

That the Internet disintermediates everything it touches we have already seen. What is not often so well understood, however, is that in doing so *the Internet drives powerful diseconomies of scale*.

The simplest way to see this in action is to look at the impact of the Internet on television.

Within a few years we will get our television over the Internet. That means that the TV stations you like to watch will be just a Web site like any other, including the one put together by the kid next door.

As information becomes cheaper along the Moore Curve and processing power moves into smaller and smaller devices, each device acquires the power of a television station. As the Internet acquires more and more horsepower, it is better able to handle all the millions of "TV stations" that come on stream.

We will discuss the implications of this in later chapters—"The Singularity" and "Network Television"—but the short of it is this: how does a TV network like CBS manage in a world where it is

ENTROPY & TELEVISION

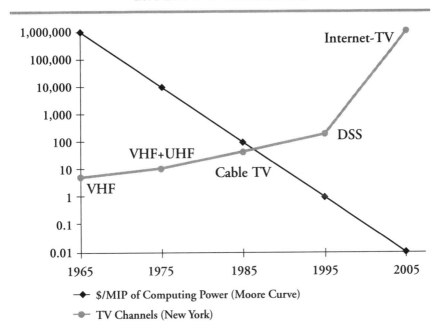

- ◆ $/MIP of Computing Power (Moore Curve)
- ● TV Channels (New York)

just another Web site among millions? How does it have hit shows in such a world? How does it advertise?

By its nature, the Internet destroys the economies of scale on which these companies were built. You can see this in the way Dell makes computers to custom order, using the Net to get the same production economies out of a single unit that another company might get by making millions of identical models. You can see this in the way Charles Schwab uses the Net to give individual customers their one-off, personal trading desk experience. The Internet does not favor any company built on scale.

For investors and managers, the message is pretty clear: don't listen to the siren call of scale economies; they are yesterdays' business. BCE, Canada's largest company, has one word printed in capital letters on the front of its annual report: "SCOPE." Scale,

BCE seems to be saying, is for suckers, a formula for value destruction. Amen.

Internet markets are a long way from consolidation. There's still plenty of time for upstarts to stake out their turf while growth is rapid and the big players scramble for strategies. Barriers to entry are almost nonexistent. Capital intensity is low.

The road ahead remains obscure. But what is clear is that yesterday's household names will not survive without completely transforming themselves. AOL is already on the way to becoming an entertainment powerhouse, far removed from its Internet beginnings.

Investors must choose from among many unfamiliar faces. In short, they must make order out of chaos.

Market Impact: local and long-distance telephone, broadcasting, cable television, entertainment, retail.

18

The Living Room Revolution

There are over a billion middle-class consumers in the world today. At the rate countries like China are developing, this number will soon be two billion. India already has a larger middle class than the United States.

The first company to dominate direct electronic access to these consumers will become the largest industrial enterprise ever known. The Living Room Market will be the biggest wealth generator of all time.

Many companies have tried to dominate direct electronic access. Most have failed, misjudging the nature of the opportunity: a Living Room dominated by dirt-cheap microprocessors and lightening fast optical communications.

Moreover, as we saw in "The Big Bang," the sheer number of computer-driven devices consumers will have in the next few years extends to the billions, with mind-boggling money making opportunities to match.

Falling information costs derailed the wealth creating calculations of many companies. Their strategies went off the track because the Living Room market they targeted is being roiled by enormous change. In this market, consumers, not their suppliers, decide what they will get and what they will do with it.

For investors, this is an opportunity akin to the railroads in the nineteenth century. But they should remember that most railroads made money selling paper, not moving people and freight. The real money was made elsewhere.

Cast your mind's eye about your home. Whose brand dominates? You don't "see" your phone company; indeed the only time you notice its name at all is on a bill. Your cable company isn't much better; all you see is its dirty signal (unless you are lucky enough to live in Canada, where the signal is excellent). Microsoft winks on and off again between crashes, if you have a PC. Network TV has a presence, unless you have a high-powered satellite dish capable of getting their signals clean and clear with CD-quality sound, in which case they refuse to serve you at all. What about hardware makers like Sony and Panasonic. These are just names on a box, though Sony is making huge moves to change this (see Part Three).

Who does have a Living Room brand? DirecTV has a clear and noticeable presence on every customer's TV, which may account in part for the problems DirecTV caused the video rental business. It probably also accounts for why CBS president and CEO Mel Karmazin—even though he says he watches "CBS from sign-on to sign-off," refuses even to answer requests to let DirecTV customers do the same.[1] Movie studios are barely noticeable as content providers on satellite, and not at all on the Internet. Some got bogged down in acquisitions.

Many have a misguided notion of market control, which they think comes from force-feeding content to their customers. NBC is going with the flow of consumer choice, providing a whole set of clearly interlinked information services like NBC America, NBC World, MSNBC, MSNBC.com, and CNBC. Though its strategy for building long-lasting customer relations through these media is unclear, NBC can choose from many options.

In the hardware business, no one has a strong position. The Living Room is divided into small fiefdoms served by a wide range of companies—makers of TVs, phones, stereos, personal computers, and computer peripherals—none of which has a position of dominance or even a good jumping-off point.

There is no dominant brand in the Living Room market today and the market is changing in Moore Time, destabilizing everyone who has attempted to dominate it.

This vacuum cannot last. Someone will step in to eliminate the vacuum, and when they do, the most powerful value engine of the new century will emerge.

Symptomatic of the many miscalculations in this market is the miscomprehension of the role of standards. All the Living Room "wannabes"—in communications, computing, consumer electronics, and entertainment—fight each other mightily to extend their private standards, such as Microsoft's CE, into the Living Room. This, they expect, will secure them brand dominance. Not a chance.

The prolonged three-way battle between computer companies, Hollywood, and consumer electronics giants over Digital Video Disk was an excellent case of the standards wars gone wrong. These three battled for years over how DVDs would or would not protect copyrights, since unlike the tape recorders of old, you can copy anything at will in its original quality. During this prolonged battle, consumers found other storage techniques, like MP3, that let them copy and move files between whatever storage facility they found useful. DVD will have its period in the market, but this will be shortened by years and by shifting consumer behavior, something we will discuss in more detail in the next chapter, "The Collapse of Standards."

Suffice it to say at this point that all that matters in today's Living Room market is Internet compatibility. If a hard drive, for example, can take an Internet download, it has met the only standard it needs to meet. DirecTV is not broadcast-standard and there is no demand for it to follow one. By focusing on DVD standards for so long, suppliers may find that they have crippled their product permanently as it is bypassed by other storage technologies. Like the Hundred Years War, this war may go on long after any one remembers why it was started.

Consumers want easy-to-use products and services that allow them to rearrange their Living Rooms the same way personal computers allowed them to rearrange their offices. Microsoft and Intel have shown what can happen when you're at the center of changes like this.

Indeed, no one sees "The Road Ahead" better than Bill Gates. He understands that the company that gets to the Living Room first, offering flexibility and control independent of TV networks, technologies, and standards, will be the company that emerges in the next century with global brand dominance and unimagined wealth.

Over the last few years, Microsoft has launched dozens of initiatives to gain control of the Living Room market, from buying WebTV[2] and launching MSNBC with General Electric's NBC, to investing in cable carrier Comcast and in AT&T in exchange for the opportunity to supply TV set-top software. Microsoft has also cast its net widely for technologies that will make Living Room displays more potent.[3]

Not one of these initiatives—not one—is targeted at Microsoft's traditional market: office computers. Nor are they pure Internet plays. They are all aimed at dominating the living rooms of the world by whatever means possible. With tens of billions of new devices into which to put its software, Microsoft's ambitions are understandable.

Microsoft has an enormous advantage: it can afford to experiment with dozens of different channels and technologies to see what works and what does not. Most important, it has no ax to grind in this market. Unlike most other Living Room players, it can go with what works.

These strengths do not guarantee Microsoft's success; we will discuss the company in greater detail in Part Three.

News Corporation sees the same future; Rupert Murdoch was determined to build global satellite access to the whole world's consuming middle class. Murdoch started building his alliances in satellite years ago and is shrewd at matching his capital-eating ambitions with cash-rich partners. His British Sky Broadcasting (BSkyB) tied up with British Telecom in 1994, an arrangement that has since been extended to include Matsushita.[4] The same year, he started StarTV for the Asia/China markets. In 1996, with Softbank, he launched JSkyB, targeted at the Japanese market.[5]

In the U.S., his strategy almost came to grief several times. Murdoch jumped into a fifty-fifty satellite partnership with MCI called ASkyB. When the MCI deal foundered as MCI's needs changed during its acquisition by British Telecom (which foundered in turn), he quickly changed partners, joining up with EchoStar.[6] This deal went the way of all flesh too, and Murdoch wound up holding the short end of the stick. He tried a couple of other deals, and after a series of complex maneuvers wound up selling his U.S. satellites to EchoStar in return for a 30 percent piece of the company.[7]

Rupert Murdoch has satellite access to every Living Room in the world. His News Corp. is the only company capable of putting an ad into every home during local prime time. It is also the only company that has powerful content, from its Fox network to its sports franchises, with which to feed those satellites.

But while he had his eye on the scale economies of the heavens, here on earth the Internet exploded onto the scene and he seemed not to notice.[8] News Corp. is playing catch up. And a hard catch up it will be. Just as he has assembled his global satellite empire after a decade of struggle, the Internet drives diseconomies right through the whole thing. We will look at Murdoch's Internet strategy in Part Three, "The TV Guide Wars."

Our rule: define the shape of the Living Room market before you place your bets. Make sure that you are investing in a value engine that works. Remember that consumers hold all the cards. They own the means of information production. They will reward those who give them what they want and will penalize those who try to lead them where they don't want to go. There will be no vanguard of the Living Room Revolution.

Market Impact: media, communications, consumer electronics, computers, real estate.

19

The Collapse of Standards

We are all used to standards. Our TVs meet certain common standards and so do things like electrical circuits for our homes. For the most part, that is the only way things can work. But the Internet has only one standard: itself.

The Internet is fast becoming the delivery medium of choice for all "software," from movies to computer programs. It is standards-indifferent: anything that can store information, whether the information is a movie, a data file, or a phone message, will do.

On the Internet, computer operating systems and hardware platforms are immaterial, a fact that threatens the market positions of firms from Microsoft to Nintendo and allows the entry of dozens, perhaps hundreds, of new competitors. The fad for MP3 files which can record, duplicate, and send music over the Net is a perfect example. It basically came from nowhere, got picked up by college students looking for a cheap way to copy and send CDs to one another, and has become a de facto medium that can be kept on any kind of hard drive and sent at will over the Internet.

When MP3 burst onto the scene, all the folks who publish and distribute recordings, and collect handsome revenues for doing so, lost control of the record production standards that assure their cash flows.

Digital Video Disk, mentioned in our chapter, "The Living Room Market," is a classic. This mass storage medium—kind of an upgraded CD for movies and videos—was supposed to have been launched years ago when the consumer electronics industry desperately needed a new product to kick start sales.

But Hollywood objected to the DVD standard developed by the consumer-electronics producers because, unlike all the mass storage devices since audio tape fifty years ago, the DVD would be able to record just about anything, with pristine digital quality. In private hands these recordings could be distributed endlessly, and for free, from personal computer to personal computer, cutting Hollywood out of the revenue stream.

Hollywood forced a delay, seriously believing that it would do what no one has ever done, set a standard for computer mass storage devices. But all the while the DVD industry was waiting for agreement with Hollywood on copyright protection, the storage market moved in Moore Time. Products close to DVD storage capacity were already available for PCs by the time the first DVD was introduced. Huge Moore Time advantages were surrendered—one reason why MP3 took off as fast as it did. VCRs using off-the-shelf hard drives are now commercially available.

DVDs have done well in the market and will continue to do well for some time, but they will never reach their full market potential because the Internet and software like MP3 will continue to make alternatives available, none of them designed to Hollywood specifications. ReplayTV now markets nonstandard systems that store and replay up to twenty-eight hours of video, leaving DVD far behind.[1]

Hollywood plays no role in the Internet and has no influence on the mass storage devices used with it. Bernoulli didn't seek Hollywood's permission to launch its popular Zip and Jazz Drives,[2] and it doesn't seek Hollywood's approval for any capacity increases it offers. Consumers don't care either, as long as they have the very latest in storage technology at their disposal.

Equally important, as communication speeds between homes increase, the Internet may reduce, or at least dampen, demand for individual storage devices of all kinds. It may be much cheaper, for example, to use low-cost machines designed to download software on an as-needed basis than to buy mass storage products like DVDs and their successors. A variety of services let PC users automatically back up their hard drives to a remote location using the Internet.

The lesson here is that the days of "standard" VCRs and compact tapes and disks that everyone uses over a prolonged period of time, rendering security to the film business and strong cash flows to consumer electronics companies, are over. The Internet has eliminated standards. Anything compatible with the Internet sells, and only for so long as it's useful.

Market Impact: Television networks, movie production houses, consumer electronics.

20

The End of Mass Markets

"Mass" markets exist because high information costs keep individuals silent. Once information costs fall far enough, consumers have the technology at their disposal to make themselves heard, one by one.

A mass market of, say, two hundred and fifty million faceless consumers is one thing. A market of two hundred and fifty million empowered individuals talking back on the Internet is quite another. Harnessing these immense forces takes a corporate commitment of unheard of vitality and endurance.

We recently switched our long distance business to Qwest. One morning while calling London, we repeatedly got a message that we were dialing too few numbers. Since we call Europe every day, we knew this couldn't be our problem, and anyway when we called Germany or France, the calls went through fine. We called Qwest's customer service and got the runaround. This was no fun, so we e-mailed Joe Nacchio, a former AT&T executive who now runs Qwest, and asked for his help. Within twenty minutes, Qwest's

116

corporate vice president for operations was on the phone! Problem solved.

Now that's one-on-one sales support, Internet-style. Doing this, Nacchio had to reverse over a century of business practice that says customers, unless they are very big, get treated en masse. Nacchio used the Internet to treat our tiny New York operation at the same level as he would have treated a Fortune 100 company in the next building to his in Denver.

While the United States market may be the most advanced today, cheap computers know no frontiers, as the governments of China and the Soviet Union have found to their cost. A China of cheap-computer–liberated individuals will be a market of unprecedented diversity and size. China will have the devil of a time dealing with the end of mass markets, the very foundation on which China's prosperity and the Communist Party were built. We expect the next generation of tigers to bypass the mass markets developed over the last century in the West and in post-Meiji Japan. Developing countries will move immediately to the highly differentiated "Internet" markets unleashed by the Big Bang, with potential consequences to match.

Equally difficult is the question of brand management. How can anyone manage a brand in a world where mass markets, mass advertising, and mass distribution techniques are coming apart at the seams? Only by using cheap information to connect with customers *individually*. This is exactly what the companies we profile, like Dell and Schwab, do.

Market Impact: media, communications, consumer electronics, computers, real estate.

21

Approaching Terminal Velocity

Terminal velocity is a function of mass and area. An object with little substance that covers a large area reaches terminal velocity at a low speed. Terminal velocity is a problem for investors when companies cannot grow fast enough to stay ahead of the cost pressures imposed by Moore's Law.

Cellular telephone service reached terminal velocity in the mid-1990s, when growth slowed and revenues per customer per month plummeted.

Cellular was built on the assumption that it commanded a premium. And for many years, it did. But the massive expansion of available spectrum and the fourfold increase in the number of potential competitors changed this assumption. Wireless today is about being a substitute for a regular phone; it's not about mobility.

Investors were slow to pick up on the distinction. We were often asked, "Can cellular companies survive if they have to beat all the other wireless competitors on price?" We told investors that the real question was, "Can cellular companies survive at prices below those paid for ordinary home phones?" In 1999, wireless prices finally reached this level.

Our model shows that wireless can reach 50 percent penetration—but only if it costs less than a regular phone to use. The average U.S. residential telephone customer pays about $67 per month for the local and long distance service. To beat this, the cost per minute of a cell phone call had to fall from between 50¢ and 60¢ to 10¢ a minute.

The trade-off is cellular usage. When wireless prices drop far enough, usage will explode, moving from less than seventy-five minutes per month per customer to an average telephone usage of over 600 minutes.

And that's why cellular reached terminal velocity. No one has a network that can handle millions of Americans using their cell phones for 600 or more minutes a month. As soon as prices fell far enough to bring calling traffic up, the network choked and profits evaporated. No investor wants this. In short, for lack of technology cellular companies could not grow fast enough to offset price cuts.

Cellular was a rich man's toy; the average U.S. cellular customer had household income of nearly $66,000 in 1995. Carriers soon ran out of people who could pay for toys, and growth rates slowed. Cellular bills had been falling 11 percent per year for a decade, and then collapsed.[1] Carriers signed up "emergency use" customers who don't make many calls.[2] These are people who get a phone and keep it in the glove compartment "just in case." While 47 percent of current users had their phones for business in 1996, 40 percent of new users bought them for safety.[3] What we saw here was the "health club" strategy: sign 'em up and hope they don't show.

Now that it is priced to compete with regular phone service, the prospects for cellular are spectacular (see "Huge Post-PC Opportunity in Wireless" in Part Three). But first, capacity must increase enormously and the technology must be available to do this. In many areas during peak hours, using a cell phone is like trying to get a dial tone in Cairo. If a significant number of customers started using their cell phones as often as they use wired phones at home, cellular networks would collapse.

The field is wide open. Today's market leaders, especially AT&T with its powerful national brand, may be tough to dislodge. But maybe not so tough; a quarter or more of cellular subscribers switch carriers (or cancel) every year.[4] Brand doesn't seem to count for much in long-distance, either.[5] There's no Coke or Marlboro in telecommunications yet. Consumers will not sustain the high margins of top brands if much cheaper and virtually indistinguishable alternatives are readily available.

There's a lot of wishful thinking going on among investors. Many hope that cellular will just muddle through somehow, lowering prices a bit here, adding some free voice mail there, and still hang on to customers. Incumbents have an advantage for sure, but this is not how competition will play out in wireless.

Now is the time to have a hard look at all wireless bets. Don't invest in something that doesn't have the capacity to meet demand. Savvy investors will be bottom fishing for players that have the right technology, and understand that they will only succeed by cutting prices fast. For those with the right structure and organization, wireless velocity is almost limitless.

Market Impact: communications, computers, consumer electronics, finance, Internet stocks.

22

Power Shift

The faster that information costs fall, the bigger the consumer surplus and the faster consumers appropriate market power.

No matter how obvious it may be that consumers have taken enormous amounts of power, investors are still being asked to support decisions by large public companies that assume consumers are dead from the neck up.

A key for successful investing in the information economy is knowing that only firms with the ability to harness the shift in power to their customers create enduring wealth.

Every example we use in this book is of a company that has designed itself explicitly to harness this power shift. The very best companies use superior organization to enhance consumer power ahead of their competitors.

Thus, the imaginative business leader isn't someone who dreams up products or services. This leader is someone who looks for power-shift discontinuities in competitor operations, examines information technologies to see how customers can better be empowered, and organizes the company to take advantage of this shift.

Failed business models assume that top products take all or that more market coverage beats less. The lesson in this book is that faster is always better than bigger and faster means allowing customers the *demonstrable* means to influence a company and its direction. Even having a faster order entry system, Dell- or Cisco-style, gives management better customer information more quickly than the competition. But the real value generator is using that order entry system to let the customer take control, perhaps by designing their own product, or by customizing how it can be used.

We saw one company that spent tens of millions to beef up its order entry system but gave up when it proved too difficult. There were just too many internal barriers to getting the job done. This company's organizational disadvantage was soon exploited by a competitor that saw the opportunity and slammed it. Within a couple of years, the competitor's market cap was multiple of this company's and it couldn't figure out why.

Market Impact: retailing, consumer products, retailing, manufacturing.

23

The Singularity

As the Internet and television slam into one another at a colossal speed, they are creating a seamless new medium. This is the Information Singularity, a shareholder value digester—and creator—of gargantuan appetite. Nothing that flows into the Singularity will emerge unchanged.

The collision of the Internet and TV is creating a seamless Information Singularity that will absorb an astonishing range of industries:

- telephone
- cable
- Internet service
- TV networks and entertainment
- consumer electronics
- financial services
- retail

- advertising
- network hardware
- computers
- semiconductors
- software
- entertainment
- real estate

A digestion of shareholder value on this scale is unprecedented. Only the invention of movable type comes close. The Reformation that followed the invention of movable type ripped through Europe and then into North America. Modern business practices, the rule of law, and even the United States Constitution were a direct result. We can expect nothing less this time.

Just as movable type destroyed medieval Europe on the one hand and built America on the other, the Internet-TV Singularity will destroy and create value on an extraordinary scale. As with the Reformation, the organizations that emerge from this Singularity will look nothing like those that went in. The value creation potential in this event cannot be underestimated.

Indeed, the Information Singularity is already reordering business models across several industries. Cisco, Dell, and Yahoo! look like prime movers. Most others, however, haven't even begun to look at its implications.

Several events show the rapid approach of the Singularity. We break these forces into two elements: demand from consumers and push from suppliers.

Consumer Demand for the Information Singularity

1. Demand for President Clinton's video testimony in the salacious Lewinsky Affair crushed the Net. In a blow for the TV industry, the ideal medium proved to be a personal computer on a megabit-plus connection.[1]
2. RealPlayer video-streaming software was the fastest growing home software.[2]
3. Nintendo games with cameras sold 800,000 units in only four months.[3]
4. Video rentals by consumers continued to decline.[4]
5. Network TV ratings continued to fall.

Supplier Push to the Information Singularity

1. NBC bought up to 60 percent of CNet's Internet portal, Snap, and announced that it would begin to offer regular TV over the net.
2. Disney bought Internet portal Infoseek.
3. Sprint, following our recommendation, announced plans for a TV-driven Internet, called ION.
4. British Telecom and its partners announced a television-driven intra-European network.
5. AT&T tried—and failed—to buy AOL, which sees itself as the next News Corp.
6. IBM, Lucent, Compaq, 3Com, AMD, AT&T, H-P, Rockwell, and Intel joined the Home Phoneline Networking Alliance to create in-home networks.
7. AT&T announced its acquisition of TCI for $48 billion, including $5.4 for At Home (followed by its acquisition of MediaOne for another $54 billion in 1999).
8. Microsoft cofounder Paul Allen began a multibillion-dollar cable company spending spree.
9. Paul Allen also agreed to acquire 24 percent of production house Dreamworks SKG.
10. AOL purchased Internet browser company Netscape.

The Singularity will devastate broadcast television. As TV began to collide with the Internet, the broadcasters' share of network viewing declined and the desperation for customers became palpable: witness the endless series of lurid "news" stories, from O.J. Simpson to Lady Diana to Monica Lewinsky. None of this, however, slowed TV's slide into the Singularity.

Rupert Murdoch brings an old-fashioned newspaperman's calculation to the process: anything that lets advertisers reach consumer eyeballs is a good thing. Murdoch is not religious about how he does this, acquiring a broad range of media worldwide. He alone can advertise to any consumer, anywhere in the world, in local prime time. This strategy is simple and unencumbered by weighty agendas, like technology. It can be understood and executed by any number of Murdoch's heirs and assigns, though perhaps not as deftly, making News Corp. a growth engine for well into the next century.

TCI founder John Malone didn't get it. Bell Atlantic gave him the opportunity to exit in 1993. He didn't take it, soon recognized his mistake, and spent the next several years doing everything possible to squeeze some equity out of the fast-imploding value of TCI as it approached the Singularity. Not a moment too soon, AT&T stepped in to take him out.

Sumner Redstone didn't get it either. Just as the Information Singularity was tearing apart cyberspace, he went back to the future, loading up on debt to buy Blockbuster and Paramount. He spent years trying to undo this mess just to get to the present. Luckily, Redstone portfolio companies are well defined and understandable to the investment bankers who must undertake the remains.

The Internet-TV Singularity gives consumer-electronics companies a new lease on life. Matsushita has launched initiatives across a broad front. It has begun transferring engineers from its PC to its TV divisions,[5] has shown televisions with 12.5GB hard drives, and has launched MediaView, a 400MHz controller that serves as a unified in-home database for several different media, from satellites to camcorders.[6] Internet-TV offers Matsushita the chance to reposition its global Panasonic brand from the world of TVs, camcorders, and stereos to the faster-growing market for post-PC devices.

Advertisers are struggling on the Internet. They will suffer real pain when the dimensions of cyberspace rupture and several hundred million "broadcasters" flood the Net with homegrown content. Advertisers understand mass markets and don't have the tools to reach markets of one. They have completely misread the enormous diseconomies of the Internet and how the Singularity will map these diseconomies onto television.

Few common carriers have planned for the Information Singularity. NYNEX, PacTel, Ameritech, and MCI took one look and exited, passing their problems on to someone else.

Level 3 and Sprint, by contrast, have rethought Internet economics from the ground up, as we shall see in Part Three.

Going into this highly disruptive period, as we have seen, no one has a Living Room brand, let alone a strong position there. Nature abhors a vacuum, and carriers, TV networks, production houses, and software companies may wake up to find that Yahoo! and AOL are already the Coke and Pepsi of Internet-TV. Part of the reason Yahoo! gets its high valuations is that it offers what broadcasters did in their heyday. But still, its financial model is not clear.

We expect three kinds of market dominators to emerge:

- new media empires built along the lines of AOL, which know how to use the Singularity to turn television into the content of the Internet.
- new consumer electronics companies, like 3Com, that know how to create new categories of human behavior like Palm, and an accompanying generation of component and software suppliers, like Rise Technologies and Broadcom.
- a new in-home, branded, and "Singularity-compliant" environment, a next-generation Yahoo!, in which consumers operate information systems from TVs to stereos and from camcorders to PCs.

Timing is critical. Today only one-eighth of middle-class homes are on the Internet. Once Internet and TV merge, 99 percent will be. On the customer side, all the important pieces are in place. Everything customers need, from mass storage to camcorders, PCs, and display devices, has long been bought and paid for. Compare the move to Internet-TV with the fifty-year-long shift from horses to cars. Going from a horse to a car meant a huge change in budget and behavior. Internet-TV requires neither. Such a happy conjunction happens rarely and presages change of extraordinary rapidity.

Market Impact: unlimited.

24

Dematerialization

When ever cheaper information is substituted for "material" inputs like labor and natural resources, large parts of industry are literally "dematerialized" and cease to exist. It follows, therefore, that investors with their money in the wrong place will be dematerialized also.

Our 1995 book, *The Total Quality Corporation,** showed what happens when the falling cost of information is applied to a broad range of industries around the world. Time and again, costs go down while quality goes up, something not thought possible in the industrial age.

We are moving into a time of virtual resources that may permanently depress the price of raw materials, forcing painful changes on developing countries dependent on these products for growth.

*McInerney, Francis and White, Sean, *The Total Quality Corporation: How 10 major companies turned environmental challenge to competitive advantage in the 1990s* (NY:Dutton 1995); see www.northriver.com for more information.

As information is substituted for oil, for example, demand for hydrocarbons may fall to such an extent that U.S. strategic interests in the Middle East are affected, introducing even more political instability in the region than there is already.

The impact of dematerialization can be devastating. Take the $39 billion global recording industry.[1] Once music is delivered via the Internet, products like CDs simply disappear. They take with them the entire industry used to manufacture, package, and deliver those products. On the Internet there is no CD and no CD manufacturing. Nor is there CD publishing or distribution. That, in turn, means no record stores. And without record stores, the traffic and buying patterns in many large shopping malls will change also. All will have vanished without a trace into a Black Hole of bits and bytes.

Six years ago, we told our clients that dematerialization of the recording industry would:

1. reinvent the business of making and distributing records;
2. slash costs and lower prices; and in the process
3. create a large consumer surplus that would
4. divert billions from existing distribution channels into cyberspace.

This sounded far-fetched to most of them, but today the ubiquitous MP3 format has allowed consumers to send recordings to each other across the Internet for free.

What, we asked in 1994, if we apply the same process to retail banking? Companies like Microsoft and Intuit have long recognized that personal computers could transform banking. Powerful PCs attached to the Internet can poll banks around the world for the best consumer deposit and loan rates twenty-four hours a day, seven days a week. Banks in one country must compete for the business of banks in another, scrubbing central bank interest rate policies and the information industry strategies of countries like Singapore. With the untold billions sloshing around in unproductive savings accounts thus liberated, banks would be at the mercy of their customers as never before. This process is now well underway.

The cost structure of bricks-and-mortar banks has been completely undermined. Branches—the banks' primary customer interface today—are being replaced by ubiquitous ATMs and increasingly by home computers. Since banks are built on their branches, the impact on employment and productivity can just be imagined.[2] Even more devastating to the banking industry will be the loss of brand and the banks' ability to control their customers' banking "experience," something central to successful sales and marketing. How do you "sell" to a PC running your bank in background mode?

E*Trade, Ameritrade, and Charles Schwab can easily become the interest-rate arbitrageurs for hundreds of millions of consumers, robbing banks of what remaining brand they have. These companies assume that a computer, not a building, is the point of sale and that geography is meaningless. They have grabbed the brand high ground just as we predicted they would, leaving legacy banks in the dust.

If all of this sounds distinctly unpleasant, it is. Peter Drucker has long argued that our biggest future challenge will be to transform service industries the way we transformed manufacturing over the last century and a half; to turn them from low-productivity/low-wage businesses to high-productivity/ high-wage ones.

Agriculture provides an excellent example of this process of transformation. Once the largest U.S. business and the largest employer, it is still the largest business, but employs only a tiny fraction of the numbers it once did. Agriculture has reached levels of productivity never thought possible when the only "real" job was down on the farm, and such luminaries as Thomas Jefferson could hold city dwellers and their banks in utter contempt.

What will make Drucker's ideas possible is dematerialization. The Black Hole in Cyberspace will be the engine of industrial transformation.

The problem is that in many cases, industry has reacted to brand erosion by taking measures that lead in exactly the opposite direction. The entertainment and banking industries, for example, have been swept by a wave of acquisitions made, in theory, to cement direct customer relationships and prevent widespread shareholder value destruction. Disney bought ABC to get new channels to market its movies and TV shows. Chemical Bank merged with Chase Manhattan for similar reasons. Others are consolidating in retail and in railroads.[3]

Our advice: carefully examine companies vulnerable to Black Hole dematerialization. Apply our Four Keys to Value Creation. If management hasn't begun to take these rules seriously, take your cue.

Market Impact: energy, real estate, manufacturing, transportation, hospitality, retailing.

25

Virtual Sex, Real Money

To see today what we mean by the Internet-TV of tomorrow, just go to your favorite Web engine and type "sex."

Pornographers have always been at the leading edge of information technology. They exploited advances in printing to create a mass market. They sold "dirty pictures," one of the first applications for commercial photography. They used 8mm film to expand the range of "home" movies. And, of course, they got VCRs off the ground before anyone else could see a use for them.

Even now, adult videos account for 25 percent of all movie rentals. The fastest growing type of adult films—already a quarter of this multibillion dollar business—is the homemade variety, produced with off-the-shelf camcorders.[1] Pay TV would be a dud without porno channels. Some 20 percent of pay-per-view revenues, and a much higher share of profits, comes from soft-core movies. Playboy's Spice and Adam & Eve networks reach more than 20 million American households.[2]

The biggest market for interactive electronic entertainment today is telephone sex. In the U.S., the sex trade pioneered "900" numbers and party lines for this application. And when things got too hot on-shore, they shifted to high-toll Caribbean locations with domestic U.S. area codes. A few years ago, 40 percent of Guyana's telephone traffic came from sex lines.[3]

Sex is a complex form of human communication. The ability of the Internet to accommodate this kind of interaction indicates its power and shows that conversation-grade video interaction, not pages of Web site information, is what will take the Internet into every home.

While videoconferencing has been around for decades, its use is limited almost entirely to businesses that spend thousands on hardware and high-speed telephone connections. Consumers never jumped at the idea of a thousand-dollar telephone that lets the kids see Granny while they're talking to her. They are willing, however, to pay $9.95 per month to watch other people have sex. Many want to let other people watch them have sex. For free.

CU-SeeMe ("see you, see me"), developed in the early 1990s by researchers at Cornell University, was the first application to make Internet videoconferencing possible. With CU-SeeMe (available commercially or as shareware), you connect to an Internet "reflector" site, essentially a video chat room. While CU-SeeMe can be used to conference with astronauts in the Space Shuttle or explorers on the Great Barrier Reef, what people really want is sex.

With a standard modem and a cheap digital video camera, CU-SeeMe sound quality is good; picture quality is poor. The video display, about the size of a Post-It note, refreshes several times per minute at best. But, when it comes to sex, people will accept poor or uneven quality. With CU-SeeMe, any amateur can broadcast live over the Net—for love or money. For those with PCs and Internet accounts, the cost is next to nothing.

Chat rooms were an early feature of on-line services and the Internet. Even before the Web made the Internet commonplace, people could log onto these sites and type messages anonymously to strangers from around the world in forums like "alt.sex.aliens." Once the Web opened up the world to graphics, enthusiasts began posting pornographic pictures. These early services were free, and capitalism abhors a vacuum.

To fill this vacuum, the world's oldest profession went virtual. Now sex over the Internet is big business, perhaps the first really successful form of e-commerce. We guesstimate that consumers spent $300 million on virtual sex in 1998, 10 to 20 percent of on-line retail transactions.[4] What is more, sex is probably the fastest growing Internet market, and the most profitable. This is all the more remarkable, considering the growth is self-financed.

Nobody in the sex business is waiting for banks to develop complex secure-transaction standards: payment is strictly by credit card. Meanwhile, investors have sunk millions—perhaps billions—into advertising-based Web models that haven't turned a dime. Pornographers have already established the marketing, sales, and billing systems of the future and know exactly how they will and will not work. This expertise will prove invaluable in dozens of markets once the bandwidth gap is closed.

While there is a special allure to sex, gambling—another "vice"—does well on the Internet too. Last year, the U.S. government decided to crack down on on-line casinos, all off-shore, that generate some $100 million in revenues.[5] Gambling is probably even more profitable than pornography, but does not require the same bandwidth.

Sex over the Internet remains primarily broadcast: a single source sends to many viewers. Most sites follow a simple formula. You become a "member" for a monthly fee (around $10), which entitles you to free pictures from a library. Then you get barraged with upgrade options: live sex, pay-per-view films, on-line games, and a variety of other activities and accessories. One entrepreneur broadcasts from home her doings around the clock—the good, the bad and the ugly. She charges $15 per year to thousands of customers who want to enter her Web site.[6]

Sex services are available from thousands of "mom and pop" sites, as well as high profile ones like *Penthouse*.[7] The barriers to entry are low: investors can build a basic Web site for $5–$10,000 (including credit card processing software). Live-video capabilities are more expensive, perhaps $200,000.[8] But remember, this is the cost of setting up a slick, interactive Web broadcasting system with worldwide reach. Fox, by painful contrast, spent many millions to set up its one-way twenty-four-hour news channel, and could not get cable system access to important markets.

The sex business shows that Internet TV will undermine *all* of the Fox financials, *all at once*. And it will undermine those of all the other networks around the world, from ABC to Deutsche Wella and NHK. Investors need to think about this.

The sex trade has shown how a shift from entertainment broadcasting to communications between peers will work. Many Web sites allow viewers to watch live sex acts (for as much as $2 per minute). Some permit actors and viewers to interact by talking or sending a simple text message. At some CU-SeeMe–enabled sites, customers interact directly with virtual hookers. At others, customers videoconference with fellow "amateurs." The site operator collects a toll only for bringing the two together and operating the reflector.

When we got our start in the information technology business nearly a quarter of a century ago, we worked for IRD, a market research house run by Ken Bosomworth. A few years later, we were running our own shop at Northern Business Information when Ken sent over a report predicting the "feel-a-phone," a robotic arm attached to a phone. We called him up to make some jocular comments about the implications of his prediction. But Ken, a man with a powerful sense of humor, wasn't laughing. It has taken us nearly two decades, but we aren't laughing any more either. Today, it is a *very* short step from two-way interactive video to the shared virtual reality of Ken's feel-a-phone. All that's missing is the bandwidth.

Interactive Internet TV is revolutionary on several levels. Many fewer viewers tune into the broadcast networks today than only a few years ago.[9] People are still watching TV, but the market has fragmented among cable channels. This fragmentation will accelerate as more viewers shift to Internet alternatives. Entropy is coring out ABC, CBS, Fox, and NBC.

The impact will be just as severe for the consumer electronics industry. New brands will be associated with Internet-TV. Sony and Phillips are not. Furthermore, with a QuickCam, Internet-TV amateurs don't need the tape or DVD storage products now being pushed by the consumer electronics industry. They pump their "art" right onto the Internet or store it on a hard drive. To use a Sony Handycam with a computer, by contrast, requires a thousand-dollar video card.

Sex on the Internet shows what Internet TV can do. Last year, a twelve-year-old boy in Illinois downloaded the hit TV series *South Park* onto his home PC and made episodes available to anyone who dialed into his web site. Between 3:00 and 6:00 after school, his site was jammed. This child:

1. turned his home into a TV station;
2. destroyed the branding of all the major networks;
3. eliminated prime time and the value of prime-time advertising;
4. took out all the big names in consumer electronics; and

5. restructured in-home communications around a jerry-rigged fast Ethernet architecture that will probably become standard at your local Radio Shack.

If this isn't an entropy-driven shareholder value shake-up, we don't know what is.

Market Impact: communications, entertainment, hospitality, transportation, finance.

26

The Total Quality Corporation

By dematerializing industrial growth and uncoupling it from the consumption of the earth's natural resources, *falling information costs have a direct impact on the environment.* What we buy today, from cars to soda cans, is made with less metal, oil, and water; what we turn on, from light bulbs to refrigerators, uses less electricity; our cars run on less gas. This is all because we can substitute ever cheaper information for other production inputs.

The falling cost of information thus puts total quality within reach. Total quality means clean production, a world where having zero waste means having zero defects. Those companies that pollute the least have the lowest-cost and the highest-quality products and services. Total quality also means that waste, or pollution, is a key indicator of cost, quality, and, most important, management problems. For investors this means that a polluter is a company out of control.

Better technology and more efficient production are partially responsible for dematerialization. But, in addition, as consumers grow richer, they spend more and more of their income on services, like entertainment, travel, and dining out. Clearly, fewer natural resources go into thirty dollars worth of cable TV shows, than into thirty dollars' worth of gas for the grill.

The information economy has swelled as computers have found their way into virtually every aspect of human activity. The raw-material content of a $250 computer microprocessor or a $500 computer program can be measured in cents. Their value derives not from any materials they contain, but from the knowledge of the producers who make them and the people who use them.

Concern about the environment—and about wasteful consumption, for that matter—is not new. But real pressure to use our natural resources more carefully began only twenty-five years ago. The first OPEC oil embargo in 1972 delivered a striking lesson to the world's consumers. While this event was entirely man-made, it was seized upon by environmentalists and neo-Malthusians as an object lesson on the limits to growth. Waiting in gas lines, everyone could consider the fragile link between industrial growth and the environment. Cheap information has broken that link, allowing us to have both.

During the past generation, pollution control laws have had a dramatic effect on air and water quality. In the industrialized world, for example, air emissions of sulfur oxides, particulates, and lead have fallen far, despite increased industrial activity.[1] In the United States, the power industry today generates two and one-half times as much electricity for each ton of pollution produced, compared to in 1970.[2] After the Love Canal disaster in the United States spotlighted the potential ill effects of small quantities of industrial by-products, toxic waste disposal was recognized as a serious problem, resulting in tighter controls. Then hysteria about garbage disposal problems resulted in new recycling requirements around the world.

Pollution laws have forced industry to reduce its use of raw materials, hastening the process of dematerialization. Less lead is used in gasoline, less mercury in batteries, less coal is needed to produce a kilowatt-hour of electricity. In the 1970s, many predicted that the world would run out of key commodities if we didn't change. Well, we did change, and most raw-material supplies are now in surplus. Industry continues to wean itself from the consumption of natural resources. "Sustainable growth," the mantra of the environmental community, is becoming a reality.

Cheap information allows managers to look at waste as an indicator of problems, a sure sign that something is wrong with what they are doing. Wherever there is waste, competitive advantage is being lost, and with it jobs and investments.

Smart companies are capitalizing on the sudden drop in the cost of information to substitute knowledge—better thinking— for machinery, labor, and natural resources. Their efforts place a premium on training and productivity, while uncoupling growth from the consumption of energy and raw materials, the source of pollution. They will survive the contest for high-wage, high-growth opportunities because they are the low-cost producers in their markets.

To invest in its workers and technology, to pay high wages and maintain good benefits, to provide the products and services that customers around the world will pay for, companies must make money. To maximize profits, managers must minimize waste.

Financial pressure, not renewed vision, is what finally forces companies to respond to market realities. They must reduce costs to survive. In this fight for survival, they can't leave any stone unturned when wringing costs out of operations. And they can't restructure their way to success without attacking the root cause of their problems.

To improve their competitive positions, not incrementally, but radically, forward-looking companies around the world are embracing the ultimate goal: they use cheap information to drive clean production. This means no smoke up the stack, no dirty water down the drain, no trash to the dump. What drives them to this goal is continual, relentless cost reduction and quality improvement.

A decade ago, many businesses thought quality cost more to make. They know now that improving quality reduces manufacturing costs. In our own experience in information technology, the low-cost producer *always* has the highest quality. The same goes for pollution. If you are worried about costs, pollution indicates inefficiency, and the opportunity to save money. If you think you can move to the Third World and pollute your way to happiness, dream on. If you think that you can somehow waste raw materials, which may be cheap, but not waste other resources, which are expensive, you are kidding yourself. Such wasteful practices indicate a sloppy organization living on borrowed time. We've seen a lot of factories, and you can eat off the floor in the ones with the lowest costs.

Cheap information shifts competitive advantage away from low-cost labor countries to low-cost information countries. To compete, therefore, low-cost labor countries for which pollution is acceptable will have to completely restructure their industries to stay in the game.

PART THREE

HOW TO SECURE YOUR PIECE OF THE PIE

With so many industries affected by the falling cost of information, investors need to know who's on first and who'll be there next. In Part Three, we look at companies in a wide range of businesses that show what to do and what not to. Their examples are illustrative of what to look for in the next quarter-century.

In general, you will need to watch for companies that move to the "edge" of cyberspace as it expands, and you will need to watch for companies that use our Four Keys to Value Creation to ensure that they have the shortest possible interior lines.

Each of the companies in Part Three follows our rules and succeeds, or doesn't and is in trouble. Example by example, you can follow the lessons learned.

27

The Brand War

By allowing consumers to talk back, the Internet is altering the relationship between customers and vendors, and turning brand into a moving target. Here we look at how Hewlett-Packard and Kodak are trying to create brand equity on a global scale in the Living Room market.

"Brand" is managing how your customer experiences your product or service. In a world of mass media and mass markets, doing this was limited to making a promise—the so-called brand promise—making sure your customers knew about your promise, and delivering on that promise.

Coca-Cola is a perfect example. The company promised a certain kind of product and refreshment, made sure you knew about it, and delivered on its promise in almost every way possible everywhere in the world.

Today, however, the cost of information has fallen to the point that customers talk back in real time. This changes the nature of brand entirely; today it is a process, often delivered remotely in your home or office, and which has to be executed perfectly on time, every time, twenty-four hours a day. Not many companies can do this. For brand managers, the risk of failure has gone way, way up. A lot of companies are unprepared, and they are losing value as a result.

To understand what the Internet is doing to brand, look at Kodak, which we profiled in "The Event Horizon." Kodak is one of the most admired brand operators in history, carefully managing how its customers experience picture-taking in many dozens of countries around the world. In the late 1990s. Kodak was under the gun: its earnings collapsed and its stock stalled in a raging bull market.[1]

Kodak's ills are symptomatic of those facing many of the world's legacy brands. Kodak was caught between two powerful forces. On one hand, a price assault by a reenergized Fujifilm was draining cash from Kodak's core photoprocessing business. On the other hand, an attack by color printer titan Hewlett-Packard and other color printer makers, like Epson, threatened to destroy entirely the need for Kodak photoprocessing.

For Kodak, a hundred years' worth of shareholder value was put at risk by the Internet.

What happened? As we saw in Part One, the Moore Curve in 1995 made information incredibly cheap and easy for the average person to control. Processing power became so cheap that the Internet exploded into markets of all kinds, ripping up assumptions about consumer behavior. The Internet replaced mass markets with masses of individuals. A classic mass marketer, Kodak didn't respond in time.

In mass markets, consumers are passive receivers of media-born brand advertising, Kodak style. By letting consumers talk back in real time, however, the Internet forces vendors to reassess brand management. Internet-born complaints compelled no less a company than Intel to recall its first-generation Pentium. For brand managers, this was the shot heard around the world.

When the interactive nature of the Internet forced vendors to replace old-fashioned brand promises like the "Kodak Moment" with entire processes delivered remotely, Hewlett-Packard smelled an opportunity.

Redefining brand as a process instead of a name, Hewlett-Packard realized that no one has a Living Room brand. It saw product names, like Panasonic and Sony, as remnants of a time when all that went into a Living Room was a TV and a stereo. And it saw the unbranded services of phone and cable companies. It also saw that none of these competitors uses the combined power of the Internet and home computers to engage customers directly in any kind of process.

Kodak, while a household name, is not in homes at all; you send out Kodak film to have it developed. Finally, H-P saw that these "name" companies react slowly because of their costly distribution infrastructures.

Thus, the way was open for H-P, an industrial company, to enter the Living Room market without facing any resistance.

This being said, Hewlett-Packard is no brand wizard like Disney or Coke. If H-P is known for anything, it is for industrial-strength computing and test equipment. In recent years, however, H-P gained dominance in printers, where it owns its segment.

To grow further, H-P decided to use its commodity technology to gobble up the profits of another industry, photoprocessing, and create a branded service hybrid capable of appropriating Kodak's prodigious cash flows.

H-P's reasoning was simple: since consumers have already bought and paid for photoprocessing services, H-P will use its printer business, where it is a global leader in price-performance, to restructure the way consumers take and print pictures. If it succeeds, it will redirect large, existing consumer budgets into its own coffers.

This cash flow will generate significant consumer surpluses—history's main generator of wealth—some part of which will flow into H-P's top line. H-P announced plans to couple its cheap printers directly to digital cameras, eliminating costly PCs and slashing the capital cost of in-home picture development. With H-P, consumers can use the Internet as an image-storing and -forwarding medium electronically sending pictures home directly from any location. What is more, they can send reproductions to friends and family at the same time. No more waiting and paying for snapshots and duplicates.

With its enormously successful disposable cameras, Kodak showed consumers that they don't need to own cameras to get their Kodak moments. H-P goes one step farther, eliminating film production, distribution, and processing altogether. In doing this, H-P wants to redefine customer service in this market. It hopes to create a new brand promise and use the Internet to deliver. H-P can create a powerful new Living Room brand, perhaps even place itself at the center of the Living Room in a way that even Microsoft may have difficulty doing.

H-P could alter entirely the economics of a Kodak moment:

- Today, cameras are cheap but film-processing lifecycle costs are usually hundreds, even thousands of times the cost of a camera.
- H-P will discount the future value of all processing expenses into a one-time consumer durable, a technology capable of developing an infinite number of pictures for the low variable cost of toner and paper. Consumers who already own H-P printers invest little or nothing.

- H-P will use the Internet to make picture development and delivery instantaneous, anywhere in the world.

Hewlett-Packard's goal is to marginalize Kodak's brand by exposing the main flaw in Kodak's promise. Kodak cannot deliver anything in a moment. H-P can.

An entire generation of legacy brands will thus be stranded as Hewlett-Packard and others change the rules of the game by exploiting the impact of Moore's Law on computers and communications. The process will repeat itself in industry after industry as newcomers redefine the meaning of "brand."

Investors need to watch their blue chips, for it is household brands that are most at risk. Kodak can lay off thousands to control costs and boost short-term earnings. But to survive and grow, it will have to answer Hewlett-Packard and the others that are sure to follow. Kodak must re-examine what it does frame by frame. Legacy brands the world over must do the same. Big brand owners have been among the strongest performers during the bull market of the 1990s.

The Internet makes brand a process, not a promise. Brand strength is in the execution, not in deliverables. Products and services alone mean nothing. Players that can integrate service into their products and processes will create enduring shareholder value through brand.

28

Advertising: Intimate Brands Kills Madison Avenue

During the 1999 Super Bowl, *America's biggest sporting event, one million television viewers left their televisions and turned their computers to the Victoria's Secret Web site.*

Intimate Brands, which owns Victoria's Secret, showed conclusively the power of the new Internet television medium over all existing media.

The *Super Bowl* is the American male's annual must-watch, pitting the nation's two top football teams against each other in the most heavily watched TV event of the year. While the *Super Bowl* doesn't even make it into the top twenty most-watched sports events in the world, in the U.S., with its huge middle class, it is an advertising gravy train. All those men with so much money to spend . . .

One hundred and twenty-five million viewers tune in. Thirty-second ads go for $1.6 million each. During the 1999 broadcast,

Intimate Brands ran a thirty-second commercial advertising an upcoming fashion show on its Victoria's Secret Web site. All Victoria's Secret's star supermodels were to appear wearing what little is needed to show their charms to maximum advantage—advantage, that is, for Intimate Brand's income statement. During the next hour, over a million viewers left their TVs, went to their computers, probably in a different room of their homes and logged onto Victoria's Secret. How much football and how many ads they missed it is impossible to say.

Intimate Brands followed this up with a campaign that placed ads in most major *business* publications—ads consisting of not much more than Tyra Banks looking . . . well, like Tyra Banks. Within about a week, Intimate Brands figures, one billion consumers had been exposed to the fashion show. One billion is one out of every five men, women, and children on the planet. Even allowing for hyperbole, this was a major success.

Intimate Brands was able to use the television network to eviscerate the *Super Bowl*'s advertising by the numbers strategy and gain an audience nearly ten times the size of the Bowl itself. Its strategy, however, spelled death for all those other advertisers who lost audience to Victoria's Secret. What do the networks do with this sort of thing? Refuse advertisers that have Web sites? Intimate Brands effectively used its *Super Bowl* ad to scrub the calculations of all the other advertisers. By investing in a mere thirty seconds.

The new Internet-television medium will replace the TV we know with millions of channels—perhaps hundreds of millions, since each home can be a Web server—eliminating the whole concept of mass advertising. On the Net, advertising means targeting audiences of one, something few existing firms know how to do.

Internet-television will offer huge new opportunities for those who understand how to use it to get consumer eyeballs and keep them. Already Amazon.com and Yahoo! are positioned as the global brands of the future, capable of carrying a broad array of new services.

Advertising is segmenting network audiences of its own accord. On cable and satellite channels with well-defined audiences, advertisers are finding new markets for customers they couldn't reach over mass-market TV networks. On the mass-market networks, falling viewership is concentrating ad revenues on a few big shows, with the result that as audiences decline, ad revenues are actually going up.

Intimate Brands demonstrated several things: the awesome diseconomies of scale available on the Internet; the ease with which other media can be co-opted to support Internet-based services; and the end of advertising as the primary pillar of brand.

This last is critical for investors to understand, as we say in "The Brand War." Intimate Brands demonstrated a superior ability to manage the way its target customers experience its Victoria's Secret products. Cheap information allows many more venues for doing this than have existed ever before.

Intimate Brands used one medium to hive off a specific audience and pull this audience into an environment that it controlled to maximum effect. Advertisers will, over the next few years, have to learn the new skills required to attract these customers, and to manage them once won over. Many of the largest names on Madison Avenue will not make the cut. And some of the more imaginative new-media people in Lower Manhattan's Silicon Alley will build great advertising empires to replace the fallen.

29

Financial Services: Schwab Cleans Up

Charles Schwab's market capitalization in 1999 exceeded that of Merrill Lynch, long the world's biggest brokerage house. Merrill has lots of people and lots of bricks and mortar. Schwab used cheap information to dissolve it all into a few servers.

From these servers, Schwab handles a third of all Internet trading. Internet trades as a percent of all trades at Schwab rose from 40 percent in 1997 to over 60 percent in 1999. One out of every twenty stock trades in America today is a Schwab trade.[1]

Schwab understands what brand control means in a way its main street competitors don't. As we saw earlier, brand means managing your customers' experience of your product or service.

Two decades ago, brand for Schwab meant selling product at a discount; today it means selling the company at a premium. Twenty years ago, consumer participation meant wholesale prices on their trades. Today it means getting the full horsepower out of computers and TVs to look, and act, like a real trading desk.

Schwab is using the Internet to reach into people's homes and offices, where it can bring them a trading environment that allows its customers to participate ever more completely in the market.

Schwab's full trading experience therefore means a lot more than discount brokerage. While a potent sales vehicle in itself, discount is only a part of what Schwab believes that its customers will need. The benefit to Schwab is infinitely more customer information and the ability to charge several times the average Internet brokerage rates. Using the Internet, Schwab gains access to a much larger share of America's investment money. Already Schwab's 2.2 million Web customers invest about $500 billion. The company is going after the $1.5 trillion in customer assets Merrill now manages.

Schwab is not completely without bricks and mortar of its own to protect. It has 275 branch offices and plans to build 200 more.[2] The firm will blend these into its Net-based services in what it calls a "social fabric" for investing: platforms for seminars, training sessions, and other tools of client education. Rather than use the Net to protect its real estate, Schwab will use its real estate to support its Net-based attack.

In this struggle for brand supremacy, Schwab and Merrill are polar opposites. Schwab has the on-line customers; Merrill has the customer assets. But if Schwab's customers like having their computer screens look like those of a broker, Schwab could turn its advantage in on-line customers into a runaway freight train that nothing will stop.

The genesis of this thinking goes far back into Schwab's history. Conceived by Charles Schwab in the seventies as a discount brokerage, Schwab was sold to BankAmerica in the eighties, and spun out—with a difference—in the nineties. At each stage in its development, the company has been driven by the knowledge that in a low-cost information world, whoever transfers the most power to customers wins. In the seventies that meant cheap trades. In the nineties it means letting your customer operate just like a broker, with full broker powers.

Schwab is far from alone in seeing the advantages for customers in trading over the Internet. There are now hundreds of Internet brokerage houses, up from twenty-four in 1997. Each of these is taking a different direction. Ameritrade is targeting no-frills customers who just like to trade and who don't want to pay for extra services like stock research. This has lowered Ameritrade's cost of doing business—it spends far less to attract a new customer than its rivals[3]—but it may also limit its appeal. E*Trade went in a different direction, spending $1.8 billion in 1999 to move into full-service Internet banking when it acquired Telebanc Financial Corp.[4]

Because it has kept customer empowerment rather than broker empowerment first and foremost in its mind, Schwab has not been afraid to cannibalize its business if that is what it takes. For the competition, this is a fearsome prospect. Most companies caught behind the falling information-cost curve—Merrill Lynch in this case no less than Compaq in its struggle for PC supremacy with Dell—must protect existing revenues.

On Wall Street, this means large numbers of full-service brokers, few of whom will be happy to see themselves replaced by a server farm in the middle of an Iowa cornfield. E*Trade dramatized this issue when it ran TV ads showing a luxurious stone chateau "that your investments helped to pay for . . . unfortunately it belongs to your broker."[5] For a Morgan Stanley Dean Witter to run an ad like this, with its 11,500 full-service brokers, would have been a human-resource disaster. This makes full-service brokerages easy pickings: they can't respond without disaffecting large numbers of their own people. This is the Dead Zone at its most vicious.

The company that will eat its own children is frightening to legacy players, deeply disturbing, psychologically, to their employees as well as to management. Time and again we have worked with companies desperate to shore up long-uncovered flanks. Management and workers together join in a desperate death struggle to plug the holes in the high-cost dike as leaner, swifter competitors use other channels to sweep around the dike, carrying everything away before them.

Some firms are lucky. AT&T and IBM got new leadership unafraid to force unwanted changes; shareholders benefited almost immediately.

Others slowly unwind as their once great names slip into oblivion, taking large amounts of shareholder wealth—usually in the form of hard-earned savings—with them.

A company like Schwab forces competitors to make hard choices: act now and suffer painful consequences, as Merrill Lynch has elected to do by embracing on-line trading; or put off the inevitable and hope that the damage won't become evident till the next watch. There is, of course, always the last CEO left standing, whose fate is public and painful. The *Wall Street Journal* is full of their stories every day.

30

Network Television: Swamped by the Internet

Network television today is just like czarist Russia in August 1914. From the outside, it has an image larger than life, with growing sales, all the big names, and big shows. Inside, the rot is deep. *Monday Night Football* contributed a staggering 28 percent of ABC's ad revenue in 1998.[1] A smart manager might simply shut down the network except for the one game. Combine it with enough Victoria's Secret ads, and you'd have a real winner. With the Internet you could do so—and that is the point of this chapter.

When the cost of information falls far enough, it allows consumers to seek a wide range of near-TV alternatives, from the Internet to PlayStation. Viewers rapidly segment themselves because cheap computing power lets them take advantage of the Internet's diseconomies of scale.

Already, viewers have pushed this process of segmentation deep into network finances, and the strains have begun to show. The

Discovery Channel has hived off affluent, well-educated viewers, reaching into 76 million U.S. homes.[2] Nickelodeon has captured 50 percent of children aged two to eleven.[3] WB focussing the twelve- to twenty-four age group exclusively. All the while, legacy TV network Nielsen ratings plummet.

With this process, the ability of the networks to make stars has collapsed. In 1950–51, Milton Berle had an 81 percent share of the U.S. TV audience. Twenty years later, Mary Tyler Moore had only 39 percent. But fifty years later, "star" Calista Flockhart has only 14 percent. Even Jerry Seinfeld, a media event in his own right, managed only 33 percent. Ten years ago, 42 percent of viewers still recognized male prime-time stars and 45 percent recognized female stars. Today that's down to 33 percent and 32 percent respectively.[4]

In 1978, the three main networks—ABC, CBS, and NBC—had about 90 percent of U.S. TV audiences. By 1997 they had 55 percent.[5] Audiences fell another 9% in 1998.[6] The worst collapse has been the most recent. It took the networks fifteen years to lose the first twenty-two points of viewership but only five to lose the next twenty. Losses like this cannot be sustained.

A TV show may never manage a top-rated "30 share" again, one point of share representing something over a million homes. But even this is deceptive: if everything with a display technology in the average American home is counted, these numbers are actually a much smaller piece of the "viewing" audience.

Operating margins have followed audiences: cable TV channels regularly outperform broadcast networks. In a 1998 survey by the *Economist* magazine of the top eighteen channels, the networks brought up the rear, generating small fractions of the returns garnered by Nickelodeon and MTV.[7]

What must be even more alarming for shareholders, Internet stocks reached higher valuations. The desperation of the media in its fight to hold on to the diminished attention of the public has become a phenomenon with a life of its own. From O.J. Simpson to Lady Diana and President Clinton's Sexgate, American TV broadcasters are searching for something, anything, to get consumer eyeballs back. Our Iron Laws of Information say this hope is vain.

Ironically, television—the technology itself, not the broadcast networks—is the application that will drive the Internet to its next level of market acceptance. For many, Internet-TV may be nothing more than watching television, with a choice of millions of channels, not just a few hundred.

As we saw in "Entropy and the Internet," network television is really no more than another Web site among millions. Once high-speed two-way communications into the home is commonplace, television stations and networks will be completely absorbed into the new medium of Internet-TV. Broadcast television, as we know it, will be a shadow of its former self.

Our Iron Laws of Information tell us that disorder in the information universe always increases. Consumers will always seek finer and finer segmentations of the market. Winners don't block this process, they attempt to harness it and profit from it.

Segmentation, indeed, is key to the growth of television. As cheap processing power allows viewers to see more of what they want to see, when they want to see it, advertisers get better returns for their dollar. Instead of spending millions for viewers they don't want to target—the mass advertising approach of the past—they can drill down to exactly those buyers they need to reach. This makes their dollars more effective. Because of its teenage focus, WB can call a show a hit when it gets only 5 percent of the viewing audience,[8] something unthinkable a generation ago.

Partly as a result, while network audiences have declined and network reliance on more focused audiences has increased, networks have discovered that their ad revenues are rising, 13 percent last year. Segmentation therefore helped networks grow their businesses. But it has helped cable companies more; their ad revenues grew by a whopping 33 percent.[9] At this rate, in a few years cable revenues will outrun network revenues.

To defend themselves against continued audience erosion, broadcast networks made the classic mistake of trying to dominate the middle ground. As audience segmentation increases, however, successful shows can account for 10 percent or 15 percent of a network's ad revenue, making networks increasingly—dangerously—reliant on one or two hits.

Contracts for these shows are so lucrative that networks are losing negotiating leverage and are being forced to pay more and more for their best ones. Time Warner, for example, got $13 million an episode for hit show *ER* in 1998, up 550 percent from $2 million the year before. The impact on profit per show was immediate. Thus, even when ad revenues go up, profits go down, miring broadcasters in an endless chase for shows killed by their own success.[10]

One alternative is to move upstream by demanding equity or revenue splits from shows. CBS now has an ownership position in its entire lineup, something unprecedented in the history of U.S. broadcasting.[11]

Downstream control over local broadcasters is a potentially bigger problem. In the U.S., geography meant that from the earliest days TV and radio signals had to be rebroadcast, giving local TV stations a point of leverage. This leverage was increased when the federal government forbade network ownership of local stations from reaching more than 35 percent of the population. Networks pushed hard for reconsideration of these regulations. This makes no sense: the Internet disintermediates networks making downstream control of affiliates less useful, not more.

Investors should look at the TV problem upside down: if TV doesn't get audiences, who does?

Broadcast.com, a startup Internet-based broadcaster recently sold to Yahoo!, says that it reaches more daytime white collar workers than NBC, CBS, and ABC combined.

Broadcast.com has the vital eyeballs of a PC-driven audience that networks can't reach. The company is hitting high-income workers when they are in decision mode, something they are less likely to be in when relaxing with a beer after work in front of a TV—if they even get the time to do this.

Moreover, Broadcast.com undermines the local role of network affiliates. It has hundreds of TV and radio stations on its site.[12] It targets local sports that the networks often ignore and for which Internet rights are cheap.

Segmentation in favor of cable broadcasters is only the beginning of the problem for legacy networks. In 1999, 39 percent of Americans' on-line time was spent on AOL-controlled sites. This was ten times the number claimed by AOL's nearest competitor, Microsoft. AOL's sales were larger than the next twenty Internet companies combined, and its $125 billion market cap was bigger than that of any media concern worldwide. Its Instant Messaging was used by 40 million. Over the next five years, AOL aims to double its subscriber base and build its "viewing" time from fifty-five minutes today to three hours, becoming a substitute for all media, from TV to cell phones and post-PC devices. Today, AOL gets about $25 a month from each subscriber (including advertising fees). It could triple this by taking a substantial portion of what its customers pay now for cable TV.

Defense of the middle market in the face of forces like Broadcast.com and AOL is no defense at all. Investors looking at markets like these have to ask: do I invest in a company that has a firm, though eroding, hold on the middle market in the hope of a brand-led recovery (it's CBS so it must be better than Yahoo! or AOL), or on what looks like a fringe company with little mainstream attraction?

The Iron Laws provide a clear answer: the fringe of cyberspace is always the place to place your bets. Broad middle markets eventually implode under pressure from the Iron Laws and they cannot long be held. It is much easier, for example, for Rupert Murdoch's News Corp. to pick off a lucrative and profitable franchise than it is for the incumbents to try to bring back the 1960s.

31

Retail: Wal-Mart Grows and Grows

Superior financial performance, rapid growth, high market share, and strong branding are all elements of enduring shareholder value creation. Investors want it all, but they have a hard time finding it. One place to look is Wal-Mart.

In only twenty years, Wal-Mart became the largest retailer in the world. Yet there's nothing new about retail: Mitsui built the first successful department store in the seventeenth century. Retail isn't particularly fast paced either. Unlike high tech, retail growth just chugs along at a few percent per year.[1] A 5 percent increase in Christmas-season sales is considered stellar. But when Wal-Mart comes to town, every retailer within a hundred miles quakes.

Newcomers to slow-growth markets like retail usually expand through acquisition—the kind of roll-up play that Wall Street loves. But Wal-Mart grew organically: it pushed up growth by doing dozens of little things right.

Acquiring Kmart a decade ago, when Kmart's velocity of capital and growth rate were crawling, would have doomed Wal-Mart to oblivion. When Amazon.com, the high-flying on-line bookseller, was looking to build back-office operations to match its front-end sizzle, it hired Wal-Mart's logistical talent, not Barnes & Noble's.[2]

During a recent quarter, sales were up 17 percent, inventories by only 3.5 percent. As a result, said John Menzer, Wal-Mart CFO, his company marked down less merchandise, lowered its labor costs on people needed to move inventory and stock shelves, and cut the amount of merchandise lost to shoplifting.

Wal-Mart's strategy of boosting earnings ahead of sales comes at the expense of suppliers and to the benefit of customers and shareholders. The Wal-Mart model scales. Wal-Mart is a $139 billion organization growing fast, just like a start-up. Wal-Mart, at more than twice the size of AT&T, looks more like go-go companies Dell and Cisco.

Wal-Mart is on the right side of history. As we have said repeatedly, information costs have fallen continuously since the invention of handwriting, gradually shifting market power from producers to consumers. Wal-Mart has harnessed this transfer of power to consumers.

Wal-Mart founder Sam Walton recognized that information is so cheap it can easily be substituted for resources like trucks, inventory, fuel, people, and most important, capital. He grew his business by substituting cheap information for other resources at every possible opportunity. Wal-Mart revolutionized the movement of atoms, organizing itself around an Intranet long before there was such a word.

We associate just-in-time delivery with manufacturing. But Walton's genius was in applying this process to retailing. By using cheap information to improve communications between buyers and sellers, Wal-Mart slashed costs by an order of magnitude. Its competitors scrambled to catch up, to which the reorganizations and restructuring at Kmart and Sears attest.

In the late nineteenth century, falling transportation costs built the Sears, Roebuck mail-order empire. With cheap parcel-post rates, Sears could undercut the prices of every general store in America with a range of goods never before seen. Railroads delivered these parcels and also made possible the great department stores of the early twentieth century.

Transportation costs continued to fall in the twentieth century, with cars coming within the reach of all middle-class Americans after the Second World War, and ubiquitous interstate highways opening up the entire country to cheap truck transport. First came the suburban supermarkets and shopping centers, then the discounters.

The arrival of Wal-Mart, however, was different. Wal-Mart's empire is not built on cheap transportation, but on using cheap information to obviate the need for transportation, handling, and storage.

Using falling information costs, Wal-Mart does what many consider impossible: *it keeps inventories low and shelves well stocked at the same time.* Furthermore, while some competitors eliminate the slow-selling items they carry to compensate for inefficiencies in their organization, Wal-Mart constantly expands its already wide selection of merchandise.

For Wal-Mart, this system means less money tied up in inventory, less spent on employees to handle its merchandise, and less spent on transportation. For investors, it means more bang for each buck invested. For its customers, Wal-Mart's efficiency lowers prices, expands selection, and makes its no-questions-asked guarantee policy viable. Small wonder Wal-Mart is now the biggest retailer in the world with no end in sight.

Beginning in the 1970s, when it was a fraction of its current size—a small, regional chain with lackluster performance—Wal-Mart invested heavily in computers. Because many of its stores were located in remote areas with poor telephone service, the company had to use its own satellite-based telecommunications network. Originally, the company used this system for routine accounting functions, as well as for training. Wal-Mart founder Sam Walton also liked to give televised pep talks to all his employees around the country.

But the real benefit of this network came when the company began experimenting with direct, real-time links between its cash registers in the store and the factory computers of its suppliers. As soon as a check-out clerk scans a customer's package of Pampers, for example, Wal-Mart's network passes that information on to Procter and Gamble's computer, where production and store delivery are then scheduled.

Sounds like common sense, but in the past, retailers tallied sales and reordered only weekly or monthly. Wholesalers, for their part, estimated the retail sales they expected, and then placed orders with manufacturers. At the plant, managers scheduled production based on their forecasts of sales. Up and down the line, large inventories buffered planners from the inaccuracies of their estimates. Basically, everyone guessed at what they needed, and then hoped they could shoe-horn what they got into the market. A costly and inefficient way of doing business.

Wal-Mart turned this process on its head, basing its orders and merchandising decisions on what people actually buy. With its elaborate computer network, the company had the information it needed to accurately, and quickly, determine what customers want, where and when. Wal-Mart took a *four to five year lead on its competitors* in just-in-time delivery between suppliers and customers. Customers themselves—not managers with their crystal balls—drive Wal-Mart production and delivery schedules.

In the past, merchandise would go into the inventory three times: once at the plant; again at the wholesalers; and a third time at the retailer's store. Much of what Wal-Mart sells, however, doesn't go into inventory anywhere. It comes right off supplier production lines for delivery to a Wal-Mart store, where it will go right onto display, to be sold within days. At other retailers, most merchandise still flows through the company's own warehouses. The stuff sits around for weeks. But at Wal-Mart it moves to an outlet within hours, if not minutes.

At Wal-Mart, the Internet is the organization, speeding decision making and improving customer service. Wal-Mart has created a powerful bond with its customers by lengthening its service cycle in a way competitors cannot match. This works only because front-line Wal-Mart employees have power to make decisions on behalf of customers. Wal-Mart employees spend less time dealing with their organization than do the employees of competitors, because there is less organization with which to deal.

Others have followed suit. Dell and Cisco extend the Wal-Mart structure right to their customers' desktops and living rooms. Like Wal-Mart, they have reduced or eliminated interstitial costs between customer departments, contributing directly to customer cash flows.

Not only does the Wal-Mart model scale, but it outlasted Sam Walton. While other companies struggle, sometimes for decades, after the passing of their founders, the Wal-Mart supply-chain management system has a life of its own, going from strength to strength.

Greater efficiency in stores like Wal-Mart has reduced the amount of truck traffic needed for each dollar of the economy, a clear benefit for the environment in terms of pollution and wasted energy. Freight ton-miles in the U.S. have dropped significantly in the last two decades. During this same period, the average efficiency of trucks (which account for virtually all traffic to and from retail stores) rose from less than eight miles per gallon to nearly eleven miles per gallon. One of the largest segments of the economy has been truly revolutionized by falling information costs.

The phenomenal growth of catalog shopping during the 1980s demonstrated that for many people, shopping is nothing but a chore. Department stores tried to revive sales by making shopping an "experience," a cross between fashion and theater. But with most adults now working, there are fewer people with enough time on their hands to cruise the malls. Other retailers, like Wal-Mart, just make shopping easy, fast, and cheap. Electronic services, particularly when combined with virtual reality—allowing a hammer to be held in your hand or a dress to be tried on, for example—may eliminate the need to go shopping at all.

When this happens, in-store shopping will become voluntary—something done only by those who truly enjoy it—rather than compulsory as it is today. The entire consumer marketing, advertising, sales, and packaging industries will be torn apart, with an impact on employment that can barely be fathomed.

In the U.S. alone, one out of four Americans is employed moving or selling goods today. Electronic retailing could reduce this number by three-quarters, or more. We have been through this trauma before. One hundred years ago, most Americans worked on farms, and domestic help was one of the biggest categories of employment off the farm. Today, only one percent of Americans are farmers, and domestic help is barely a category at all. The falling cost of information will have the same effect on retailing worldwide.

32

Computers: Dell Breaks the Moore Time Barrier

When the personal computer market slows, Dell not only grows, it becomes more profitable. What is Dell's secret? *Like a plane breaking the sound barrier, Dell moves faster than Moore Time, thus accumulating seemingly market-defying advantages over its competitors.*

Moving this fast, Dell adds real value for customers and builds value for shareholders by doing so. In 1998, Dell was the twenty-eighth most valuable company in the world, far outranking Ford and GM, companies with thirteen times the sales.[1]

The problem of competing in Moore Time, as we saw in Part One, is *miss a year in Moore Time and competitive advantage goes elsewhere at exponential rates.* In Moore Time, a two-year product plan can turn what was a competitive advantage of months, even years, into a disadvantage of decades. Dell offers one of the best examples of how to compete in Moore Time.

Dell doesn't stay ahead through new technology or even new products. It sells someone else's—Intel's. Dell's secret is no secret at all. Dell simply adheres to the age-old business wisdom of Konosuke Matsushita, that the competitor closest to customers takes all.

Dell sells direct to customers—not through retailers—to eliminate anything that might get between it and its customers. When a customer calls or orders over the Internet, Dell's system does not even begin to order parts until the customer's credit card number has cleared. Once Dell has the cash, which takes a second or two, the parts are ordered, the machine is assembled, often to custom requirements, and the system is shipped a few hours later.

By integrating distribution into manufacturing this way, *Dell gets paid ten days before incurring expenses.* Most of its competitors get paid between thirty and seventy days *after* incurring expenses, giving Dell a huge competitive advantage.

Dell has reduced its number of suppliers from more than two hundred five years ago to less than fifty today. It insists that its suppliers warehouse parts within fifteen minutes of its factories.[2] As a result, inventories run at seven days and inventory turns at fifty-two. Dell also has almost no parts store and no upstream exposure to major product changes by key suppliers like Intel. When processor generations change, Dell changes on the fly.

Selling through the Internet automatically broadens Dell's customer base to anyone in the world with a computer. In addition, through this system Dell can sell anything from high-end servers to TVs. It will be much easier for Dell to fill its distribution pipes with a range of new products than it will be for the existing producers of those products to change their distribution systems to match Dell's ability to generate cash.

Dell may have discovered the distribution strategy for the twenty-first century. What gives this strategy legs, moreover, is that it is a system. Michael Dell could drop dead tomorrow and his system would continue intact.

For Dell, there are several great advantages to being structured this way. For starters, direct selling generates no inventory pipeline. With every shift in computer price-performance, competitors get stuck with months worth of stock in their dealer chains that must be sold off at firesale prices to clear the channel for new products.[3] This takes time, undermines brand, unsettles dealers, and moves customer focus away from new products and onto the fire sale.

With no dealer channel to support, Dell's undiscounted retail prices are everyone else's wholesale prices. While others scramble to squeeze margins to support dealers, Dell gets full markup and probably then some.

Dell's ideas are not always leading-edge. Dell's goal of cutting the number of times a hard drive is handled by someone from thirty to fifteen (human contact is the point at which most flaws are introduced), would be laughed at in most Japanese factories, where such a part would probably never be touched at all.[4]

Indeed, one of our clients asked us what it had to do to be like Dell. We very quickly discovered that our client's gross margins were much better than Dell's, while its net was nonexistent. It was a superior manufacturer in every way, but its costly multilayered distribution system soaked up every penny it made. Our client had become a bank whose sole purpose was the financing of its dealers' inventories.

What distinguishes Dell is that it manages change on two axes at once: distribution and manufacturing. Others, by contrast, are used to moving on a single axis: manufacturing. All the plant changes in the world mean little to customers unless they result in changes in distribution.

To see just how devastating Dell's formula is, compare it with Compaq when it was preparing to buy DEC in late 1997.

Between the third and fourth quarter of 1997, while Dell was getting paid ten days before incurring expense, Compaq slipped from getting paid ten days afterwards to twenty-six days. That moved the gap between the two companies from twenty to thirty-six days—over a month's worth of cash—in Dell's favor. Worse still for Compaq, it was buying a company that got paid fifty-four days after incurring expense, putting the combined companies forty-eight days—almost seven weeks of cash—behind Dell.

How long would it take to overcome a forty-eight day disadvantage? Dell faced the same question in the mid-nineties when it found itself an also-ran in the PC business and was looking for ways to compete effectively. The answer: it will take years for Compaq just to get to where Dell was in the late nineties. To get to where Dell is today or will be tomorrow may not be possible because, translated into Moore Time, these competitive shortfalls are almost infinite.

Buying DEC was clearly the wrong thing for Compaq to do. Yet it might have been done for the right reasons. We stressed in "Competing in Moore Time" that the only antidote to increasingly compressed cycle times is to prolong customer service relationships. The accepted wisdom was that buying DEC gave Compaq DEC's first-class customer service organization. On the face of it, then, acquiring DEC was the right thing to do. The problem is that Compaq may be measuring service the wrong way.

Rather than build a large, people-heavy service organization, Dell used cheap information to eliminate people, integrate distribution into manufacturing, and generate cash, the life blood of all business.

By moving back up the Moore Curve to acquire DEC, Compaq has forgotten the cardinal rule of information mechanics—that each point on the Moore Curve unleashes a market an order of magnitude larger than itself. By this logic, the bandwidth engines of the future will be in hundreds of millions of homes, not tens of millions of offices. As with the collapse of France in 1940, Compaq has taken itself out of the play for the next big market, leaving the field to Dell.

33

Software: Goodbye, Mr. Bill?

Bill Gates has a simple problem: how to move Microsoft from the market for hundreds of millions of PCs that Microsoft dominates to the market for tens of billion of post-PCs that no one dominates, or even understands. Gates has a secondary problem almost as large: good post-PC software is invisible, as it is on a Sony PlayStation. How can Microsoft stay visible, and brandable, in the Big Bang markets of tomorrow?

The alternative is to settle back into a personal computer market that will gently slow down to the low single figures at which the world's middle-class consuming population increases.

Gates's ability to answer these two questions, therefore, will determine whether or not Microsoft is a growth stock for the twenty-first century.

The PC market that Gates so adeptly commandeered was a new one with very few competitors, and most of those from one industry—computing. By contrast, the post-PC business, as we saw in "The Singularity," comprises dozens of legacy companies from dozens of industries, as well as the usual array of start-ups.

In addition, the post-PC numbers are so large, and the wealth to be made so obvious, that Microsoft will have none of the advantages it had in the PC business of going into a market the future of which so many, including IBM itself, doubted. Everyone will want their piece and all the big players, from media juggernauts to consumer-electronics empires, are staking their claims. None of these will simply bow out because Microsoft enters. On the contrary, they all see the Big Bang as an opportunity to expand their brand presence at the expense of Microsoft.

Post-PCs run on a babble of mostly proprietary operating systems, like 3Com's PalmOS and Sony's PlayStation. They don't need common software—they just need to communicate. If they can access the Internet, that's probably good enough. In addition, in the view of leading Sony executives (who should know), Microsoft operating systems are too difficult to use in living rooms.[1]

There is no reason why video-game players, pagers, cars, phones, TVs, and network computers should not be Internet nodes running independent of Microsoft-type operating systems. Nothing prevents post-PC contenders from trying to achieve software dominance. Already fights are underway to control software for cell phones, set-top boxes, digital TVs, and even appliances. Perhaps a time will come when your VCR can ask your breadmaker to crunch a few gigaflops in between the rising and baking cycles. If so, Microsoft will probably not have much to do with it.

So far, Microsoft Windows CE, a knocked-down version of Windows 2000,[2] is not the post-PC operating system of choice. While some palm-top PCs use CE, the most successful such device, 3Com's Palm Pilot, does not. CE's size takes a toll: CE computers are bigger, more powerful, and more expensive than their competition. CE-powered machines cost between $300 and $1,000. Post-PC devices generally cost under $300. Like PCs themselves, CE is a jack-of-all-trades and master of none.

Alternatives to Windows CE are abundant. Ericsson, Motorola, and Nokia joined forces with Psion to develop a new operating system for hand-held wireless devices. They will pay $10 to $15 per cell phone for their software.[3] Sun is advocating Java as the post-PC operating system of choice. Sun charges around $5 for a cell phone or set-top box,[4] although TCI is paying only $1 per box.[5] This is not a financial model that will work for Microsoft, which charges about $25 per unit for CE.[6]

Java's little brother, Jini, is designed for "plug & play" communications and distributed processing between post-PCs. Sun is busy signing up consumer electronics and computer vendors. Sony and Philips have their own OS called Home Audio/Visual Interoperability. Microsoft responded with Universal Plug and Play.[7]

If CE is too bulky for post-PCs, Windows is out of the question. Windows 2000 (which merged NT 4.0 and Windows 98 into one platform) has 20–30 million lines of software code. By comparison, a Lucent 5ESS telephone exchange, the backbone of the American telephone network, has some 25 million lines.[8] Windows NT 3.1 (circa 1993) had 6 million lines; Windows NT 4.0 has 17 million.[9] A typical cell phone has just 2 to 3 million lines of code.

Yet despite its heft, Windows faces stiff competition to run the network. Unix dominates carrier-grade markets such as phone companies. The up-and-coming operating system for serious networking is Linux, a Unix derivative. According to the *Wall Street Journal*, Linux is "simple, lean and fast"—in short, everything that Windows is not.[10] Microsoft is locked in a PC prison, an Alcatraz from which it is unlikely to escape.

Interestingly, CE shares one important trait with its post-PC rivals: it runs on non-Intel microprocessors.[11] After Intel killed them in PCs, consumer-electronics companies focused on applications-specific designs of their own. Hitachi, for example, is a leader in chips for hand-helds and set-top boxes.[12]

The number of post-PC products like computer games, cellular phones, television set-top boxes, Palm Pilot hand-helds, digital cameras, camcorders, burglar alarms, and other computer-powered devices sold in the United States already exceeds the number of PCs. The post-PC era is well under way as is the erosion of Microsoft's position in it.

We include in post-PCs anything with the processing power of a personal computer. But these post-PCs—even the toys—aren't toys. Nintendo 64 and Sony PlayStation have more horsepower than the average home PC.[13]

The post-PC era does not mean the death of Microsoft. On the contrary, the PC market remains robust. Nevertheless, the action is shifting elsewhere. Just as IBM and DEC were unable to adapt their organizations to meet the needs of PC customers, so Microsoft may find itself maladapted to the post-PC world. Strange as it may sound, Microsoft could quickly find itself stuck in a Dead Zone in the post-PC race.

We've seen this before. For years, IBM tallied in its annual report the relentless and rapid increase in mainframe capacity demand. The only problem was that prices fell faster than demand rose—and the glamour moved elsewhere.

For many, this is a new dawn. During the past decade, all would-be information-technology players danced to the Microsoft tune. Now, the field is wide open. Barriers to newcomers remain low. For every type of post-PC device, the scramble is on. Newcomers and familiar faces alike are jockeying for position. This includes Philips, Sony, Matsushita, and many others that were never able to crack the PC market in any meaningful way. But others are moving to the fore; no one has a lock on post-PC standards. As we saw in "The Collapse of Standards," entropy in post-PCs will make any attempt to impose standard software meaningless.

Communications is the only thing post-PCs have in common. Naturally, therefore, Microsoft is moving to control the points of network access, like the set-top boxes that will connect TVs to the Internet. The weakness of this strategy is that those that own the networks, like AT&T, the phone companies, and even Microsoft cofounder Paul Allen, are fully aware of the brand value of those access points. Microsoft invested $5 billion in AT&T—which certainly helped AT&T's balance sheet after its acquisitions of TCI and MediaOne—but will AT&T allow Microsoft brand dominance in the Living Rooms of its customers? Doubtful.

It is entirely possible that Microsoft has already lost the brand momentum in post-PCs and many have to settle for the invisible role of supplying the customized software that supports the post-PC brands of others. This is probably the outer limit of what AT&T would accept. No one else with a brand as big would accept any more.

Paul Allen's strategy is an interesting contrast to that of the company he cofounded. By acquiring cable companies, he is acquiring a brandable platform that, unlike software, is an annuity paid by customers every month forever.

Consumers will look for dial-tone simplicity. The PC industry has done a remarkable job of shifting service costs onto the backs of its customers. Businesses accept the demands of running PC networks. So do the 25 percent of consumers with PCs and Internet connections. But most of the consumers who will buy post-PC devices (and already have phones, TVs, and VCRs) will not accept PC-grade service.

Unlike Nintendo 64, PCs—and the computer networks that

connect them—crash every day. One reason post-PCs work so much better than PCs is that they do only one or two things. They already meet the Granny Test. Granny doesn't want a computer-savvy twelve-year-old systems administrator to turn on her TV. And she won't need one for the post-PC devices she will use.

34

Phone Companies: The Next Penn Central

The Internet has turned traditional telecommunications investments, the bluest of blue chips, into a shell game. Phone companies the world over are slowly liquidating a hundred years' worth of shareholders' equity, only shareholders don't know it yet. In this environment, where velocity of capital is the key to value creation, successful players will maximize financial flexibility by unlocking the full value of cash flows and hidden assets.

Phone companies are excellent examples of large amounts of shareholder value locked in the Dead Zone. Their organizations are deep, integrated, and overmanned—the exact opposite of Cisco, a company we will look at in another chapter. For agile competitors, these companies will be easy pickings. Without a radical overhaul, and soon, they will share the fate of Penn Central, something no number of megamergers will forestall.

Phone companies can learn something from Ryder.

Ryder owns and operates truck fleets for its customers. While it's known for truck rentals, Ryder evolved its business from renting to leasing to full-service leasing, and finally to what it calls "integrated logistics." With a full-service lease, Ryder owns the trucks and maintains them, even painting them with customer logos. Integrated logistics goes much further: Ryder is completely responsible for all or part of a customer's supply chain.

Ryder allied itself with Anderson Consulting and IBM to expand its reach further into customer operations. Integrated logistics became its fastest-growing line of business.[1] Fedex is doing the same.

EDS already owns and operates huge corporate and government computer and communications networks. So does IBM, which also leases PCs to big customers for a flat monthly fee. IBM will replace the computers as frequently as every two years.[2] This solves a big problem: if you buy a computer, you must depreciate it over five years, even though it's worthless after two or three. For phone companies the problem is even bigger: regulators traditionally have required them to depreciate their assets over decades.[3]

Phone companies could sell their networks to an investment syndicate, lease back what they really need to control customer experience of their network, and continue to operate them as before. This is how the airline industry works. Lessor GE Capital owns more aircraft than British Airways or United Airlines.[4] Unloading the network would unleash large amounts of capital and has the potential of turning the old phone company into a powerful new generation of high-capacity/low-cost carriers. Those blue chips could become the shareholder value engines of tomorrow.

They could also go the other way. Unthinkable though it may seem, nationalization of the telephone system in the U.S. is a real possibility. Politicians respond to voters, who don't like paying high prices for lousy service. New York State "nationalized" the Long Island Lighting Company, a major electrical utility. The state swamped the market with $7 billion in debt to take over LILCO.[5] New York "socialized" the difference between what LILCO carried on its books and what it was worth to another utility. Most of the difference is for "stranded assets," particularly the Shoreham nuclear power plant, built but never turned on. Brooklyn Union Gas bought LILCO's "right priced" assets; New York taxpayers were left holding the bag.

Many local U.S. phone companies are getting squeezed into the same corner. Their high payout ratios make their shares near-debt instruments. And their entire capital structure is geared to regulated rates of return they no longer have. This is bad enough in itself, but these companies are paying for equipment that won't be worth much, if anything, when alternate means of access get turned up. Most of their plant will become stranded. Carriers—or, more accurately, their investors—will be stuck with investments they can never recover.

The Pennsylvania and New York Central railroads revolutionized communications in the United States during the country's period of most rapid industrial expansion. The New York Central made Cornelius Vanderbilt the richest man in America.[6] Less than a century later, Penn Central, a combination of both assets, was a wreck, a ward of the state.

Despite decades of underinvestment that made it vulnerable to truck competition, once formed in 1968, Penn Central immediately embarked on a diversification program that took it into real estate, pipelines and other areas unrelated to its core business. Two years later, the company was bankrupt; in 1976, the U.S. government purchased its rail assets, forming Conrail.

By the time the government acquired the railroad, the only thing of any value was its real estate (of which the Penn Central Company naturally kept as much as it could).[7]

What happened to Penn Central could easily happen to phone

companies the world over. Like the Penn, many have suffered from prolonged underinvestment that makes them vulnerable to competition. Also like the Penn, they have neither the cash flows nor the asset values to justify their debt exposure.

The problem for the Penn was that, over time, its options diminished. The longer management waited to exercise these options, the less room it had to maneuver, until finally it had none.

Still, it took fifty years for the Penn to come undone. The shareholder value of phone companies, by contrast, will evaporate in Moore Time.

The number of CEO's who have understood this calculation is tiny. One of the very few who has is Ivan Seidenberg, former CEO of NYNEX and now CEO of Bell Atlantic. NYNEX carried a load of debt in 1995, but the company played a smart game. By cutting costs fast, Seidenberg was able to boost earnings and command an offer from Bell Atlantic in 1996 of twenty-one times earnings. This is a handsome value for a company with one of the most difficult infrastructures in the world to manage.[8]

Pacific Bell, by contrast, commanded $16.7 billion from SBC, a multiple of only sixteen and a difference of $5.3 billion, or 32 percent compared with NYNEX. Part of the reason is that Pacific Bell's debt burden was so much greater than NYNEX's.[9]

MCI and MFS both had debt ratios in the 25 percent range, and they were acquired quickly as a result. MFS was sold in 1996 for $14.4 billion, a handsome premium of twenty-five times 1995 sales and 54 times losses.[10] The reason for their relatively low debt is that neither had a large local phone network to support.

What is prematurely aging phone companies is the Living Room Revolution. This revolution is destroying the value of one of the carrier's few points of leverage—access to customers. Consumers will want lots of bandwidth, and they will want it cheap.

Providing this bandwidth and the services to use it will be the biggest market in history. If phone companies cannot transform themselves fast, the Living Room market will go elsewhere.

Phone companies have to sell their assets while they are still worth something. When the Bells started merging a few years ago, their undepreciated plant was valued at about $125 billion dollars. Over 40 percent of this was "outside plant," mostly those last miles of copper wire (and the gear that keeps them humming) that run from phone exchanges to homes and offices. In sum, the Bells carried about $1,000 per customer-line on their books in undepreciated plant.[11]

Those assets may be wasting fast, given the threat of competition and new technology. But they still represent an annuity of unparalleled value. On average, each phone line threw off almost $300 per year in cash.[12] That's an excellent return on $1,000, and a good return on the nearly $2,000 originally spent to install each line. Returns start to deteriorate when you look at what they were spending to add new phone lines: $5,000 or more. You can do better with Treasuries.

Clearly, there are big risks right over the horizon. But the phone companies still have assets of enormous value. And they still have a range of options for realizing the value of these assets. Measured in Moore Time, however, they won't last long.

The options available to the phone companies, therefore, will dwindle fast. Five years from now, the value of their assets will have diminished hugely.

The worst option may be merging with another carrier, today's preferred method of survival. Merging local networks does not change the economics of the network. Again, Penn Central, itself a merger, is instructive.

Phone company mergers simply combine low-level access to the kitchen wall; they bring these companies no closer to the Living Room than they were before. To us, this is rather like merging horse stables and feed lots in order to take advantage of the coming age of the automobile.

Like the railroads, the phone companies have a lot of real estate. When their networks reach the end of the road, as the Penn discovered, that may be all that's left of any value. Today, real estate is just a fraction of the undepreciated plant on their books, but there are many hidden assets. There are buildings, towers, vaults, rights-of-way, and other properties that are carried at cost, even though many were purchased decades ago. In some cases, the real estate may be worth selling separately from the telecom plant.

Financial transactions on this scale are not for amateurs. The opportunities are enormous, and so are the risks. Managing residual values and technological change on top of market swings is not easy. When the airline industry stalled in the early 1990s, GPA Group PLC, the aircraft leasing maverick, went into a tailspin. In a classic vulture play, GE capital picked up the pieces.

These questions are being forced by another. Harnessing the Living Room market will require an expensive network upgrade. One phone company CEO came to us with a plan to fund such a plan that required him to turn off his dividend flow for nearly a decade. He asked us, "Do our shareholders have the nerve to go along with this?" Our answer, of course, was "No."

In the mid-nineties, Ray Smith, then CEO of Bell Atlantic, faced the same issue when he told investors that by acquiring TCI he hoped to give the combined firm the multiple of a Microsoft. In return, he told them, they could expect little, if anything, in dividends. A wholesale shift in shareholder profile like this—from widows and orphans to high risk—is fiendishly difficult to engineer, especially on such a scale. The deal collapsed and Smith's plan was never tested.

Today, we believe, the answer is large-scale deleveraging. Write-downs will be required, certainly, but the companies that emerge on both sides of the transaction will be stronger, better valued, and will have a firmer equity footing than before. One will be the low-capacity, legacy network managed for cash flow. The other will be a high-capacity network managed for growth. Deleveraging will unleash the large amounts of equity needed for the construction of new networks. It will infuse the industry with the new blood needed to harness the Living Room Revolution.

35

Industrial Sales: Cisco Systems

Cisco Systems is one of the best examples of a company that uses all the recommendations we made in our first book, *Beating Japan*, and has the sales growth to match. Cisco uses superior interior-line advantages to get to customers faster than competitors laden with more complex organizations and lower velocities of capital. Cisco teaches investors that today the big do not beat the small; rather, the fast beat the slow.

Look at the 1999 data: 55 percent of orders were not touched by anyone; sales were up six times over 1994 but sales support staff had only doubled.[1] Cisco made 70 percent of its $11 billion plus sales over the Internet, making it one of the largest Internet commerce players in the world. This company is practically hollow inside. It sells highly engineered industrial products without the expense of touching them or supporting them.

Founded in 1984, Cisco became the fastest growing company in history. Its products are industrial: routers for the Internet. But it sells nearly $8 billion of these over the Internet, accounting for fully one-third of all Internet commerce in 1998.

Things weren't always so rosy.

Cisco's products are, in themselves, not that interesting. They are the rails of the Internet, near-commodities made by several others. Normally you would think that a company like this is vulnerable to price competition and would live under severe margin constraints. Indeed, that is exactly what the market was looking for in early 1997 when Cisco's shares dropped 34 percent between January and March.[2]

The press talked about "Cisco's Crunch Time" and "Cisco's Skid."[3] By 1997, some 85 percent of Internet routers were supplied by Cisco and the company had grown an average of 80 percent a year over the previous four years. The main complaint seems to have been that revenue growth from routers would grow only 30 percent. The naysayers started jabbering.

Two years later, Cisco was a hard-charging giant. Its sales more than doubled and its market capitalization soared. Cisco's turnaround has enormous lessons for investors in the information economy.

What Cisco does is to seek leverage where others don't look, and to secure proprietary advantages by doing so. For example, Cisco spends large amounts of time on improving the way phones are answered and people hired, all to reduce costs and use technology to the hilt. The result is good customer relations, fast growth, excellent returns, and a high market cap.

Cisco's advantages are not its products but the way it uses information technology to support those products. Competitors are easily suckered by such an approach. Seeing sales success attached to a competitor's product, they rush out to spend billions to enter the market. More often than not the buyer wakes up six months down the road with a huge headache from an acquisition that is failing. Shareholders take the hit.

At the very moment analysts and the press were slamming

Cisco, it managed to increase productivity 22 percent using the Internet.[4] Cisco solves seven out of ten customer technical questions over the Net. According to its CEO, John Chambers, this allowed Cisco to move a thousand engineers out of technical support and into product design, giving the company huge competitive advantages. Indeed, by 1997, the company was saving $350 million on an expense line of $1.5 billion and was improving the price-performance of its products in line with the demands of Moore's Law.[5]

Cisco uses all four of our Keys to Value Creation to unlock growth. Cisco's results: it is ranked first or second in fourteen of the fifteen markets it serves. In three years its market capitalization nearly tripled.

In many ways, John Chambers is the Konosuke Matsushita of our time. He has taken Matsushita's fundamental assertion that to contribute to society, a company must do everything possible to close up the gap between itself and its customers. Using our Keys to do this, he has given shareholders wonderful returns.

Cisco doesn't hook customers on its hardware, nor even on its software. Instead, it hooks them on the way it uses information technology to do business, a very different proposition. The company is organized around networks, not an organization chart, giving the firm flexibility and responsiveness. CEO Chambers keeps in direct contact with fifteen key customers around the world, getting voice mail updates from them directly each day.

Cisco and its suppliers work on an order simultaneously, without actually talking to each other or their customer. Customers place orders over the Internet, outside contractors "see" the same order over Cisco's Intranet and ship the same day. The company books and bills, often without seeing or touching a thing. This way of doing business is so successful—Cisco outsources 70 percent of its production—that it has quadrupled production without adding plant, and cut new product introduction time by two thirds, to six months, a very short period. Overhead costs are eliminated in the same way: millions of pages of health benefit and other employee information are on the Net.

Cisco attributes to this use of the Internet its ability to "collapse time,"[6] allowing the company to take on more and do it more quickly than the competition. For example, noting that U.S. small businesses with networks increased from 1.4 million to 2.1 million in only the two years from 1997 to 1999,[7] the company launched its attack. There is plenty of room for growth; more than 70 percent of small businesses still don't have networks. Sales to this sector increased from $170 million to 1996 to $2.2 billion in 1999.

Collapsing time goes far beyond supplier interaction. The CFO can, at any time of day or night see sales and margin data no more than twenty-four hours old by region, country, customer, or even by salesman. He can close his books within a day at the end of each quarter and will soon be able to close them at the end of each working day of the year.[8]

The advantages are enormous. Cisco gets the highest sales per employee in its business but spends a tiny 1 percent of sales on its finance department. When downturns occur, as one did a few years ago in Japan, the company claims to see this coming before its competition, giving it three full quarters to adjust its footing while others keep pumping iron straight into the loss column. Equally, its accounting system allows it to see upturns before others do and to take advantage of these more quickly.

To make our rules of organization work, Cisco became a model inside-out company, using the network to allow it to operate at high enough speeds to get ahead of the curve. This has allowed the company to design itself to unusual criteria: change rather than stability; the shape of the network rather than the shape of the organization chart; a web of interdependent partners; and the pursuit of constant technological advantage.

Lesson One for investors is to look for companies that use the information to enhance the "personal touch," not replace it. Cisco consistently uses the Internet to enhance its ability to get closer to customers, employees, and strategic partners. The distinction is vital: wholesale substitution of information for people leverages neither the people nor the information.

36

Intel: Where the Chips Fall?

The Big Bang presents much the same problem for Intel as it does for Microsoft. The sheer number of places into which you can put the kind of superfast microchip in which Intel specializes is increasing at an exponential rate. For twenty years, Intel dominated one such place, the personal computer. Today there are dozens more places, from games to TVs and camcorders. And where there are only so many hundreds of millions of personal computers, there will be many billions of new opportunities.

The trick for Intel is to be in them.

But where Intel has all the advantages of market dominance in PCs, in post-PCs it has, in effect, gone back to the minors. Ahead is lots of hard slogging to get back on top. This may not take long. But it might take forever.

Intel is well adapted to the manufacture of chips for expensive PCs. The price of PCs sold in the United States was remarkably constant for two decades—about $2,000[1]—giving Intel a huge boost during most of this time. But the company had to scramble to supply chips for sub–thousand-dollar PCs. By 1997, cheap PCs accounted for a third of the market, and Intel was losing this sector to arch-competitor Advanced Micro Devices.[2] Intel began to feel the pain: its share of the PC market fell 10 percent in 1998, falling three times faster in the fourth quarter than in the first quarter.[3] To close the gap, Intel introduced its Old Navy line of less powerful, sub–thousand-dollar PC chips, called Celeron.[4]

In post-PCs, the company is not a big player. By early 1998, post-PC chips cost between $10 and $40.[5] A year previously, Intel's average price was $220; its cheapest Pentium was $87. The problem, moreover, is that post-PC applications need more powerful chips, not less.

The impact on component suppliers will be profound. These companies, long in Intel's shadow, have a real breakout opportunity. They include Japanese, Korean, and Taiwanese giants, as well as numerous smaller American companies. In PCs, Intel takes an enormous share of total profits because of its lock on standards. In the future, as we saw in "The Collapse of Standards," the only standard required will be the need to communicate. For the most part, this means the Internet.

This is not a pretty picture. Left untouched, Intel could find itself making the slowest chips for the slowest market, a recipe for value implosion.

Intel is being torn several ways at once: the growth market is in areas like toys and TVs, where its presence is limited; prices in the market it dominates—PCs—are plunging; cycle times in the fastest growing markets are fractions of those in the PC business.

A natural first reaction for Intel is to defend its home turf—the PC—which it is doing vigorously. The PC market will continue to grow for many years, no doubt about it. And Intel will see plenty of opportunity there. But making the transition into broader markets will not be easy. Intel will have to transform itself into a platform for post-PC devices in an Internet-television world.

Here Intel has been caught on the horns of a dilemma: does the company try to turn its basic PC platform into something more powerful, say by including TV capabilities, or does it shift into new markets with completely different economies? The first move is defensive and the second is offensive. There are weaknesses in both. PCs may become less important, making defensive moves there redundant. And the second move is into a market unlike any Intel has dealt with before, and which is growing at exponential rates in so many areas that it is hard to see how Intel can harness even a fraction of them. And which fraction?

Between these horns, Intel's competition is moving in quickly. Advanced Micro Devices struck early in low-priced PC chips.[6] Then a whole series of hot consumer-electronics products, from digital cameras to DVDs and PlayStations, ripped through the market with no "Intel Inside."

To ensure its place in the information markets of the future, Intel is driving across several fronts. It is moving to broaden its expertise in "hybrid applications" chips.[7] Its stated goal in the late nineties was to bring to home devices a single chip with the animation quality of *Toy Story*. That's serious processing power: *Toy Story*'s creators used 117 Sun workstations for each frame, and it would have taken a single then-current Pentium forty-three years to render the movie's full seventy-seven minutes.[8]

Intel bought Chips and Technologies in 1998 for $420 million and is launching new graphics chips that the two developed together. These circuits are designed for PCs, however, and these remain relatively expensive. As we will see later on, Sony has sold 50 million of its under–two-hundred-dollar PlayStations in only twenty-four months, roughly the total number of PCs sold by all suppliers worldwide between 1980 and 1990.

Both products are disposable: PCs are virtually useless after two years and rarely support new software after three years; and toys like PlayStation are so cheap they are often junked after a year or less. The differences between PC and post-PC cycles place enormous pressures on chip suppliers like Intel.

Where an Intel chip for a PC might be priced at about $200, an entire Nintendo 64, chips and all, sells for less. Processors for markets like these will have to sell in the $5 to $20 range, a huge leap for Intel to make.

Intel has identified key weaknesses in Internet access, and is offering a variety of solutions to help quicken the pace at which we get images over the Internet.[9] There is huge merit to this, not the least of which is the recognition that bringing a highly visual, TV-like component into the PC is essential to the continued success of both the computer and the Web.

But, having done this, Intel annoyed Internet publishers with what they saw as a transparent attempt to get Internet customers to upgrade their computers to the latest Intel technology. Internet users are familiar with notes on their screen telling them that such-and-such a page would be better seen or used with the latest version of Netscape Navigator or Microsoft Explorer. But these software packages are usually free or virtually free. Intel proposed notifying Internet customers that sites using its Web-enhancing technology would be better used if they went out and replaced their computer with the latest Intel-based machine.[10] This did not go over well.

The nature of the PC is such that it must support decades of software, forcing chip designers to accommodate a lot of costly overhead, much of it completely redundant and useless to a post-PC manufacturer. The Nintendo 64 gets tossed after a Christmas or two, and with it go its software and any obligation by its chip designers to accommodate that software. This gives Intel competitors a huge advantage over the company and forces Intel to seek new ways of competing.

At its core, Intel is a high-volume manufacturer, and it must keep those volumes coming. To protect its margins, it has moved upmarket into high-priced servers. These are largish computers which "serve" information to other computers on the network (their "clients"), and which naturally cost more than a commodity-like PC. Similarly, Intel is expanding into larger systems—usually "board level," that is, literally a single board full of chips and circuits—giving the company more control over how its core processors are used and the ability to profit from pools of value further downstream from its chips.

The move into board-level assembly has taken Intel down some new roads. In 1999, the company paid $780 million for Dialogic, a maker of add-on cards for servers that integrate a range of telecommunications services, such as phone calls into office computers.[11] This will enable Intel to expand its sphere of influence beyond computers to a whole range of emerging multimedia facilities in the home and office—and hence the number of places it can put its chips.

In a more complex move into services, Intel is expanding its interests in the telecommunications market as a whole, investing $200 million in Williams Communications, a long-distance carrier.[12] This will enable Intel to sell services from its servers—to create an annuity stream from its chip operations, in effect—and control some of the infrastructure necessary to do this.

Intel also has moved downmarket into home networks and consumer-electronics products like digital cameras that will connect to them.

What this adds up to is a company moving quickly away from its personal computer base into an enormous range of multimedia opportunities. "Intel Inside" is becoming something Intel wants to put on everything from the office communications system to the home camcorder and everything in between.

Compounding the complexities of Intel's moves to harness the post-PC Big Bang market are its relations with Microsoft, long the supplier of operating systems for Intel Inside personal computers. On the one hand, Intel has to maintain costly chip overhead for ancient software code from the earliest days of personal computing that no one but Microsoft needs. On the other, Intel can't, shouldn't, and won't wait for Microsoft to set the agenda in post-PCs the way it did in PCs. As we saw previously, there is no reason to believe that Microsoft will dominate the post-PC business. However, while Intel has its own strategic needs, it cannot afford to offend Microsoft unnecessarily.

Tensions, nevertheless, have emerged between the two. The integration of TV into the Internet has provoked some of the deepest divisions between the companies.[13] In 1997, Intel backed digital cable-TV standards set by Network Computer Inc, majority-owned by Oracle, a relentless Microsoft foe.[14] Intel has licensed the video compression technology of Real Networks,[15] a Microsoft competitor in the providing of video—TV—to personal computers.

On its side, Microsoft has had to back the multimedia technology for inexpensive PCs of Intel's archenemy Advanced Micro Devices.[16] When AMD's share of the market more than doubled and its position in the low-priced PC segment verged on dominance, Microsoft naturally decided that it couldn't afford to be left out.

The risk lies in the fact that Intel must spend huge amounts of energy to protect its back door in personal computing while the front door is opening to a range of opportunities which are growing too fast for the company to harness. In late 1997, for example, then CEO Andy Grove told *Business Week* that he wanted to attack the broad market of homes without PCs—some 60 percent of the total—and that this could be done without becoming a producer of high-volume twenty-dollar chips.[17] Well, months later, the twenty-dollar era arrived, forcing Intel to scramble to catch up and Grove to talk about being at a "strategic inflection point" with a "cost imperative that will force us to re-engineer in ways we should have done long ago."[18]

For investors, the big question posed by Intel is this: can a company manage its way along the Moore Curve, balancing cash flows from one segment against the margin pressures of another? History suggests it will be hard slogging.

37

Megamerger Mania

Common-carrier debt stands in the way of the Internet—and the U.S. economy—achieving full potential.

Five years ago, we predicted that only three of the big eight U.S. telephone companies (the seven Baby Bells plus GTE) would remain by the end of 1999. With the merger of Qwest and US West, exactly three remained: Bell Atlantic, BellSouth, and SBC.

Our reasoning in 1994 was simple: in a world where information costs are in a free fall, debt- and cost-laden common carriers have limited options. Consolidation is one of the few options and therefore is inevitable. Expect lots more. And expect yet another round a few years from now.[1]

Never mind that most acquisitions are duds. Big deals keep the wolf at bay. At the height of financial speculation in the 1980s, junk bonds bankrolled department store and consumer goods consolidations. A decade later, they paid for telephone and cable companies.[2]

We are admirers of Sol Trujillo, CEO of US West. Under his direction, this Baby Bell has refocused on its core business, while initiating an aggressive broadband Internet strategy for the future. He "gets it." We often use US West as an example of smart repositioning. By merging with Qwest, Trujillo may be able to extend this vision beyond his western territory to other domestic and international markets.[3] The problem is how he will pay for it. US West ushered in the era of equity-free telecom equities. With its spin-off of MediaOne in 1998, US West pushed its debt ratio to 92 percent.[4]

Investors are applying extraordinary pressure on telephone companies to boost revenues and maintain dividends. They want the double-digit growth of Internet and computer plays, not the low single digits eked out by carriers. To grow this fast, telephone companies must cash in on broadband markets for entertainment and communications. But that costs money—big money.

With lots of new optical fiber underground and underwater, Global Crossing and Qwest could use the acquisitions of US West and Frontier, respectively, to help fill their big pipes. While debt service costs stay the same at best, retail prices for bits moved through those pipes are plummeting. These local operators are bit stream catchment basins to make up the shortfalls. But, telephone company local revenues, now local operators' most predictable source of cash, will also come under pressure from wireless and cable alternatives.

AT&T paid top dollar—$110 billion in total—for TCI and MediaOne's 16 million cable customers, doubling the going rate of $2,500 per subscriber.[5] Most of these must be upgraded with two-way cable and telephone connections—adding perhaps another $1,500 each.[6] If it were to borrow $6,000 per customer to pay for all of this, AT&T would have interest charges of $30 per customer per month (at its current borrowing rate). This is about what it now receives for basic cable service.[7]

Of course, AT&T didn't borrow all $110 billion, but it did

borrow a lot of it. In the quarter it closed on TCI, AT&T loaded an additional $20 billion of debt (including short-term loans) on the balance sheet, boosting its debt ratio to 38 percent. Some of this was assumed TCI debt, some new. AT&T completed the biggest corporate bond deal of all time. Investors lined up to buy these notes. The price tag for MediaOne was $54 billion in cash and stock. Paying with stock is good, since shareholders can't foreclose. But they can get tired of dilution. At least Microsoft's $5 billion investment in AT&T boosted the equity side of the ledger.[8]

Maybe AT&T can double or triple what it gets from each cable customer, with premium movie channels, Internet access, and telephone service.[9] Others with this kind of market power, like Standard Oil, Intel, Microsoft, and even AT&T during its stewardship of the Bell System, provided steady price declines to maximize total demand. They weren't greedy. By contrast, most telephone and cable companies have raised prices in brazen defiance of Moore's Law.[10]

What will happen to AT&T's plans if real competition comes to the cable market? What if customers use At Home to get TV over the Internet? What if satellite becomes a real competitor?

Long-distance and cellular prices are now in free fall. Iridium is a good illustration of how an explosive cocktail is made by combining debt and collapsing prices. When it was conceived a decade ago, Iridium planned to charge $5 per minute for global mobile telephone coverage. This made sense when international calling card rates were several dollars per minute. Since then, new fiber-optic capacity on major overseas routes has driven prices down by two-thirds, with even bigger cuts expected. Scrambling to recover, Iridium cut charges to $3 or less in 1999. Not surprisingly, customers were few, and well short of levels required by its debt covenants. Iridium entered technical default on more than $2 billion in notes and lines of credit. Its junk bonds (with a steep 14 percent coupon) fell to $17.[11] By August 1999 it was bankrupt.

In 1998, AT&T Wireless boosted demand sharply with cheaper calls and simplified billing called "Digital One Rate." As a result, AT&T added nearly two million wireless customers, keeping up the pace in 1999. Unfortunately, the carrier also squeezed all the profit out of the business; net income from wireless dropped from $424 million in 1997 to $3 million in 1998—and only 10 percent of customers had switched to the new Digital One Rate plan by year end. Just as profits dried up, AT&T had to double capital expenditures in 1999 to $2 billion. Demand flooded the network and resulted in busy signals and disconnected calls.[12] AT&T budgeted a total of $11 billion for network upgrades in 1999, up sharply from 1998.[13]

Maybe AT&T will not be squeezed this hard in cable, which has one key advantage over telephone: it offers entertainment. People will stop feeding their kids before they cut off the TV—long after the phone gets disconnected (even longer after they stop calling home on Mother's Day).

Anglo-Saxon financial engineering has found its way to Europe. In 1999, Olivetti paid $32 billion for 52 percent of Telecom Italia, a company about seven times its size. To raise the money, Olivetti broke AT&T's record for the biggest corporate debt issue ever.[14] While it's not easy to unravel a deal like this, we estimated that the new Olivetti would have a debt ratio north of 70 percent, right up there in US West territory.

In the good old days of inflation, monopoly, and regulated rates of return, debt was cheaper than equity. Government franchises made utility bonds look like sovereign debt. Telephone tariffs were simply pegged at levels that covered interest payments, built networks, and gave investors predictable dividends.

If telephone companies used leverage aggressively, cellular and cable operators pushed it to the limit. The concept was simple: why pay taxes when you can pay interest?[15] Interest expense is tax deductible. That's why cable companies have no profit. Creative Wall Street analysts invented the concept of EBITDA, a proxy for cash flow from operations, to value companies that have never returned a nickel to investors as dividends. Today everybody wants a balance sheet that looks like TCI's.[16]

Junk bonds work great when a government franchise guarantees your pricing power. They work during periods of inflation, which favors debtors. And they keep on working during periods of financial euphoria, like this one. But information technologies are driven by deflation and competition, the twin enemies of heavy debt loads.

Any carrier that wants to offer high-capacity broadband to its customers must pony up billions of dollars, with no assurance of success. Moreover, to encourage edgy investors to keep their chips on the table, carriers must maintain dividends. The first whiff of dividend cuts can send investors heading for cover. US West had a dividend yield of nearly 4 percent, multibillion-dollar capital expenditure budgets already in place, and minimal free cash flow.[17] There isn't a lot of spare change here. Where will the money come from for massive broadband upgrades?

Normally, investors will exchange current returns and steady dividends for future growth, with the payback in capital gains. But investors are not confident that carriers can make such an exchange possible. Telephone investments were once as good as gold. Before long they may look more like the loans to Latin American governments of the 1970s (or gold in the 1990s). Indeed, in the face of low-cost alternatives in carriers' traditional markets, aggressive cost cutting will barely keep them above water. They don't have the internally generated funds needed for big new initiatives. They depend on expansive capital markets.

In a time of declining prices, debt does not make sense.[18] Even so, some companies issued new debt to buy back shares. Few issued new equity in telecom, except for IPOs.[19] By contrast, the giants of computers have used the bull market to keep debt very low. Intel and Microsoft are debt-free and don't pay dividends. They are banks. In 1999, Microsoft had a cash reserve of $20 billion.[20] In telecommunications, Equant is one of the few carriers with little or no debt. AT&T had wrestled its debt to the ground, but has reversed course sharply with its cable acquisitions.

AOL wisely kept debt low. This allowed the company to invest $1.5 billion in Hughes Electronics for broadband satellite services for its customers. AOL is even more dependent on plain old telephone service than AT&T, which has an agreement to provide cable modem connections from At Home, its own cable-based Internet service company.[21] With lots of borrowing capacity and little interest expense, AOL's options are open.

Many European telephone companies used their remaining monopoly-generated cash flows to clean up their balance sheets. British Telecom has minimal gearing. Deutsche Telekom, France Telecom, and Telecom Italia all lightened their debt loads considerably. Telecom Italia maybe went too far—investors complained about its lack of leverage. Olivetti probably solved that problem once and for all.

The best option for carriers is deleveraging, which we have long advocated. Smart carriers have started. BellSouth and Bell Atlantic sold their cellular towers to Crown Castle in deals totaling $1.3 billion. BCE sold 20 percent of Bell Canada to Ameritech for cash. With this payment, BCE could cut its debt ratio to about 20 percent, just where it wants to be in this uncertain industry.[22] We expect there will soon be large-scale securitizing of carrier assets.

Debt is the one force powerful enough to delay the Information Singularity, which will occur when the Internet and television slam into each other at a colossal speed. If common carriers had conservative 20 to 30 percent debt ratios today, most of the world's middle-class consumers would have television over the Internet already—and Qwest's and Global Crossing's pipes would be full.

For the industry, the most likely alternative to deleveraging is government action. Regulators can either nationalize local telephone operations, taking the bad stuff and leaving the good for investors (as they did with Penn Central and LILCO), or they can end predatory pricing, as the United States did for the railroads in the 1880s. Then, as now, cutthroat competition threatened the interests of bondholders.

For the economy, the alternative to deleveraging is recession. Information technology drove the 1990s boom.[23] We don't think that consumer Internet connections can grow 30 percent per year or more at current modem speeds. Today's Internet has limited entertainment value. The PC market is also near saturation until faster networks unlock the Internet's entertainment potential: a three-hundred-dollar PC cannot connect to the network any faster than a thousand-dollar PC can. Price cuts alone, therefore, will not reinvigorate the PC market. Consumers are not looking for second-rate PC simulation. They want—and will pay for—first-rate entertainment. They want point-and-click simplicity. Not until real-time, full-motion video and CD-quality music is available will Internet growth return to its torrential pace.

The Internet may have already overshot its mark at current speeds. A recent survey indicated that people are not using their PCs or the Internet.[24] We attribute this to the "encyclopedia effect," parents buying computers to facilitate their children's education. Most people realize, once they own a PC and have spent some time surfing, that the Internet may have its uses, but it's not particularly educational, and it's definitely not entertaining. For investors and everyone else, the debt gap must be filled.

38

Consumer Electronics: Sony Beats the Rap

Sony is a classic example of the last half-century colliding with the next half, full force.

A maker of consumer electronics products, from stereos to TVs, Sony made its bones during Japan's resurgence in the decades following the Korean War. Cofounder Akio Morita, an urbane and charismatic man, made a name for himself and his company worldwide as a provider of high-quality consumer capital.

Sony got hit from two sides. First, its products became commodities, made as easily and less expensively by others in countries from South Korea to Thailand. Second, consumers wanted more for their digital dollar, and more Sony didn't have. By 1994, sales of personal computers in the United States had moved ahead of those of televisions for the first time[1] and Sony was left on the sidelines, watching control of its hard-won Living Room brand move to others like Microsoft and Dell.

This is the same old story that has belabored Japanese industry for over a decade and which we profiled in our first book, *Beating Japan:* companies driven by their own highly integrated product divisions trying to shoehorn products into customers that they don't even know. All over Japan, companies run like this have suffered major reverses, forcing the nation to abandon decades of business practices that generations of Japanese had come to regard as sacred. For many, change has come too little and too late. The massive layoffs now coursing their way through Japan's blue-chip companies simply presage a final wind-down of some of the best names in many businesses. Things have become so bad for many companies that their overseas employees have no jobs to go home to.

The Internet caught Sony flat-footed just as Akio Morita became very ill. Sony has been quick to respond, creating a seamless "brand architecture" that shows all its products interworking, from camcorders to laptops. It has grasped the threat of Internet-television to its core home products and has demonstrated its camcorders as Internet broadcasting devices for the home.

Just look at Sony's Mavica, the leading digital camera, which had sales in 1998 of over one million in the United States alone. Although clunky and expensive, consumers love the Mavica because it communicates easily with a PC or printer. Communications here means "sneaker net." You take a standard floppy disk out of the Mavica, walk across the room, and stick it in your PC.[2] This was how we "networked" our Radio Shack TRS-80s twenty years ago. Simple, but it works, and it got Sony into the Living Room market early.

Even more farsighted, Sony has realized that its real competitor is not Panasonic, the company with which it has fought tooth and nail for market share in just about every country in the world for five decades, but Microsoft. For Microsoft to succeed, it must dominate the software and service environment in which the world's billion middle-class consumers live. For Sony to prosper, it must do exactly the same thing. This brings the two head to head in a furious battle for consumer loyalty.

Moreover, the numbers are staggering. As we have shown before, those consumers will buy several of the post-PC products that Sony wants to sell them. Sony was tops in their minds once before and wants to be there again. This time, however, there is formidable competition. And not just from Microsoft.

As we saw in "The Living Room Revolution," the home, where the Moore Curve is hitting hardest, throwing off a vast new array of products and services, is one great big brand void. Fighting to fill that void are a vast array of computer companies, media empires, software companies—and, of course, Sony.

Looked at this way, the news for Sony is both good and bad. On the good side, there is more opportunity in the Living Room market over the next decade than today's Sony could fill in a century or two. On the bad, Sony is a fallen Living Room star in need of serious burnishing. There are only so many TVs people can buy, and the world's consumer market, while large, is not growing at the rate of, say, the Internet.

When Morita became ill in 1995, he passed the reins to a relative unknown inside Sony, Noboyuki Idei. Idei moved quickly to realign the organization in the late 1990s.[3] Sony is not an old-line Japanese company based on the Japanese samurai clan system, as is a Mitsui or an NEC. Created after the Second World War by up-and-coming entrepreneurs, it has always sold itself on its American ways. Below the surface, however, is a different story. And this was the core of Idei's challenge.

Behind the glossy ads, Sony is as Japanese as any company with highly autonomous product divisions competing for shelf space in dying retailers. Morita tried to do an end run around Sony's consumer-electronics competitors by buying Columbia pictures and CBS Records, gaining media it planned to use to force-feed the market with its preferred technologies—digital technologies like minidisk and DVD.

One of Sony's smartest moves was to create a brand architecture. "Brand architecture" is a fancy term for making different products look and feel the same. This has the effect of making you feel "it's a Sony" when you look at a Sony product or pick one up. The company soon started advertising together hugely different products made by unrelated divisions. Thus, its popular slimline PC, the Vaio, is often pictured together with its latest camcorders. Everything is color coordinated and looks as if it fits together. Consumers see a united Sony with a broad, all-capable line of Living Room products.

Another brilliant move was to redefine the role of television. Most of us sit and watch TV. It's such a passive, low-definition medium that Marshall McLuhan called it "cool."[4] Sony's PlayStation has completely reinvented how TVs are used: today a TV can be connected to a PlayStation for hours at a time without a single broadcast or TV ad being seen.

Not only does PlayStation eliminate the role of TV networks and advertisers in the minds of Sony customers, it weds consumers to Sony software and places them firmly in a Sony environment. Indeed, it's as if Disney World came to you, rather than you going to Disney World. Sony has managed to transform your living room into a Sony World, as it were, a place where you live, eat, and breath Sony.

PlayStation is a big threat for Microsoft, AT&T, Yahoo!, AOL, and many others. More powerful than a PC, it does not have "Intel Inside," nor does it use Microsoft software or offer AOL-World. Intel insiders call it "the Death Star."

PlayStation is not the only product of its kind; Nintendo makes the impressive Nintendo 64. What makes Sony different is the sheer number of machines that it sold—some 50 million in only a couple of years.[5] This take rate is extraordinary; the personal computer took a good fifteen years to get this far. PlayStation and products like it are the vehicles for growth in the future.

Another linchpin to Sony's thinking is a realistic appraisal of consumer buying patterns. While Microsoft must protect its big base in PCs and try to make the Living Room PC-centric in order to keep pumping PC and PC-like software, Sony works with a clean slate.

Sony thinks that processing power will be embedded in everyday products which will be sold for everyday prices. Consumers should just be able to plug them into each other or into the network and expect results. Microsoft, on the other hand, expects customers to buy extra hardware loaded with enough proprietary Microsoft software to run their TVs, stereos, and other entertainment devices. Sony has placed the smarter bet: buying computer networks is not much fun.

There are plenty of acronyms in this business of connecting machines, and in the main they are not important. What is important is the ease with which a product can be used and the price-performance consumers get. Sony wants to offer a brand architecture and an underlying hardware and software package that is simpler than anyone else's. As a rule, this is the kind of thing that wins: all things being equal, simplicity takes the cake. IBM could not shoehorn its complicated mainframe operating systems into small personal computers, leaving the PC market wide open for Microsoft. Sony clearly recognizes the same weakness in Microsoft a generation later and is moving to take advantage of it.

Sony is right to hit this market hard. Microsoft may not be the challenge it is cracked up to be (see "Software: Goodbye Mr. Bill") but Dell certainly is. Dell could turn its direct-distribution guns on Sony, which still relies on costly retailers for the bulk of its sales, far sooner than Sony could counterattack Dell in its PC heartland.

Indeed, this simple calculation haunts everyone in the consumer-electronics business: no matter how good their products, Dell has the potential to be more profitable in any market they can name, and to get to that market faster.

The biggest risk to Sony is the sheer disposability of PlayStation. At around $130, the product can quickly be dropped for something else, as the endless generations of devices at the top of the game hit parade—Sega, Nintendo, Sony—make clear. This is why Sony's brand architecture is so smart: Sony wraps PlayStation in something bigger and more embracing than PlayStation itself.

To prevent the company from backsliding, Sony decided in 1999 to cut 10 percent of its workforce, cut its seventy factories to fifty-five, and regroup ten internal companies into four independent units. Says Idei, "If we'd stuck to our present corporate model, Sony would probably go the way of other large Japanese electronics makers."[6]

To escape the pull of the Black Hole in Cyberspace and to reestablish Sony's position in the Living Room, Idei had better stick to his guns.

39

Automotive: Nissan

An early inspiration for this book came from Nissan Motor. In a visit to its Smyrna, Tennessee, factory, we first recognized the relationship between information, knowledge, quality, and waste, and saw this relationship implemented on a massive scale. Nissan makes cars and trucks at Smyrna, located twenty miles south of Nashville. The scale of the place is breathtaking: a low, vast building more than a mile across, occupying more than five million square feet, or thirty-three acres.

In a hotly contested market like cars, survival means relentless cost reduction. Manufacturers can turn down the screws on employees and suppliers to produce incremental savings. However, to gain lasting advantage by reducing costs permanently, they must rethink production, if not their entire business, every day. Unfortunately, managers cannot use traditional methods to evaluate new ideas.

Shifts in thinking, by definition, defy measurement. They take the relentless application of information technology to the entire process of car making to root out pools of cost, eliminate unnecessary inventory, reduce cycle times, and cut waste to the bone.

At Nissan, we saw one gigantic operation where management used every means possible to substitute information for other resources. The result was no waste, nothing up the chimney, just cars coming off the production line. Nissan was the best example we had ever seen of using information to ensure that zero waste means zero defects.

Purchases of raw materials and components make up three-quarters of the total expenditures of car manufacturers like Nissan. Labor costs are relatively minor; at the most efficient plants, 5 percent or less of total production costs.[1] For many manufacturers, the cost of carrying inventory (parts, work-in-progress, and finished goods) often exceeds all other expenses, and can spell the difference between profit and loss.[2]

The problem is that scarce cash has been shelled out for all those spare parts and half-finished cars that are gathering dust in the factory. That money could be used for better purposes, like selling cars, developing new ones, or paying dividends. If managers can reduce what's in the pipeline at any given time, they can improve velocity of capital dramatically. And naturally, if they throw away less of what they buy, they are better off.

In eliminating waste, Nissan has in effect zeroed in on inventories. If the company was to reduce production costs every year, reducing the costs of raw materials and components had to be its first priority. According to a Nissan executive, "What we are talking about here is twenty-first–century materials handling."

If parts and materials are the biggest expenses for a car manufacturer, better organization is the easiest way to reduce costs. In cars, as in most manufacturing businesses, automation is an expensive alternative. Car manufacturing is not highly automated. In fact, industry-wide, automation of final assembly is surprisingly limited.[3] While robots do some tasks such as painting and welding very well, people do complicated and varied tasks better. Indeed, at first glance, car assembly today does not look all that different from the way it looked at Henry Ford's Rouge River plant.

Small changes that make the process easier also produce large savings. The key is to simplify. We have visited many factories around the world—in North America, Asia, and Europe—and most of them were a mess. Racks of parts and unfinished goods, dirty floors and cardboard boxes full of coffee cups: this was the norm. The most efficient plants, always operated by extremely successful companies, appear simple, with clear layouts and no clutter. Efficiency and simplicity go together.

If the plant is a mess, the company is a mess and performance reflects it.[4] Sloppy operations indicate poor management. On the basis of these observations, we concluded that there is a high correlation between plant cleanliness and market share. When the factory is well organized, when there are wide aisles and lots of elbow room, employee safety and morale benefit. So do quality, efficiency, and productivity. As someone at Nissan put it, "If the plant is a mess, a worker doesn't care if one more bolt drops on the floor; if it's spotless, he will be careful." Smyrna was clean and well organized.

Managing the flow of raw materials into Smyrna is a staggering job. Some ten thousand parts that go into Nissan's cars and trucks are purchased from others, but the material staging area at Smyrna is a tiny part of the plant. By switching to reusable containers for virtually all the parts its buys, Nissan simplified the way it assembles cars and trucks. Instead of having a lot of people unwrapping and disposing of boxes, and others feeding them into the right spot on the assembly line, parts come straight into work areas in the right quantity, in containers that are easy for the line workers to use. What's more, there are smaller quantities of parts in the reusable crates than in the throwaway ones that they replaced, so there is less traffic handling materials and less congestion on the line. These changes made housekeeping much easier, and cut parts handling significantly. And since parts did not have to be unwrapped, labor costs were reduced.

Work stations on the assembly line had been fifteen to twenty feet long, with big boxes of parts needed for each of, say, twelve colors. Nissan made the containers smaller, the right size, and engineered for each job. Workers spent less time walking and more time working because of the new containers. Labor costs, even if a small part of the total, still count—every cent counts in this market. With less wasted effort, less goes into each car. But most important, controlling the flow of parts in this fashion also reduces parts inventory. In the beginning, some suppliers were apprehensive about delivering half- or quarter-truckloads of parts (the "milk runs," Nissan called them) instead of the full loads they were used to. But these suppliers came around.

In two years, there was a 40 percent reduction in parts inventory at Smyrna. This kind of savings, companywide, would have freed up as much as $400 million at Nissan, the same amount that Nissan spent to put a new model into production. And while the entire reduction in parts inventories was not due to reusable containers, better and simpler materials handling was a big factor.

Fewer parts and less clutter had other indirect, but real benefits. Less handling means better quality. A worker grabs a windshield out of large delivery tray, and swings it into place on a car in one motion—the only time it is touched in the plant. Before, it would have been unwrapped, moved to the production line, then lifted into place: there were three opportunities for the worker to break or scratch each one. Custom-designed crates protect parts better. Tire rims, for example, arrive in big plastic eight-pack pallets, each rim in its own slot. Before, they came on plywood sheets, stacked up and then shrink-wrapped; not only was there a lot of garbage, but the plywood was expensive, and the rims could rattle around inside getting dented.

Smaller production runs became possible. Faster delivery of smaller quantities of parts right to the production line made it easy to switch from one car model to another. That meant that Nissan could match production more closely to demand; for example, the company might want to minimize the number of cars it made with standard transmissions and no air conditioning. If nobody wanted them, they would end up sitting on dealer lots until sold at steep discounts. Car companies also appeal to consumers by giving them a larger number of options and models to choose from. To do so and still make money, the company had to keep production flexible.

Less space was needed for each car produced by Nissan. When it opened, Smyrna had 3.4 million square feet to make 250,000 vehicles per year; by the time of our visit, the plant had grown only about 50 percent in size, but vehicle capacity had nearly doubled and engine assembly and parts stamping had been added. That meant about one-third less space was needed per car produced. For each car that rolled out the door, this meant a smaller investment in bricks and mortar, lower real estate taxes, less heating and cooling.

Safety also improved. Wider, less cluttered aisles reduced the chance of accidents. Without packages to be unwrapped, there were far fewer injuries from box knives than before. All this added up to lower medical and worker's compensation costs, fewer sick days, and better employee morale.

Smyrna, which can make 450,000 vehicles per year, is the biggest car manufacturing facility under one roof in the United States. The real work of industry is done in places like this, where steel and other raw materials are turned into everyday products—in this case, those icons of American culture, automobiles. Under twenty-foot ceilings, the scale of things looked awesome, from the huge stamping presses to endless overhead conveyors. Activity was ceaseless; forklifts went back and forth; partially assembled cars moved along their tracks; robots moved with inhuman motions, welding and painting. Everywhere, workers moved quickly and with determination.

A factory this big should produce a lot of waste, and it used to—as much as a small city. What's more, operations here once sent tons of paints and solvents into the air or down the sewer drain every year. Today, it's a different story. Nissan has nearly approached the goal it set for itself: no smoke up the chimney, no fifty-five–gallon drums of toxic chemicals to storage, no garbage to the landfill.

During the past decade, recycling became a reality for most American households. At home, Americans have grown used to sorting their trash into a half-dozen piles and listening to homilies from their children on the evils of ozone depletion, rain forest destruction, and pitching out newspapers with the coffee grinds. But in the U.S., as in other developed nations, businesses, not households, account for most waste. In recent years, industry has contributed over 80 percent of all solid waste produced in the U.S.[5] In other words, we don't see three-quarters of the garbage we produce—and pay for. This mess results from the products and services we buy, before we buy them. The application of information, by eliminating large amounts of production waste, has the potential to slash prices and generate large consumer surpluses.

When Nissan decided to rethink its production in order to eliminate waste, from unneeded inventory to garbage, the challenge it faced was extraordinary. Perhaps even more daunting than the engineering and management challenge was that greatest of forces: organizational inertia.

Although, like all traditional operations of its size, the plant was generating waste on a monumental scale, the direct costs of this waste to Nissan were low. At the same time, the potential for disrupting production for the sake of efficiency was a strong argument against change. Making cars is an immensely complex process. Thousands of parts must be brought together at just the right time by thousands of people. Production lines are like tightly wound clocks, put together over months and years. You don't mess with them unless there's a compelling reason, and Nissan, in a tough market, was in no position to throw money around.

To avoid disrupting its existing production lines, Nissan decided to focus its efforts on the Altima, a midsized, four-door sedan. By staking out new ground with the Altima, the company avoided the risks of disrupting its ongoing business, but it added a new element of risk. The Altima was to be a bold move into a segment of the market in which Nissan's performance had been disappointing. The first Altima rolled off the production line in June 1992 after three years of preparation. Annual capacity was 200,000 units, a little less than half of Smyrna's total output. Since most environmental damage at a car plant is caused by painting and parts packaging, this was where the most radical changes were made in the Altima's production line. The lessons learned with the Altima were gradually applied to other production lines.

When the Altima was conceived, Smyrna produced twenty long dumpsters of waste *every single day.* Four years later, this figure was down to just two daily landfill-bound loads; another year later, it was down to about one. To give an idea of how much this represents, if each employee threw out four soda cans per day, one dumpster would be filled. Another way to look at solid waste is in terms of the amount per car. When the program began, Smyrna generated 180 pounds of trash per vehicle; four years later the plantwide average was down to 30 pounds; another twelve months on, it was down to 14 pounds per unit. Plans called for this small volume of trash to be reduced a further 90 percent. These were plantwide figures; even less was produced for the Altima.

Nissan's switch to reusable containers for parts and components that it buys from other suppliers was the main factor in this dramatic reduction of waste. Eventually, 98 percent of the 9,750 parts Nissan bought came in reusable containers; the balance were delivered in containers that could be recycled.[6] Before, parts containers were simply trashed.

Buying clout helps when you want to make suppliers change. Globally, Nissan made nearly three million vehicles annually, so it could throw its weight around. Suppliers were responsive to Nissan's suggestions, to say the least. Furthermore, many of its suppliers had been doing business with Nissan for years, if not decades, so relations were tight. To some extent, supplier changes were made by fiat; Nissan simply said, "This is the way we are doing business." The stick that Nissan wields was obvious; the carrot was long-term contracts that gave suppliers stable, predictable revenues and cash flows.

Despite Nissan's purchasing power, any big change involving suppliers, if it is to be successful, requires selling them on the benefits and working closely with them. To get results, Nissan sometimes paid higher prices, sometimes lower. Typically, for example, it might cost the supplier $7.50 for a throwaway package and $10 for a reusable one. Suppliers had to figure out how to make reusable containers pay. To some extent, Nissan simply shifted its waste problem to suppliers. Those that delivered their parts using unrecyclable materials (like foam, for example, as blocks between stacks of windshields) were required to take their own garbage back. This proved a strong incentive for them to change.

Masterminding the return of thousands of reusable crates was no small task. Nissan hired some managers from another car company to run the container handling system. This competitor had tried to switch to reusable crates, was unable to manage the logistics of getting them back to suppliers, and ultimately abandoned the idea. Nissan, with more patience, has benefited from this rival's failure.

The idea was to eliminate waste altogether with reusable containers and supply management systems. Nevertheless, for a very small number of parts, the company will accept delivery in recyclable containers, like those made of corrugated cardboard which can be baled up and sold for scrap. For example, the factory receives enough fuses in one cardboard box to last for two weeks; it just doesn't make sense to have special containers for such small parts that are ordered infrequently.

For process wastes, like trimmings from plastic moldings and metal stamping, Nissan has relied heavily on recycling. There was a ready market for steel, which can be reused to make more steel. Originally, the company simply gathered up trimmings into loose piles and threw then into a truck to be hauled off to the scrap yard. Then, Smyrna purchased a machine for crushing scrap metal into small cubes, which fetch more on the recycling market than loose trimmings.

Plastic was another story. Sometimes unpainted plastic trimmings or defective parts can easily be ground up and reused for the same purpose. Generally, however, reuse was difficult because plastic is easily contaminated. For example, trimmings from plastic bumpers cannot simply be ground up and turned into more bumpers because the paint gets mixed in with the plastic and makes it inflexible. Nissan began to send painted plastic scraps to a company that turns them into plastic lumber, parking stops, and other items Nissan buys back at inflated prices. Nissan was stimulating demand for its scrap by specifying the recycled content of the plastic products it buys. Here, again, was where buying clout helped: Nissan asked Rubbermaid, for example, to use scrap from Smyrna in the garbage cans and other products Nissan buys.

To avoid "cascading" (whereby plastic is recycled into less valuable products until it is finally worthless), Nissan was trying to reuse plastic for its original purpose. If you are spending a lot of money to produce high-quality plastic, you don't want to pay someone to take it away to make park benches. Until the Altima was introduced, Nissan only made bumper parts at Smyrna; then it began to also make plastic gas tanks. At its labs in Japan, Nissan figured out how Smyrna could shred and reuse multilayer plastic gas tanks. And the labs also developed a process for removing paint from bumpers so they can be recycled as bumpers.[7]

These kinds of high-tech fixes were expensive. To simplify its task, Nissan also reduced the number of plastics used in its cars (the proliferation of plastic types itself makes recycling difficult), and redesigned some parts to use plastics that can be reused more easily. But the real opportunity for savings, and the next challenge Nissan has set for itself, is to "design out" process waste. Changes in manufacturing as well as in car design are necessary.

By reducing the number of parts, by designing parts that are easier to make, by operating machines to closer tolerances, and by reducing defects (i.e., fewer parts that need to be scrapped), Nissan can stop a lot of problems before they start and avoid a lot of headaches: no waste, no need for complicated recycling technologies—and no need to worry about the vagaries of the scrap markets.

Once the waste monster was tamed at Smyrna, Nissan turned to the next biggest mess, the paint shop. With traditional painting techniques, cars and trucks are painted by workers (or robots) with spray guns, but only about half the paint reaches the car. Most of the rest evaporates into the air, and some residual amount finds it way into the drains on the floor as sludge. Paint contains petroleum-based chemicals, called volatile organic compounds (VOCs), which are a major component of smog. Twenty years ago, VOCs overwhelmingly came from motor vehicle emissions and flue gases from power plants. These sources have been cleaned up, but the smog persisted. So in the late 1980s, the government started casting around for other sources, like paint shops, which once were considered marginal contributors to the country's poor air quality.

Half a million vehicles take a lot of paint and, in the bad old days, created a lot of VOC emissions. So, beginning with the Altima, Nissan switched to water-based paints, which have only a tiny fraction of the petroleum in them that the old paints did. The change was not easy: Nissan had to develop new paints and a new application system. The biggest concern was finish quality. Other car makers had switched to water-based primers, but kept oil-based finishes for the final coat, to hedge their bets. Nissan decided to switch over completely for the Altima, and claims it was the first car company to go to a hundred percent water-based paint for any model.

Nissan did not want to spend a lot of money on a new paint shop while still wasting half the paint it sprays on its vehicles. So the company's engineers chose a state-of-the-art electrostatic system, which gives the surface to be painted an electrical charge so that it attracts the metal in the paint like a magnet. Unfortunately, this system would not work with the water-based paints; Nissan's paint suppliers said it simply could not be done. Other technical difficulties had to be overcome as well; for example, cleaning the new system proved much more difficult than the old. But after considerable wrangling with suppliers and the complete reformulation of all its paints, Nissan eventually got the system to work. VOC emissions were down 75 percent compared to the old process.

Another byproduct of the painting process is sludge, the residue that collects from the paint that doesn't get on the car. By switching to electrostatic painting, Nissan greatly reduced the amount of sludge it produces. And, by using water-based paints, the paint shop produced sludge that was less toxic than if oil-based mixes were used. A small amount of sludge remained, which would normally be landfilled. Nissan built a $4-million incinerator to dispose of paint sludge (even water-based paints contain some hydrocarbons that can be burned), as well as wood and broken shipping pallets which cannot be reused. Some other solvents may also be burned. This incinerator was an expensive way to dispose of a substance like paint sludge, which was not considered hazardous. But there were a number of benefits. There was less potential legal liability than in sending it to a landfill, from where it might come back to haunt the company later. Landfill charges were avoided. And costs were partially recouped by using heat from the incinerator to help heat and cool the plant. Capturing energy that would otherwise be wasted helped Nissan reduce the amount of energy it took to make a car by 35 percent over the previous two decades.

Paint is not the only source of VOCs in car manufacturing. Many oil-based solvents are used for cleaning. Nissan experimented with citrus- and water-based cleaners for its machinery and in the preparation of sheet metal for painting. In addition, Nissan switched to "closed loop" systems, which permit solvents to be reused many times before being returned to suppliers. Solvent packaging has also changed. For liquids, refillable containers of up to six hundred gallons are used, which eliminates the need for cleaning. In the past, fifty-five-gallon drums created storage, cleaning, and disposal headaches. In total, Smyrna recycles or sells back to its suppliers 92 percent of the hazardous materials it uses in production.[8]

Then there were the direct savings. When it originally switched to returnable containers, Nissan expected to lose money, but the change has turned out to be a break-even proposition. First, of course, bills for trash handling and disposal were down. By reducing its volume of landfilled trash by 95 percent, Nissan dramatically reduced its trash disposal costs. In tipping fees alone, the plant cut operating costs by some $5 million per year. Furthermore, collecting, compacting, and loading a trainload of garbage a day took a big organization. In just eighteen months, Nissan was able to eliminate five positions for rubbish handling, a savings in the hundreds of thousands of dollars per year.

On the direct cost side, Nissan had to set up a special department for handling the return of bar-coded, reusable plastic crates for incoming parts. With this complex system, much of what Nissan gained from less unpacking, it lost in crate handling. Recycling cardboard and other materials also required a sizable collection system.

When these easily identified costs and savings were tallied, Nissan concluded they were a wash as far as the bottom line was concerned. So while it breaks even on direct costs, Nissan benefits from production economies and quality and safety improvements that management does not even try to quantify.

Nissan used the same criteria to finance this project as any other capital investment; but it never undertook any project on a strictly financial basis. There was no strict policy that all investments must show a 30 percent rate of return, for example. Other considerations, like safety and quality, also came into play. Each project was judged on its own merits.

When Nissan installed its new electrostatic painting system, for example, the savings on paint alone were large. With the old system, 50 percent of the paint sprayed on a car went into the air or down the drain; with the new one, only 10 to 20 percent was lost. At $70 to $80 per gallon of paint, the savings covered a lot of investment. At the same time, the finish quality of its cars improved and environmental costs and risks went down. For other investments, like Smyrna's incinerator and plastic recycling program, the benefits were long term.

Adding up all these benefits—some small, some large, some easy to quantify, some not—Nissan believes that its investments were worthwhile. This deliberate approach to process management, which produces consistent results (in this case 10 percent cost reduction per year), is the very essence of *kaizen,* the system of continuous improvement made famous by Japan's large car companies. Perhaps more to the point, the Altima was a new product launch success: sales exceeded expectations in the first year after introduction, raising Nissan's U.S. market share significantly.[9]

Nissan successfully substituted information—and the knowledge of its workers—for other resources, thereby boosting its financial performance. While the cost of its cars went down, their information content went up. This is how wealth is created in the information economy.

40

Commercial Real Estate: Cyber Termites

The growth of the U.S. economy in the 1990s was driven by the breathtaking speed with which American business substituted information for other resources such as labor and capital. With the Internet, companies can minimize their need for physical assets. We expect real estate to take a pounding.

Like a cybertermite, e-commerce is eating away at the distribution edifice that evolved over the two last centuries. The financial risks for property holders is just beginning. Retailing dominates urban and suburban landscapes worldwide. More people are employed in the retail and wholesale business than in any other.[1] The future will look entirely different.

Dell used the Internet to eliminate a layer or two from PC distribution. It forced competitors to shuffle from fire sale to fire sale as they try to burn off inventory in unsustainable distribution pipelines. All those PC stores that proliferated in the 1980s went the way of Commodore and Osborne.

Remember the earlier example of the Japanese executive living in Tokyo who told us how he orders his computer equipment from Cyberian Outpost at prices far less than he would pay in Tokyo's Akihabara electronics district. What does that make Akihabara property worth?

Charles Schwab is having the same effect on Wall Street. The financial sector employs seven million Americans in 628,000 establishments.[2] All these banks, brokerage firms, and real estate agents have lots of bricks and mortar. Of the ten largest on-line brokers, only one is a traditional Wall Street player.[3] Schwab, the largest on-line brokerage house, does most of its total trades on line.[4] In 1999, Schwab's market cap topped that of Merrill Lynch, that great provider of Main Street storefronts.

Real estate is a vulnerable sector. The amount of commercial space per American tripled during the past half-century. From the end of the Second World War until 1960, commercial real estate construction expanded in line with population growth. Then, in the sixties, it kept up with output per person. Since 1970, it has grown faster than population and economic output. Once the bull market began in the early 1980s, commercial real estate exploded. As space expanded, so did the number of people in it.

Internet termites are boring away at commercial real estate in other ways. Of course Wal-Mart has decimated Main Street USA. Wal-Mart is built around an Intranet that minimizes inventories. With less inventories, Wal-Mart needs less store space. A few years ago, Wal-Mart used 10 percent of its stores for inventory, compared to 25 percent for retailers as a group.[5] In 1998, Wal-Mart reduced inventories just as it reported record sales and profit growth.[6] Wal-Mart sells far more per square foot of building than its competitors. In a sense, at $139 billion in annual sales, Wal-Mart is the biggest e-commerce company in the world.

Like books, CDs are easy to sell over the Internet.[7] But consumers are going one step farther with music, eliminating the CD altogether. We saw that computer-savvy students download music in MP3 format and store it on their hard drives. Diamond Multimedia sells a Walkman-like portable player that does for music what the Palm Pilot does for data. No CDs, no music stores, no record companies. That's a lot of real estate—and people.

Travel faces the same pressure as real estate. Some $1.6 billion worth of travel was booked on line in 1998, less than 1 percent of total sales. But far more people use the Internet to do their research before booking with a travel agent. Furthermore, the power of the Internet to auction airplane seats and hotel rooms could devastate profitability in those sectors. With high fixed costs, these organizations make their profit at the margin.

Americans purchase more than a quarter of all new cars with the help of the Internet.[8] Few of these purchases are calculated into the e-commerce numbers, however, since final purchase and delivery takes place at a dealer. Those using Internet car buying services like autobytel.com and Microsoft's Carpoint have disintermediated their local dealers and taken much of the remaining profit out of dealer sales. No wonder this sector is consolidating at breakneck speed, eliminating the independent dealers that populated every town in America.

Even the most ebullient forecasters place e-commerce sales under 5 percent of total retail trade in the next few years, up from less than 1 percent in 1999.[9] But actual sales on the Internet are misleading. The impact of a 5 percent loss in sales is huge for retailers with gross margins of 3 percent. Furthermore, these figures don't include the tire kickers who find out what their used cars are worth on line, and then go beat up their dealers. Consumers are empowered by the information they find on the Internet, even if they buy—for now—at traditional stores.

Dell Computer, like other Internet innovators, has eliminated large sectors of commercial real estate, from warehouses to retail outlets and even factories. Dell's sales are more than thirty times its investment in property, plant, and equipment, or PPE. By contrast, traditional manufacturers have PPE turns well under ten times. Less equipment, less factory space.

Like their retail and manufacturing counterparts, office workers need less space. Telecommuting is already affecting commercial real estate. Through telecommuting, IBM reduced its office space for its North American sales force by 75 percent in 1999.[10] Nearly one-third of AT&T managers work at home part of the time, 10 percent full time.[11] Today, an estimated 14 million Americans telecommute.[12] Once broadband DSL and cable connections are available, the ranks of at-home white-collar (white-bathrobed and -slippered?) workers will really take off.

Telecommuters may want more space for their home offices. Maybe we (or our children) will live in converted strip malls. In the 1970s and 1980s, old factories in New York were converted to loft apartments. In the 1990s, vacant downtown office buildings were reclaimed for residential use. In the future, perhaps this process will occur not just in nineteenth-century city centers, but in twentieth-century suburbs.

The overhang of commercial space could devastate prices (as it did in New York). A large share of personal net worth is tied up in real estate. For most people, their home is their biggest asset. Pension plans allocate a significant share of their investments to real estate. One way or another, a high proportion of people own real estate. They own their own homes, and they own commercial real estate directly or through investments and retirement plans. Perhaps the great REIT (real estate investment trust) boom of the 1990s was a way for smart money to shift this risk to the great unwashed.

The surge of sales on the Internet in December 1998 spooked the REIT market.[13] Homeowners are more vulnerable than businesses. Real estate has represented a declining portion of the balance sheets of U.S. companies for over a decade. Businesses have been passing these risks on to others at a healthy rate.

The idea of real estate even having commercial value is itself a product of the Industrial Revolution. With the development of London in the eighteenth century, real estate became a liquid investment. Previously, land was a power base given to nobles— and taken away—by their king. After three centuries of development, real estate is now bought and sold like any equity. The Internet will change this equation in ways that are impossible to anticipate. The impact on the landscape and employment will be just as profound.

At the turn of the last century, one in three Americans worked on the farm. Today, agriculture is still America's largest industry, but only one in a hundred Americans are farmers. One in four Americans works in the retail and wholesale sectors. With the help of the Internet, retail productivity will soar and employment in these sectors will plummet. Absorbing this change will be a major economic challenge in the first half of the next century. What will your children do?

We know where the damage is being done. It's not so clear where new value will be created. The fundamentals for Internet investing are excellent. We are at the dawn of the "virtual economy." Information and communications will be substituted for real goods and transportation on a scale never before seen. Because virtual resources are nearly free, the opportunities are nearly limitless. But don't look to the cyberfollies that topped the stock charts.

Whatever the real prospects for the virtual economy, however, Internet investments must generate a profit sooner or later. No matter how important, the Internet in itself is nothing special as an investment. So far, investors have been remarkably patient, if not foolish. Nobody knows what a profitable Internet company looks like. We may find out soon. Investors must ask themselves what will happen when access to capital is shut off for high-flying, loss-generating Internet plays.

In the nineteenth century more money was made building and using the railroads than running them. Plenty of companies profit from e-commerce, but they are not Internet plays. Charles Schwab, Dell Computer, and Wal-Mart are not in the Internet business. All, in fact, sell commodities. But they use the Internet to do it best. They use the Internet to obviate the need for real assets, and produce stellar returns for their investors as a result.

Cybertermites have been eating away at the core of U.S. business for some time. The reforms introduced by President Carter a generation ago completely restructured the movement of goods and services in America, allowing the dismemberment of the transportation industry. The resulting flexibility in distribution has allowed the Internet to rip through business after business unchecked. Commercial real estate will not escape the termites' bite.

41

Games: Nintendo Uber Alles

Video games move in Moore Time the way nothing else does. The market for them is unforgiving. One year Sega is on top, the next it's Nintendo or Sony. There is no saying who will take top position or when. Games and consoles are completely disposable.

The kids who buy games seem to put no value in their store of software the way businesses do; they just junk it and move on to the next hot system. Prices are so low that what makes it under the Christmas tree one year is gone the next. It's as if a Microsoft is everything one month and nothing a few months later. Games are the best example of the roiling violence of the Singularity. Few firms can tolerate stresses like these; most will have to learn.

The 20-billion-dollar video-game market is now larger than the first-run movie business.[1] Individual game software regularly outsells the biggest films. But volatility is high. Only a couple of years back, Sega was the undisputed leader. Today it is a distant third behind Sony and Nintendo.[2] To promote its Dreamcast game console and get back into the game, Sega budgeted $100 million. It has to. In the five years since its Sega Saturn console was launched, it sold only 5 million game consoles. Sony sells that many consoles in a few months.

Games suppliers are designing their products to become the network hubs of every home in the consuming world.[3] Consoles will play DVDs, decode digital TV, and surf the Web—all for a couple of hundred dollars. They won't have Microsoft and Intel inside and they will outsell the entire personal computer base built up over twenty years in only a year or two. Effectively, these games are shutting Intel and Microsoft out of the high-growth end of the post-PC business.

Nintendo's N-64 software allows a degree of interactivity never seen in a TV broadcast or in previous generations of TV games. N-64's games are still crude, but if you load the James bond 007 game you will be drawn into your TV, literally, in a way that nothing has drawn you before.

For starters, if you, as James Bond of course, shoot one of the bad guys in the elbow, he bleeds in the elbow. Bullet marks appear onscreen exactly where you put them. What you shoot at breaks. You move through four dimensions in a remarkably realistic way. You can be attacked from all quarters, even from behind.

Players get to participate in a James Bond game in ways that were not possible in past games or in movies. The net effect is that N-64 has moved from the realm of children's games into mainstream entertainment, shifting the moorings of the fifty-year-old TV and film industry.

What does this mean?

First, N-64 has killed the passive nature of TV, what Marshall McLuhan called its "cool" quality. The new TV is a "hot" medium requiring constant human interaction to work.

Second, by splitting the TV "audience" into two—the "cool" audience that sits back and watches regular TV and the "hot" audience that gets involved with James Bond—N-64 has killed the advertising-by-the-numbers business. TVs can be on for hours at a time with not a single commercial—not even an Internet banner—reaching the "hot" audience.

Third, N-64 takes up to four players and is begging for full Internet-TV to turn it from sensational into explosive.

Fourth, N-64 takes eyeballs away from PCs, the Internet, network TV, and movies of all types, and does this all at once. In other words, by injecting themselves into mainstream entertainment, games suppliers are displacing *all* forms of media, not just "cool" TV.

These systems are the "new" TV. This medium does not require digital TV, HDTV, a PC, or large amounts of mass storage to work. Systems cost only $200, making them disposable generation to generation and classic examples of the devices now supplanting PCs in home entertainment.

Sony estimated in 1999 that one in every six U.S. homes had a Sony PlayStation. Sony sold 2.9 million PlayStations in December 1998. Nintendo sold 1.4 million N-64s in the same month. Between the two, these companies had penetrated between 4 and 5 percent of all U.S. households in that month alone.

The "new" television in video games is interactive and network driven. It is unleashing stupendous amounts of bandwidth and will redefine the post-PC universe. The "new" TV will revolutionize television viewing habits, make enormous bandwidth demands on carriers, and force the pace of change in consumer electronics. This will drive the venture business, of course, but it will also drive more mergers and determine the worth of those that have already been completed.

42

The Huge Post-PC Opportunity in Wireless

By applying the power of Moore's Law, wireless will move from exclusive, upmarket luxury to everyday necessity for dozens of Post-PC devices. How this challenge is met will drive large amounts of shareholder value—up or down—the world over.

This is a huge opportunity for investors, but only if wireless carriers can get their costs under control, as we saw in "Terminal Velocity." Right now, wireless prices are falling faster than costs. Wireless carriers must finance big network investments just as prices are collapsing.

To build markets, wireless carriers are cutting prices dramatically. Customers are responding in spades. To make these cuts pay, carriers must get the price-performance of their network hardware back on the Moore Curve, harnessing the relentless reduction in computer costs. Simple, robust, and cost-effective wireless network elements are necessary.

We have long argued that wireless would be a good investment *only* if price-cutting got brutal. Black Hole pricing will force wireless carriers to pick up new technologies capable of pushing costs to the point where Internet-type pricing is possible. New technologies will allow cellular carriers to build their networks for less than $100 per customer, a cost reduction of more than ten to one over a new wired connection from a cable or phone company. Investors should follow these opportunities carefully.[1]

Today's telephone and wireless networks are built on costly telephone exchanges engineered for one-dollar minutes, not one-cent minutes, and not at all useful for post-PC products. Cellular was built on the assumption that mobility commands a premium; and for the high-income customers who could afford these premiums, it did.

While cellular demand is strong, it's only part of the wireless story. The number of cellular phones, computer games, television set-top boxes, Palm Pilot hand-helds, digital cameras, camcorders, burglar alarms, and other computer-powered devices shipped in the United States now exceeds the number of PCs.

What all post-PC devices have in common is communications. Post-PCs are driving up demand for network connections. Most of these links will be wireless. Post-PCs, therefore, have changed the wireless equation. Today, wireless is about communication for the masses, not mobility for the few. In mass markets, market share is built on price and bandwidth. With their high costs, wireline operators cannot afford a fourfold increase in connections. Wireless will fill the gap.

Low-cost plus mobility will be a winning combination for business. There are seven million commercial establishments in the United States, about four million with more than four employees. These companies have communications systems to connect employees to local area networks, PCs, and peripherals. Traditionally, wireless was used only when mobility was essential, because of its high cost. Low cost, ease of installation and maintenance, and potential for voice data integration will make wireless the leader. 3Com, for example, announced a wireless net-working plan that lets people stay connected while they move around offices with their laptops.

There are a hundred million American households. Essentially, all have telephones and TVs, three-quarters have VCRs, and half have PCs. Few have any way to connect their post-PC devices with each other or the outside world. For example, consumers that add At Home Internet service to their AT&T cable TV need a way to connect their PCs (in the den) to their TVs (in the living room). Wireless will be their first choice. The cost of rewiring a home is simply prohibitive.

There's no need to spend thousands on copper wires to reach the majority of the world's population—the billions of villagers who have never made a phone call. Wireless will bring them telephone, cable television, and a first-rate suite of other services.

Responding to brutal price competition among cellular carriers, consumers around the world bought 51 percent more cell phones last year compared to the year before.[2] In most places, however, a cellular call still costs several times as much as a regular one. In the United States, where mobiles are now cheaper to use than wired phones, 20 million new subscribers signed up in 1998 alone. More than 30 percent of the population now uses them.[3]

Low prices bring in new customers and they boost usage. In the U.S., minutes of use per phone per month are rising sharply. There's still a long way to go: Americans use their cell phones only a third as much as they use their home lines.

Growth will accelerate as American consumers realize that a Sprint PCS phone is now cheaper than the wireline alternative from their local phone company. When you move into a new home, why have anything else? Maybe keep one line for computers (and a cable modem could soon replace even that). Prices are also reaching a level at which kids can take over. Teenage girls made AOL a success—this is where they "hang" with their friends. They also made PHS a success in Japan—and killed it when they moved on to something else.

Phone companies have invested heavily in cellular, a natural extension of their wired business. In Europe, cellular is still priced as an upmarket service, not as a wired substitute. Last year a cellular call cost five times as much as a wired one.[4] As a result, calling volumes were low, less than 150 minutes per month.[5] To keep demand growing, carriers will have to cut prices sharply. This process is well underway in the United States and Canada.

The good news for cellular is that consumers respond to price cuts. The bad news is that carriers did not make money at 10¢ per minute and few have the infrastructure to handle the wireline-like call volumes that low prices unleash.

Carriers must build new networks to meet post-PC demand. Now that prices have fallen through 10¢ per minute for airtime and long-distance, they cannot afford to add capacity the way they did when they charged a dollar or more. They need radical price-performance improvements from their infrastructure suppliers. Carriers need easy-to-buy, easy-to-install, easy-to-maintain equipment that will rapidly expand their coverage to meet post-PC capacity requirements.

We saw earlier how AT&T boosted wireless demand sharply with cheaper calls and simplified billing, added nearly two million wireless customers, and squeezed all the profit out of the business.[6]

Carriers need to wring more revenues out of their investments. Annual revenues are only a fraction of their investment in property, plant, and equipment. Under severe pricing pressure, North American wireless operators are struggling to do as well as traditional telephone companies (such as the U.S. Bell companies). In high-priced markets, like Italy and Japan, carrier performance is better.

The long arm of Moore's Law will soon reach wireless. Unlike fiber and copper wires, wireless does not require any ditch digging. Whatever the impact of Moore's Law on electronics, digging ditches still costs more than ever, placing wired companies at a disadvantage.

Cell tower base stations are a good example. To meet demand, the cost of these sites must fall below $1,000 and the bandwidth potential of these sites must expand well beyond voice calls. When the cellular networks were built, base stations were priced like large computers.

Since then, prices have fallen quickly, but they have a long way to go. As the wireless network extends its reach into the post-PC home, the number of base stations must grow by an order of magnitude. Base stations will become consumer electronics devices. Consumerization will take the number of cell sites into the hundreds of millions.

AT&T is field testing "personal" base stations at the endpoints of its cable television network, letting the company offer in-home, multichannel wireless connections. Thus linked, AT&T customers can use their cell phones at home or away. AT&T can do an end-run around phone companies and harness all the customer revenues, from cable to long-distance, the Internet, and local calls. Adding AT&T's TCI and MediaOne customers to the mix, AT&T can reach 62 million American households this way.[7] Personal base stations could generate the post-PC cash flow AT&T needs to upgrade its new cable assets to handle Internet-TV.

Many carriers will be run aground by plants they can't maintain, price to market, or write off. These companies are like the American railroads. In the 1960s, such icons of industry (and stock markets) as the New York Central and the Pennsylvania Railroad were bankrupt, many think, because of the postwar combination of Interstate highways and universal car ownership. Actually, railroad passenger traffic peaked in the U.S. in the 1920s as the first federal highways unleashed intercity buses. By the 1950s, the mighty Pennsylvania paid more in taxes to the state of New Jersey than it made in revenues. Wireline voice traffic probably peaked some time ago. Investors must consider their wireless options carefully.

43

Agriculture: Buena Vista Uses Information to Grow Wine

Eighteenth-century French philosophers, known as the Physiocrats, theorized that manufacturing (to say nothing of trade and finance) adds nothing to the wealth of nations; manufacturers are simply parasites living off the surpluses generated by farming. Even Adam Smith, the first modern economist, conceded to his French contemporaries that, "Farmers and country laborers, indeed, over and above the stock which maintains and employs them, reproduce annually a neat produce, a free rent to the landlord . . . [their labor] is certainly more productive than that of merchants, artificers and manufacturers."[1]

Today we believe that wealth is generated on and off the land. Nevertheless, agriculture remains one of the largest and most productive industries in the world—a tiny proportion of Americans can feed the whole country and a good part of the rest of the world. One of the most successful agricultural activities of the past generation has been wine making.

As the French have known for some time (long before the Physiocrats formulated their economic theories), wine making may be the ultimate business, a kind of alchemy which turns 25¢ worth of grapes into $25 worth of wine. And of course, the French are not alone in believing that good wine cannot be valued in financial terms only.

Agriculture is the oldest information-intensive industry on earth. It was the early application of knowledge to the cultivation of grasses that produced the grains that enabled civilization to get its start. These created surpluses that drove the earliest city-states and empires. Later, agricultural surpluses financed the industrial revolution.[2] Today, agriculture is more information-intensive than ever.

Agriculture is about survival at one level, and good living at another. As an industry, farming is in direct contact with the earth—for good or bad—in a way that is unlike any other. Similarly, the farmer's land—one small part of our environment—is literally his biggest asset. For this asset to show a return, it must be properly maintained. The farmer must in every sense be a steward of his land. Organic farming is one way for the farmer to enhance the value of his biggest asset and give consumers what they want. But many doubt the commercial potential of organic farming, particularly for large agribusiness.

Giving consumers what they want in agriculture is no different than flying a very big jet plane: to get it right, a lot of information must flow to and from the right places. Get it wrong, and the thing simply falls out of the sky. Not much opportunity to glide!

Buena Vista Winery, the largest estate winery in Carneros, one of California's most fertile grape-growing districts, is located at the end of a long, dusty dirt road, about ten miles from the town of Sonoma. A visit there a few years ago forced us to think about the question of how information—not computers and fancy technology—affects an industry on which we all depend for our survival.

Founded in 1857, Buena Vista in its current, prosperous incarnation dates from 1979, when the winery was acquired by the Moller-Rackes, a German wine-making family. It was moved in 1984 from the edge of Sonoma to its 1,360-acre estate in Carneros. Buena Vista grows its grapes employing organic methods. Strictly defined by the California Certified Organic Farmers, an independent regulatory group, the rigorous certification process began here in 1989.[3] For Buena Vista, 1992 was the first vintage year the winery could label some of its wines "grown organically."

While one of the most advanced, Buena Vista is by no means the only winery with organically certified vineyards. Only a small percent of the wine grapes in California are organically grown, but a much larger proportion of vineyards have some of their acreage organically certified.[4] A few years ago, industry giant Gallo, for example, began experimenting with organic methods on thousands of acres of its vineyards.[5] And there are numerous small wineries that specialize in organic wines.

Information-intensive methods helped Buena Vista focus on its true mission: to grow good grapes that make good wines. And focused you'd better be to survive in the wine business. There's a popular image of wine making as an expensive pastime for entrepreneurs from nearby Silicon Valley looking for a gentrified way to spend their untold millions. For all its airs, however, wine making is a cutthroat industry with a long list of problems.

In many ways, wine making suffered the same fate as personal computers in the late 1980s and early 1990s. After a booming decade, demand started to slack off. Health-conscious Americans began drinking less. In the United States, per capita wine consumption fell by about 10 percent between 1988 and 1993.[6] Demand measured in dollars continued to grow, however, because wine drinkers switched from cheap "jug" wines to more expensive varietals. This move upmarket saved many American wineries, including Gallo, the world's largest wine producer, which successfully repositioned itself as a quality leader. By the mid-nineties, Gallo's top-of-the-line cabernet sauvignon commanded $60 a bottle.[7]

At the same time, a host of new competitors rushed in to get their share of the action. Cheap imports from Australia and Chile began to pour into U.S. wine stores. Many French and other European wineries with deep pockets staked out their claims in northern California, joined by all those Silicon Valley tycoons looking for ways to stay busy when they retired. To make matters worse, the best grape-growing areas suffered years of drought. Then the region was rocked by two grapevine diseases which forced the replanting of thousands of acres, a process that will continue until every grapevine in northern California is replaced.[8] Not much room under these circumstances for sloppy management.

It was under such a cloud that Buena Vista proposed to go organic. The idea was to improve vineyard management by going back to basics. As one Buena Vista manager said, "There's an old saying in the wine business that fine wines start in the vineyards. Good grapes make for good wines. By going organic, we have to focus on the grapes; it makes you a better manager of your vineyards. We can focus more on the vineyards." This change forced Buena Vista to ask, "What is it that we do?" The answer, deceptively simple, is "Grow grapes for wine."

When the process began in 1989, Buena Vista could not make a compelling business case to management for the change. There were no clear financial benefits, better wine, or even clear marketing benefits. But Buena Vista did know that organic methods require farmers to pay more attention to their crops and land.

"What do we do best?" is not an easy question to answer for any business. And customers will invariably have a different answer from managers. Why do customers buy? Sounds silly, but most companies don't have the faintest idea. Knowing what customers value about a firm is the flip side of knowing what customers want. To sell their products, managers must know what customers need. But if they don't know what customers value about them, they will find themselves constantly missing the mark in advertising, new product development, and strategic direction. Managers who don't know what customers value about them won't know where to focus their energy. Furthermore, what a company does best is also where it makes the highest return. The bean counters may be skeptical at first, but they will like the results. They did at Buena Vista.

A. Racke Co., founded in 1855, is an old-line, family-owned German firm and one of Europe's leading wine and spirits merchants. Management—from headquarters in Germany to the vineyards in Carneros—led the switch to organic at Buena Vista. Commitment right from the top down, through every level of management, helped make this change work. What does not work is the "Gamelin system" of issuing environmental directives from the head office. (Field Marshal Gamelin will forever be infamous for resisting the German invasion of France in 1940 from the comfort of his GHQ near Paris, many hours distant from the front. Every morning, he methodically sent orders by courier to his commanders in the field, who usually received them after their positions had been overrun.) Few recognized, as Buena Vista did, that information-driven organic agriculture is an opportunity to make sure farming doesn't suffer the same fate that befell France a few decades ago!

When Buena Vista first considered going organic, its bet was by no means a certain one. Traditional accounting and forecasting methods are ill suited to measuring the benefits of process changes. These changes require a leap of faith by leaders willing to take risks. The Buena Vista team gambled, and made the switch on faith. They could not make a dollars-and-cents business case on a computer spreadsheet, but they were confident that it would pay in the long run. Having commitment to this idea at the top, as well as owners with a long-term view, made such a bet possible.

In many ways, vineyards are well suited to information-intensive organic farming. Generally, wine makers do not need to worry about the appearance of their grapes. Some fruit, like peaches and table grapes, must look perfect, or consumers won't buy them. And compared to other fruit, like pears and apples, grapes have relatively few insects predators. Consequently, wine making is generally less chemical-intensive than other kinds of farming. Nevertheless, Buena Vista, like other vineyards, once used chemicals to deal with a number of problems.

Mold and mildew can spoil the grapes while they are still on the vine. To eliminate the need for fungicides, the vineyard crew changed the way they pruned and trellised their plants, and they adjusted the spacing between rows to allow air to circulate better. By trimming back the vine leaves, they allowed the wind to dry their grapes (and even blow some insects off). Fortunately, the Carneros region, where Buena Vista is located, has good breezes, minimizing mildew problems. The shallow clay soil cannot support large leaf vines that attract many bugs. Other grape-growing regions of California, like the San Joachim Valley and the North Coast, have more problems with pests and mold.

Then Buena Vista tried to eliminate pesticides. First, they introduced ladybugs to counter some predators. Then they planted cover crops such as clover, oats, and peas between the vine rows. These harbor the predator insects that eat the bugs that attack the grapes. Ground covers also add nutrients and keep down weeds, reducing the need for fertilizer and herbicides. Elsewhere in the vineyard, natural landscaping kept undesirable bugs down. A compost mixture of pomace (what's left of the grapes after the juice has been squeezed out) and manure replaced synthetic fertilizer.[9] When necessary, soap-and-water mixtures were used to discourage pests.

All this sounds pretty simple, but organic methods vastly increase labor costs. By the estimate of one vineyard, growing grapes organically increases costs as much as three times over chemical practices.[10] At another vineyard, hoeing weeds costs two-thirds more per acre than spraying them with herbicides.[11] At Buena Vista, there was more mowing, pruning, and tending the vines, all labor-intensive activities. Previously, they just sprayed everything with herbicides and fungicides once a week or once a month. Daily or weekly tending became necessary.

Other costs rose as well. The vineyard had to purchase new equipment, like tillers and cover-crop seeders.[12] And the cost of organic certification itself is high. Detailed records must be kept, and the certification organization charges a fee and a commission on the value of the crop.[13] Nevertheless, at Buena Vista they concluded that these costs were both manageable and overshadowed by other considerations, such as the price per ton of grapes in Carneros, the highest in California. Savings on chemical purchases are increasingly large, since government regulation of pesticides has raised their costs dramatically. Still, these savings were not enough to offset the increase in labor costs. "So," we asked one Buena Vista manager, "how do you preserve your margins? This is a competitive business." The response: "We have a three- to four-year lead on this, so we can fold it into the overall price."

With information-intensive methods, Buena Vista found that the consistency of its crops improved. Here, we're talking cash flow. As one Buena Vista manager told us, "A couple of bad years, and you're dead in farming." The vines themselves were heartier. In addition, they found that wines grown organically were easier to ferment. Fermenting can be tricky; the process can halt midway, and the wine maker has to get it going again. Organic grapes are cleaner and ferment more smoothly, making the job of wine production easier. Smoother operations and greater consistency lower costs in the long run.

The consensus among those growing grapes organically seems to be that costs rise at first, but then decline after several years. The spokesman for one vineyard experimenting with organic methods told us, "It is 20 percent more expensive in the beginning, for the first couple of years, but after the second to third year, you get more consistent grapes and you have lower input costs." One reason may be that the soil gets worn out by chemical farming. Marcus Moller-Racke, Buena Vista's chairman, told *California Farmer,* "In Germany the soils are depleted. Everyone uses synthetic fertilizers. It's almost impossible to grow organic grapes."[14] Healthier soil leads to healthier plants, consistently high yields, better grapes—and, hopefully, better wines.

The fate of agriculture affects us all. Most directly, we all have to eat. If the food supply is reduced by natural disasters or tainted by pesticides, everyone feels the effects almost immediately. But farming is also a big industry. Agriculture employment has fallen steadily since industrialization began in the nineteenth century, but agriculture remains a huge business. America's two million farms employ more people than all the manufacturers of automobiles, electronics and computers combined.

For the past four decades, agricultural exports have led America's growth in global markets. The U.S. is by far the world's largest exporter of food, quite literally feeding the world; in Japan, some three-quarters of food imports are American. Recently, however, U.S. farms started to lose their edge. In the late 1970s, the U.S. share of food exports shot up to nearly 30 percent, but then plunged back down to about 20 percent after 1985.[15]

Stiffer competition was the cause. Many other countries began heavily subsidizing food exports. Europe, in particular, poured billions into subsidized farm exports, and may soon displace the U.S. as the world's number one exporter. In addition, farmers around the world have adopted the high-tech, chemical-based farming practices that built American agriculture. Many countries, including some Third World countries like Mexico and India, transformed themselves from big customers to tough competitors in a generation. If the huge farms of Russia ever hit their stride, the world will be swamped with cheap food which will further erode America's share of the pie.[16]

While Europe has given the U.S. a run for its money, the fight has taken its toll on European agriculture. In Germany, for example, agriculture's share of GNP has slid from 9.5 percent in 1950 to less than 1.5 percent in the 1990s. Between 1980 and 1990, full-time agricultural employment fell from 394,000 to 260,000.[17] Agriculture is under stress throughout the industrialized world.

We all lament the decline of great companies, but the fall from grace of agriculture may have a bigger impact on our pocketbooks. This is an industry that needs to be turned around, to be reinvented as the car and computer industries were. Information-intensive farming may be the catalyst for this change.

The list of problems caused by modern farming techniques is endless, from the accumulation of pesticides to soil erosion. Continual tilling removes topsoil and silts up nearby rivers. Fertilizers "burn" the soil and cause lakes to be choked with algae. Over the past two decades in the U.S., the amount of fertilizer used rose by a third to nearly two tons per square mile of arable land.[18] Pesticides turn underground wells into toxic waste sites. Irrigation destroys natural water flows. And while we have large surpluses, the quality of our food is in question. Residues of pesticides, fertilizers, and feed additives permeate everything we eat and drink. For many, particularly those with small children, this is alarming.

There is also the bigger question of nonsustainable agriculture. Farmers are destroying the local ecology in a number of areas. South of San Francisco, in the fertile Salinas Valley, irrigation of fruit and vegetable farms may have reached its limit. Overpumping of underground wells has drawn in sea water, tainting the water supply for farmers and everyone else.[19] In the heavily irrigated valley of the Sacramento River in northern California, rice farmers grow in the desert a crop native to monsoon-flooded jungles. The cost is high for taxpayers who foot the bill, and also for the river's wildlife which suffers from diverted water flows.[20] In Florida, the Everglades have been polluted by fertilizer run off from sugar farms. This huge swamp is a unique ecological treasure and a critical source of water for all of Florida, including not just its farmers, but also its industry and city residents.[21]

Falling information costs may restore the fortunes of agriculture and eliminate a lot of environmental damage in the bargain. In an experiment run by Rhone-Poulenc, Europe's largest agricultural chemical maker, a wheat farmer in England saw his gross margins jump when he abandoned conventional farming.[22] John Reganold of the Washington State University Department of Crop and Soil Sciences compared sixteen conventional organic farms in New Zealand. He concluded that the organic farms had better soil quality and were just as successful financially as their conventional counterparts.[23] In Germany, the fabled vineyards of the Rhine and Mosel have been hard hit in recent years due to tough competition and changing tastes; the sweet Rieslings of Germany have lost favor to the drier chardonnays of France and California. Some German vineyards have responded successfully by experimenting with new grape varieties grown organically.[24]

Organic farming places renewed emphasis on the quality of soils, plants, and produce. Quality is particularly important for wine makers, since wine is sold by the ounce, not the ton. Unlike a dairy farm, Buena Vista has to look beyond sheer quantity. If organic farming improves the quality of its product, a vineyard can charge a higher price. If it also lowers costs, so much the better. Any farmer—any businessman—can benefit from lower costs and higher quality.

Information opportunities are great for those developing biological alternatives to chemical farming. One by one, governments are banning pesticides and herbicides because of the damage they cause to foods and the environment. For those chemicals they keep on the "approved" list, regulators raise the burden of safety rule compliance to increasingly onerous—and costly— levels. New methods that obviate the need for chemicals without tainting food in the process will find ready markets. This new industry will grow most quickly in those countries where the demand for organic foods is strongest.

Agriculture is one of America's most productive industries, but American farmers may have gone as far as they can through the application of ever increasing amounts of capital and chemicals. Information-intensive organic farming may become the cutting edge of competition worldwide. This shift requires more greatly skilled management and labor, but reduces costs by substituting knowledge for pesticides, herbicides, and fertilizers at a time when consumers are demanding foods that aren't tainted with chemicals. Organically grown foods taste better, as anyone who's tasted a homegrown tomato in the summer knows. At the moment, most farmers compete on price alone since their products are, quite literally, commodities. Selling quality is a lot easier.

To go organic, managers at Buena Vista discovered that more than a shift in the way they grew grapes was necessary. They had to rethink the whole process of making wine. In particular, they had to retrain their workers, involving them more in the management of the vineyard.

Using conventional methods, Buena Vista's workers just drove around spraying everything. To farm organically, they had to understand what was going on. Which rows need to be mown this week to keep beneficial insects around the vines? How should the vines be pruned to take advantage of prevailing breezes? In short, the workers had to be trusted to make decisions that managers had previously made exclusively. One manager explained it to us this way: "When we started out, we expected the workers to say 'you guys are crazy' because it was so complicated. But they didn't. They embraced the new system. They are more like craftsmen, more involved in operations." He went on, "If you had to choose between a job that involved high-tech chemical methods and one that was environmentally sound, what would you do?"

Turning labor from a liability into an asset: this is what the information economy is all about. The great strides made by the manufacturing sector in the past decade come in large measure from empowering the work force. The challenge now is to reinvigorate other sectors of the economy. With millions of workers, mostly low-paid, agriculture is a good place to start.

For the past few generations, the best jobs for those aspiring to a middle-class way of life were in factories. Rapid productivity increases resulted in good pay, but also reduced the number of jobs available. While manufacturing has accounted for a steady share of total economic output for the past couple of decades in the U.S., employment in this sector has fallen steadily, and will keep going down. And so it is throughout the industrialized world: fewer workers are needed to produce more and more goods. When industrialization began, manufacturing jobs paid poorly. But rising factory wages drew workers off the farm by the tens of millions. Now, by applying knowledge to farm work, by substituting information-intensive organic procedures for chemical solutions, agricultural productivity and wages can be raised.

44

Network of the Future: Sprint's Big Bang

The first shock waves of the Big Bang hit Sprint hard. The Internet exploded, changing all Sprint's assumptions about how it was to grow and make money. In 1996, we published our analysis of Sprint and said that it had no alternative but to rip everything up and start over again. Two years later, Sprint CEO William Esry announced a "Big Bang" of his own, following our assessments almost to the letter.

Immediately after the Big Bang hit, Sprint reported that Internet bandwidth demand was doubling every three months.[1] Then, Sprint suddenly hit terminal velocity. The mainframe-based telephone exchanges that controlled Sprint's networks had been conceived in the 1970s when large computer architectures reigned supreme and the millions of Internet-driven PCs that now dominate so many markets were just a gleam in Bill Gates's eye.

Overnight, affordable processing power had fundamentally changed how networks like Sprint's are structured and the type of information they carry. The Internet has no central exchange or hierarchy. It simply links computers at the edge of the network.

These have all the information and power they need to operate autonomously.

By contrast, Sprint's telephone customers were connected by devices with little or no intelligence that are dependent entirely on the central exchange for service. Compared to the Internet, this is inflexible, unreliable, and hugely expensive. In effect, Sprint was designed to fight a First World War in which millions of troops were massed under a central control that could not be exercised. The Internet is like a blitzkrieg of independent commands designed to move quickly and effectively and which communicate with one another by radio.

It may seem bizarre that the Internet can be so much cheaper than a phone call, since the Internet is overlaid on the telephone network. The difference is pure economics. For historical and political reasons, telephone calls are priced on "average costs." To determine its average costs, a carrier sums up expenses and divides by the number of units sold. The Internet is priced closer to "marginal costs"—the additional cost of adding one more unit.

For telephone companies, like other utilities, marginal costs are extremely low except during times of peak demand. For Sprint to handle one more call during the middle of the night when its plant is nearly idle costs it essentially nothing. To handle one more call at four in the afternoon when capacity is at its limit could cost thousands, perhaps millions. A study done for Teleport Communications Group (since acquired by AT&T) put phone company marginal costs at 0.2¢ per minute.[2] So, charging us a penny per minute to connect to the Internet still leaves lots of profit.

Cheap personal computers allowed Sprint's customers to "right-price" Sprint services well ahead of Sprint's ability to cut its own costs, completely undermining Sprint's network architecture and driving it to terminal velocity.

To deal with this, in mid 1998, Esry made his "Big Bang" declaration, the Integrated Optical Network. In its simplest form, this high-powered network will be driven by many small routing devices instead of a few very large ones, making it more reliable and more powerful at the same time—just what Wal-Mart does for its stores.

Sprint's Big Bang architecture will push prices to a fraction of what they cost today,[3] or well below 1¢ a minute. With its Integrated Optical Network, Sprint may leapfrog other phone and cable technologies, and bring television to the Internet.

Sprint's ION reinforces what we have said often in this volume; that the futures of television and the Internet are inseparable. Within weeks of Sprint's Big Bang announcement, AT&T put down $48 billion for CATV giant TCI.[4] Soon it put down even more for MediaOne.

In turn, Sprint may tie the core of its new network to high-powered wireless distribution,[5] which is key to the post-PC world as we describe in the chapter "The Huge Post-PC Opportunity in Wireless." Through wireless, Sprint could avoid the costs AT&T faces in buying cable properties and then converting them for two-way use.

For TCI, NYNEX, Ameritech, and Pacific Bell, by contrast, the integration of TV into the Internet made the risks of staying in far greater than the benefits of selling. Esry's announcement heralded a process about which we have issued warnings for years: a major shift in shareholder value from those who are behind the Moore Curve to those who are ahead of it.

Media empires, as we have seen, are already plagued by declining market shares as the number of TV and near-TV sources of information and entertainment rapidly grow. These empires remain wholly unprepared for the merger of television and the

Internet into a single medium, or for the hundreds of millions of "broadcasters" that are about to flood their markets. ION completes this shift.

Consumers are not waiting. Some are experimenting with fast Internet around the house, and a few are even spending real money to rewire their homes with it.

ION, therefore, will not come a moment too soon. There will be technical problems, of course. There usually are when companies take the lead. But the need for a fully integrated Internet-TV medium is pressing. Those that fall behind in providing it will almost certainly go over the Event Horizon.

45

Transportation: Lufthansa

Lufthansa influenced us early in our thinking about how information can be substituted for other resources. At the time, we were looking at the use of cheap information to drive high-quality, low-cost manufacturing. Lufthansa inspired us to think of service businesses in the same light.

Changes in European and world air travel markets in the early 1990s hit Lufthansa hard. Engineered for the gentlemanly days of flying, when markets were carved up among flag carriers like the spoils of war and prices were fixed to accommodate the least efficient player, Lufthansa found itself holding low cards in a high-stakes game. This reversal was immediately reflected in Lufthansa's financial statements. Despite buoyant growth in revenues, the airline lost DM 444 million ($300 million) in 1991, then DM 373 million ($225 million) in 1992. After a decade of strong growth and unbroken profitability, Lufthansa was in free fall, headed for a crash landing.

Lufthansa was the prey, not the predator.

It was not alone. During the 1990s, one big company after

another was blindsided as the rules of the game changed. One day they were unassailable market leaders, the next day they were on the ropes. The causes are varied: deregulation, technology shift, globalization. The results are the same: loss of direction, red ink, layoffs, and retrenchment. As often as not, those at the top eventually get the axe after a prolonged period of denial, indecision, and in many cases outright panic. Ultimately, management accepts that costs are completely out of line with those of competitors, many of them upstarts. For each of these hard-hit dinosaurs, survival means improving efficiency while boosting quality and service.

Three of the world's largest carriers—American Airlines, British Airways, and United Airlines—were slugging it out for world domination. Survivors of fifteen tough years of deregulation at home, these battle-hardened competitors had slashed costs and were crowding Lufthansa's markets. At the same time, a recession hit Europe particularly hard, with airline-passenger traffic declining for the first time in history. Demand fell, capacity increased, and prices plunged. To top it all off, the value of the German mark soared, raising the price of everything Lufthansa bought at home. Lufthansa began to look like another great name from aviation history now vanished from the skies: Pan Am.

Declining prices are nothing new to the airline business; they have been falling in real terms since 1960, when jet aircraft first entered commercial service in large numbers.[1] But this time Lufthansa could not keep up; its expenses were spiraling ahead of ticket prices. With deregulation, the German flag carrier had to compete on price, but found itself carrying costs up to twice that of its leanest rivals.[2] Wages and benefits were high, productivity was poor, and Lufthansa was simply flying with too many empty seats. Change exposed Lufthansa to severe pressures. Like a 1940s test plane approaching the sound barrier, the company was ready to burst apart.

Despite all these problems, the fundamentals of the airline business appeared good—perhaps better for Lufthansa than for most others. Worldwide passenger traffic grew 6 percent per year in the 1980s, and industry observers expected demand to grow by at least 5 percent per year over the next decade, more than twice as fast as the economy as a whole.[3] While worldwide traffic dipped in 1991,[4] Lufthansa passenger volumes continued to grow. The collapse of the Soviet Union created enormous opportunities for Lufthansa (and the rest of Germany) as the new gateway to the East.

Lufthansa naturally wanted to be one of the survivors in this business. But in the early 1990s, it was only the eleventh largest airline in the world, and the third largest international carrier. In an industry where half a dozen competitors, at most, would become truly "global," Lufthansa was vulnerable. It had a big and rich home market, and a strong position on major routes through-out the world. But the outlook in 1991–92 was bad, and until it put its house in order, Lufthansa was not going to capitalize on any of the opportunities it enjoyed. Outside Germany, aggressive competitors—especially the Americans and the British—were slashing prices on Lufthansa's most profitable routes. These gate crashers were grabbing share while Lufthansa's financial woes mounted. The airline had lost control of its fate.

Juergen Weber took over the controls at Lufthansa in May 1991, becoming chairman just when the red ink began to flow. An engineer, previously the airline's chief technical officer, Weber had to slash costs, and fast.

His solution: use information to identify and eliminate pockets of cost throughout the airline's operations. He lowered the company's operating and capital outlays significantly. At the same time, he improved service by zeroing in on what customers value and shedding the rest.

Weber's plan began to pay dividends almost immediately. Within a year of his appointment, costs per seat-mile fell while traffic volume went up sharply. By the end of his second year, despite continued problems in the airline business, Lufthansa turned the corner, showing a profit in the second quarter of 1993. For the whole of 1993, loses were cut by two-thirds.[5] Even more impressive was the company's performance in terms of fuel consumption, noise pollution, emissions, and waste of all kind.

In many ways, Juergen Weber's hands were tied. Germany is a big market, but it is not an easy place to do business. For a company like Lufthansa, the government sets the rules—lots of them, and tough ones. Increasingly, successful Germans are finding this environment oppressive, and a steady stream of big companies are packing their bags. Among car companies, Volkswagen shifted production to Spain, while BMW and Mercedes opened new plants in the U.S. But Lufthansa was stuck at home. Service providers such as airlines must make locally what they sell. Weber could not cut and run. He had to be creative.

Weber told an interviewer that 80 percent of Lufthansa's costs were out of the company's control, including fuel costs, airport charges, and interest payments for its fleet. He added that he had the "most control over personnel and capacity utilization."[6] Yet, in the short term, Lufthansa's power to affect even these costs—particularly labor costs, which alone account for one-third of the airline's expenses—was severely circumscribed.

Government-mandated benefits in Germany are generous, and labor unions are notoriously militant. Germans enjoy the highest wages in the world—and the longest vacations. Massive layoffs, so readily employed as a recourse by American managers, don't play well in Germany, where they are unusual and extremely costly. Lufthansa receives no public subsidies, having been partially privatized in the early 1980s (the government retained just over half its shares). Government-mandated benefits had to be covered from cash flow.

Lufthansa's—and Germany's—prospects looked bad enough that the company negotiated with the unions to cut some 5,500 positions over two years, bringing down the workforce 11 percent from the end of 1991.[7] Wages were frozen for 1993, and productivity concessions were granted by the unions. In short, Lufthansa got its employees to work more for less money—almost unheard of in Germany. Nevertheless, these concessions came at a high price in terms of severance pay. The wage bill continued to rise in 1992 and 1993, albeit at a slower rate than would have otherwise occurred. There was a limit to how much the airline could extract from the unions, particularly if the German economy turned up.

Airport charges in Germany (including landing, terminal, and air traffic control fees) are exorbitant, twice as high in Frankfurt as in Paris and four times what they are in London.[8] Lufthansa's chairman figured he could save DM 500 million ($310 million) in airport charges if he were operating out of the U.S.[9] This figure was more than the company's total losses in 1991–92. In 1992, when Lufthansa was struggling to bring its finances under control, airport charges went up 16 percent. Air traffic control fees alone jumped 33 percent,[10] despite notorious inefficiencies in the European air traffic system that produces thousands of hours of holding time in the air for Lufthansa every year.[11] Those delays cost the airline hundreds of millions of marks, more than its losses in 1992.[12] Since airport and traffic control operations are monopolies, Lufthansa had no direct control over this expense, its second largest after wages.

Oil prices are entirely out of Lufthansa's hands, but the strengthening of the mark helped keep fuel costs down, since oil is priced in dollars. In the short term, Lufthansa could only hope that the price of oil in German marks would keep falling. In the long run, however, the airline can have a real impact on its finances by raising the fuel efficiency of its fleet. In 1992, a critical year, Lufthansa spent DM 1.2 billion ($1.5 billion) on jet fuel, 10 percent of its expenses.[13]

New planes can cut fuel costs dramatically. The Airbus A340, the first of which was bought by Lufthansa in 1993, reduced jet fuel consumption by one-third, compared to that of other long-haul aircraft. For example, on the 2,800 mile flight from Munich to Chicago, an A340 burns an estimated fifty-four tons of fuel, while a DC10-30 with the same number of passengers consumes seventy-four tons of fuel. One-third is a big number: in 1992, Lufthansa's entire loss was less than a third of its fuel bill.

By maintaining one of the youngest fleets in the industry, Lufthansa boosted fuel efficiency radically. Between 1970 and 1990, the amount of jet fuel it took the company to transport a passenger one mile fell by half. But, as the performance figures for the A340 demonstrated, there remained considerable scope for further savings. A 13-billion-mark ($9 billion) fleet modernization plan for the first half of the 1990s[14] reduced operating costs, and the airline grounded or sold the older, inefficient aircraft in its fleet. The savings went right to the bottom line, with fuel outlays declining by 5 percent in 1991 and 11 percent in 1992, despite rising traffic. Without any other changes, this course alone would put Lufthansa solidly back in the black.

Compared to existing long-distance planes, the A340s reduced exhaust by up to 85 percent. Noise levels were cut in half, reducing Lufthansa's outlays for airport fees.

Noise is a big problem for Lufthansa. In Germany, landing fees are set as a function of noise level (the only other country that does so is Sweden). Lufthansa spent DM 2.5 billion ($1.5 billion) on airport charges in 1992, even more than on fuel. In 1993, the airline outfitted forty of its Boeing 737-200s with "hush kits" to reduce noise levels by up to 80 percent. The savings were real: a 737 with a new hush kit paid only DM 805 to land, compared to DM 2,415 without them, a savings of two-thirds.[15] New planes reduced landing fees even further.

When we visited, Lufthansa Technik was the largest third-party aircraft maintenance supplier in the world. Located on the edge of the Hamburg airport, away from the passenger terminals, the Technik center faced a runway crowded with planes from around the world, waiting to be serviced. Among the many grimy, sprawling buildings was a spanking new hangar with two enormous bays, each big enough to accommodate two jets at the same time. This was the Lufthansa Technik paint shop, completed in 1992, where planes are stripped of old paint and refinished, a process which must be repeated every five or six years to maximize fuel economy. This hangar was part of an 800 million-mark ($500 million) expansion of the Hamburg overhaul center.

Lufthansa used its "Aquastripping" process to remove old paint. In the past, teams of workers applied two and a half tons of chemical strippers to each plane. These solvents were dangerous: to apply the stuff, workers had to wear what looked like space suits. Contaminated work clothes, along with the used stripper and the seven and a half tons of water per plane that were needed for the process all had to be treated as hazardous material. Disposal costs were significant.

In Aquastripping, by contrast, a large Aquastripping nozzle feels its way along one section of an airplane fuselage, manipulated from a computer console. Aquastripping relies on water under high pressure to remove paint. Chemicals have been essentially eliminated, while 97 percent of the water is recycled. After extraction from the air and water in the hangar, only the old paint remains, which is incinerated.

The benefits of Aquastripping to Lufthansa have been significant. Material and disposal costs were slashed. Worker safety was enhanced. Quality was better: Aquastripping took off the outer coat, and left the primer layer, reducing the damage to the metal underneath (and saving paint, since another primer coat is not needed). Best of all, one man could do the job faster than thirty using the old method and the payback was fast.

To regain its competitiveness, Lufthansa needed more information-driven efficiency improvements like this, since labor made up a third of its costs. Lower fuel costs and landing fees helped the bottom line, but were not enough. Labor productivity had to go up.

Lufthansa needed more from the capital it invested. There is little point in increasing fuel economy by 50 percent if planes are running half empty, and Lufthansa "load factors" (the proportion of seats filled with paying passengers) have been low.[16] Lufthansa could do more to repair its finances—and the balance sheet—by filling its planes and flying fewer of them, than by buying more efficient jets.

Better returns from labor and capital require additional investment, to be sure, but most of all, they require better management. The idea here is simple: use information systems to figure out a way to get passengers around with fewer planes. Don't just buy better planes; get rid of some planes altogether.

This approach paid dividends. Lufthansa eliminated some routes entirely to save cash, but also rethought its route structure. The airline had relied on a complex "hub and spoke" strategy in Germany, where more than a fifth of its revenues were generated; for example, a flight from Berlin to Hamburg might take you through Frankfurt. This approach, poorly adapted to the German market, was replaced by direct flights with smaller planes.[17] Such changes helped the airline carry 7 percent more passengers in just one quarter, with 3 percent fewer flights. The company had been trying to build market share by adding flights—and flying them with empty planes, a losing strategy.

Lufthansa did for service what Wal-Mart does for its stores; it substituted information for planes, and improved service to customers at the same time, since everyone prefers non-stop flights to sprinting between gates at a hub. The bottom-line benefits were large.

Lufthansa developed an onboard system that monitored aircraft performance (including exhaust, fuel consumption, and noise). Data was recorded on a cassette, then run through a computer on the ground, providing feedback for maintenance crews. For example, the system might tell maintenance workers that the fourth bolt on the third engine should be looked at because that engine is using 4 percent more fuel than necessary. With the A340, the system maintains contact with maintenance computers on the ground throughout flight. The system provides in-flight feedback to the pilots, helping safety and lowering fuel consumption.

Lufthansa's flight monitoring system—the first to be developed and perfected—helped its planes operate more safely and inexpensively than before. But the airline also needed to fill up its planes. The simplest way was to discount fares across the board, but that's a tough game, as many airline failures show. For high-cost players like Lufthansa, discounting alone is not a viable option. A better approach is to charge full fare when you can (for business travel, for example), then selectively discount seats that would otherwise be empty.

American Airlines wrote the book on "yield management systems" (those that generate the highest ticket price possible for each available seat) during the rough-and-tumble 1980s, when deregulation swept the U.S. airline industry. Its reservations systems became the most profitable operation at American Airlines.[18] Moreover, by eliminating the need for airplanes and the fuel they burn, this computer network has probably done more to reduce aviation energy consumption than any other innovation.

Lufthansa brought such a system on line in 1993. Considering that one new jet costs $100 million, the potential savings from yield management are enormous. In the first quarter of 1993, Lufthansa's load factors rose by six percentage points after languishing for years. With more than 230 jets in its fleet, a sustained 6 percent increase in capacity utilization could obviate the need for fourteen aircraft. That's a lot of money. Sam Walton would have been proud.

Again, like Wal-Mart, Lufthansa managed to maintain—if not improve—customer satisfaction during its retrenchment. Polls consistently ranked Lufthansa among the top five carriers, and among international business travelers, the German airline comes out on top.[19] With many of its information-driven initiatives, Lufthansa not only cut costs directly, but also improved service. By rethinking what service really means, the airline focused better on what customers really want.

Recession in the early 1990s exposed the high cost structure of many European companies, like Lufthansa, which were forced to compete on world markets. During the booming 1980s, Europeans had felt that they had the tiger by the tail. The building of the single European market, the fall of the Soviet Union, and the way society seemed to work all added to the euphoria. But the mood turned sour once the recession of the early 1990s arrived. Endless reports showed that Europe had lost its edge, that Europeans could not turn good ideas into profit, that costs were too high. As if to prove the point, many national champions, particularly in high tech, were looking for the exits. Suddenly the safety net that Europeans took for granted seemed to drop away.

As unemployment lines lengthened, Europeans realized that something had to give. High-profile layoffs (like Lufthansa's) showed that there was a simple, if harsh, way to bring costs back in line with those of American competitors. But many Europeans were searching for a third way, one which preserves Europe's highly developed—and expensive—social net. Pantomimes of American business strategies are probably doomed to failure anyway.

European manufacturers have been exposed to fierce competition from the U.S. and Asia for some time, but service industries, such as the airlines, went relatively unscathed until the 1990s. In the airline business, as we have seen, the walls of protection finally came down. For Lufthansa and its continental European rivals, the threat came primarily from the U.S. and Britain. But matching these competitors was not enough. With higher wage rates and benefits, Europeans were unlikely to win discounting wars in the airline business (or any other). Rather, to succeed, European companies needed to change the rules themselves, to turn the tables on their challengers.

Certainly there was over-manning at Lufthansa and other European airlines, particularly on the ground and in management positions. But lasting efficiency improvements that do not undermine service came from boosting productivity, not bashing labor. In the first few years after it sank into the red, Lufthansa successfully used its information-driven program to flag pockets of cost that could be eliminated, raising the productivity of both labor and capital. For Lufthansa, this approach has proven hugely profitable. By 1998, sales reached DM 227 billion, load factors were at an all-time high, and profits reached DM 2.5 billion—many multiples of its losses from a decade earlier.

46

Fiber Optics: The *Titanic* Sails

The world communications network—much of it brand new and seemingly indestructible—is steaming straight toward a price collapse of *Titanic* proportions. This collapse will drive a complete reordering of the communications business. Investors need to place their bets with care.

Today, communications demand is constrained by high prices. In the United States, long-distance prices have indeed fallen—by more than half since AT&T's divestiture of the local phone companies in the early eighties.[1] But a phone call carries just 64,000 bits of information a second, the same as it has for a hundred years. Price-performance has stood still. As a result, over the decade, total U.S. long-distance traffic grew by less than 10 percent per year.[2]

Slow growth numbers like these would kill most companies in the computer business, where Moore's Law price-performance improvements are a daily occurrence. Of course, computers are not free, and like long-distance calls, the average PC has remained remarkably constant in price over the years, at around $2,000.

Only recently has the popularity of computers costing less than $1,000 started to place real pressure on this average.

Computer prices may have been flat, but, unlike phone calls, every year you get much more for your money. Compared to the first PC we bought, the latest one has a modem that's 100 times faster and a microprocessor that's 150 times faster. It has 1,000 times the memory and 15,000 times as much disk storage. All of this isn't gravy; Microsoft certainly takes its tithe. The current version of Word, for example, requires 100 times as much memory as WordStar did in 1980. But that old computer now looks like a Model T; the phone is the Model T we're still driving.

As chips get cheaper, people buy much more computer power. PC makers have passed this price-performance benefit on to customers. Computers are also the basic building blocks of the telephone network, but for people making long-distance calls, there's been little improvement to show for this. Consumers are being ripped off, big-time. These numbers are about to change, and when they do, this *Titanic* will sink, taking a lot of folks down with it.

Most of the drop—such as it is—in U.S. communications has come out of the hide of the local phone companies. The FCC required these to lower the fees they charge the long-distance companies for use of their networks. What the long-distance companies actually net from this has fallen much less.[3] Some private-line rates for business have fallen by more than 90 percent since the Bell System was broken up in the early eighties, but this has not been enough to offset the large retail dialing market. For the long-distance companies, operating margins have doubled in the 1990s. Prices flat, computer costs falling: this is good work if you can get it—and hang onto it.

Judging by the number of solicitations they receive at home at dinner time, Americans may think the communications business is getting more competitive. Lots of newcomers are attracted by fat margins, but carriers have yet to begin real price competition. During the mid-1990s, retail prices were actually creeping up. Even at the wholesale level, long-distance companies were boosting rates sharply.[4]

Supply and demand explain these trends. Price cuts took place between 1985 and 1990, when long-distance capacity quadrupled, network utilization plummeted, and prices fell. Then the pressure came off: between 1990 and 1995, capacity grew by only one-third,[5] despite a robust economy and booming data traffic. Utilization rates rose quickly, and topped optimal levels.[6]

The big communications rip-off is at the end. Huge amounts of new long-distance capacity are coming on line in the United States. We measured the capacity potential of just four new fiber networks, as a multiple of AT&T's existing network.[7] We got the equivalent of eighty new AT&Ts. Internet traffic is growing, but not this fast.[8]

When average prices fall below 10¢ a minute, the impact on today's carriers and their investors will be profound. Although AT&T maintains that most of its traffic comes from discounted minutes,[9] the company's standard tariff for interstate calls was 26.5¢ per minute in 1998,[10] a rate paid by some two-thirds of its residential customers. By acquiring MCI, WorldCom got a boatload of fifteen-cent minutes that were clearly unsustainable.

Long-distance companies pay a few cents to the local phone carriers where each long-distance call begins and ends.[11] These local access charges are falling, leaving lots of room for more price cuts from today's levels.

While domestic prices have been flat in the United States until recently, prices on international routes have plummeted. A couple of years ago, we negotiated a new volume-based agreement with AT&T which included 35¢ per minute for calls to Britain, a good price at the time. In 1999, when we switched to Qwest, our rate went down to 12¢ to Britain with no volume commitment.[12] Soon after, a flyer came under the door (along with a Chinese take-out menu) offering 9¢ per minute.

Overcapacity is driving down prices. At the end of 1996, only 37 percent of total available transoceanic fiber was in use.[13] Resellers, which buy spare trunks, moved into the market in large numbers and cut prices fast. By 1998, new carriers accounted for more than 40 percent of international calls from the United States and more than 30 percent of the international calls from Britain.[14]

Fiber capacity grew 18,600 percent between the United States and overseas locations during the first seven years of the 1990s. Just one of the new transatlantic cables has enough capacity to carry all U.S. domestic traffic.[15] Regulation alone keeps the cost of calls to Europe higher than domestic ones. The next round of transatlantic construction, coming on line in 2000–2005, will boost network throughput by another factor of ten.[16] If something doesn't happen to unleash consumer post-PC traffic by then, there will be a lot of blood in the water.

Regulators are giving a push. The FCC requires that U.S. carriers pay their foreign counterparts in developed markets no more than 15¢ per minute to terminate calls. Less-developed markets will follow.[17]

A couple of years ago, a study reported that if only 6 percent of long-distance phone calls were carried over the Internet, all U.S. long-distance profits would disappear.[18]

Right now, data traffic is growing much faster than phone calls, but is nowhere near its potential. Growth in data is barely offsetting the shift to the Internet. For example, if you send a Microsoft Word file by e-mail instead of faxing it, you increase your data traffic by a cent or two, but cut your long-distance costs by a couple of dollars. The Internet has a long way to grow to make up for revenue shrinkage like this.

For the moment, though, demand is constrained by slow lines to people's homes. Until this changes, supply will stay ahead of demand. Few consumers can tap into the Net at speeds greater than 56,000 bits of information a second, which is only fast enough to fill a still Internet page very, slowly. Sheer computer power maximizes the utility of these speeds, but without more bandwidth into the home there are limits to the traffic available to fill all the new pipes being built.

The stall in the capacity of ordinary phone lines threatens to dampen computer demand, and may force computer makers to slash prices to a small fraction of their current levels just to keep their plants open.

The stage is set for a collapse in long-distance prices. "Ultimately, voice will be free," Nathan Myhrvold, Microsoft's visionary chief technology officer, told the World Economic Forum in Davos, Switzerland, in 1998.[19]

Some carriers will do well by the *Titanic*'s sinking. Level 3, for example, came to market with a cost structure designed for these conditions. NTT, a company with no international infrastructure to weigh it down, invested $100 million in Teligent[20] and another $100 million in Verio, an Internet company consolidation play founded by top telecom venture capitalist, the Centennial Funds.

Internet companies that don't own capacity, like Verio, will do well because their cost of operations will drop. Local phone companies can thank their lucky stars—or better still, their regulators—that they never entered the long-distance market. If they had, they would go down with the rest.

The biggest losers will be long-distance carriers in the U.S. and overseas. Their cost structure is all wrong and their ability to respond is limited. The overseas carriers have the most to lose because they are the target of the bulk of new capacity. Today's carriers won't disappear, however. The poor are always with us.

The long-distance *Titanic* has set sail. On board are some of the biggest shareholders in the world. Soon they will see the true worth of their investment as brittle rivets are tested against the shearing forces of Black Hole price-performance.

47

The TV Guide Wars

Once a television network is just another Web site and every home is a TV station, we will need help managing what we watch. This is the ultimate portal opportunity and explains why portal companies like Yahoo! get such high valuations. But the portal landscape will change radically.

Big media has discovered the Internet, and there's a run on portals. Television networks, movie studios, newspapers, and magazines are staking their claims. These companies can see that traditional media are losing audiences to the Internet, and they want to ensure continued access to their customers.

They are staking these claims on faith. Right now, the portal revenue model is a joke. Portals make their money from banner ads, and there are too many banners chasing too few viewers. The potential number of banners is quite literally limitless. And no matter how powerful the portal, competitors are just a click away. At current access speeds, the Internet may have already overshot its mark. Not until TV is available on the Internet will ad revenues take off. And TV means broadband access that no one yet offers.

CNET is the premier on-line portal for information technology. Like others, CNET charges advertisers for access to its viewers, of which it has more than eight million per day. These viewers are decision makers, making CNET uniquely positioned to tap into the trillion-dollar IT market. Projected 1999 revenues were $100 million,[1] about what AT&T spends on advertising in a slow quarter.[2]

Sportsline.com is regarded as a category killer. It has a first-mover advantage, a well-defined market, strategic relationships with key partners like CBS and AOL, and a committed audience of American sports nuts. Projected 1999 revenues were $60 million.[3]

Even Yahoo!, the granddaddy of portals, was aiming for 1999 revenues of $500 million.[4] That's a lot of banner ads, but it's also not far from what CBS took in from thirty-second spots during last year's NFL football season.[5]

Advertising is a 200-billion-dollar market in the United States. TV accounts for a quarter.[6] In total, the Internet accounted for maybe 1 percent of expenditures last year, about what GM spent on television.[7]

Consumers spend hours every day watching TV, but only minutes in front of their PCs. Everybody has a TV, but less than a third of American households are on line. And those with connected PCs are using them less, if recent consumer surveys can be believed. We attribute this to the "encyclopedia effect": parents buying computers to facilitate their children's education. Most people realize, once they own a PC and have done some time surfing, that the Internet may have its uses, but it's not particularly educational, and its definitely not entertaining.

As their viewing choices have increased over the decades, people have found more time for TV in their day. Cheap computing power has driven a rapid increase in the number of channels available to viewers. From just a few in most markets (and just one or two in many countries), the number of channels has jumped into the hundreds for digital cable and satellite subscribers. The step up to millions of Internet-TV sites will be like nothing ever seen before.

Advertising is growing as a share of GNP. Ad expenditures were especially buoyant during the 1990s expansion. But the pie is being cut up into smaller pieces as television, radio, newspaper, and magazine audiences splinter. Wait until the Internet gets rolling. Millions of choices means millions of media alternatives for advertisers. We call this "market entropy," and it cannot be stopped.

To many, the intersection of TV and the Internet means that you can browse the Web while watching TV. This means you can get baseball statistics while you watch the game on ESPN, find out about your heartthrob while you watch *Buffy the Vampire Slayer,* or make a purchase on the Home Shopping Network with a few clicks on the remote.

Useful, perhaps, but basically more of the same. And this is not where we are going. The Internet will bring an unlimited number of TV channels to every home. Viewers will be able to select any channel broadcasting from anywhere in the world, be it the BBC evening news or the Tasmania–New South Wales cricket test match finals. Entire film libraries will be available on line. What's more, every home will also be a TV station, capable of pumping live camcorder traffic onto the network. Given trends currently underway, we believe this is inevitable. What's not so clear is how people will find what they want and how they will pay for it.

Organizations have great difficulty making these kinds of shifts. Yahoo!—even the personalized My Yahoo!—is like an electronic newspaper based on static screen shots. Indeed, one of the virtues of Yahoo! is that it is optimized for slow-speed modems. This means lots of text and minimal graphics. A fast-loading, text-based interface made Yahoo! a winner in the slow-speed world of home telephones attached to a modem. What will make it a winner in an Internet-TV world?

Newspapers didn't dominate broadcasting. We have little reason to think that these first-generation portals will make the transition from text to video. As we watch the big media players rush in, we are reminded of the Japanese investors who bought Pebble Beach and Rockefeller Center at the top of the 1980s. Sayonara shareholder value.

Not everyone is paying top dollar, of course, and a lot of the new currency is play money. Last year, Disney picked up 43 percent of Infoseek at a price well below market.[8] Then Disney bought the rest with paper—and not Disney paper, but new currency issued for Go.com, its Internet tracking stock.[9] And while Infoseek may be a legacy portal, Disney recognizes where the Internet is going. CEO Michael Eisner knows that broadband networks will make Disney content more accessible to his customers.[10]

TV Guide is well positioned to be the dominant portal in this new era. The TV Guide franchise was built on the magazine, the best-selling weekly in the world, with 12 million paid subscribers. Now the company also provides TV Guide channels for cable and satellite television, including AT&T's TCI and News Corp.'s properties. In the United States alone, TV Guide reaches 100 million homes.[11]

A couple of years ago, TV Guide had one of the top Web sites, but it has slipped off the charts.[12] Its site, www.tvguide.com, is simple and easy to use: you enter your zip code, and it brings up today's listings. This is a long way from Internet-TV; still, few have a franchise this strong.

For digital cable and satellite, the TV Guide channel can be customized, much like My Yahoo! The idea is to manage television, not simply to shift printed pages onto the screen. Parents want to screen for their children by ratings, for example. Viewers may want to sort by time, content, or source. Links with next-generation VCRs will permit simplified recording for "time-shifting." And the programming channel can be used for pay-TV selections, and ultimately for video on demand. The next step to a direct Internet connection is not a big one.

The set-top box is valuable real estate, and TV Guide is slugging it out with a variety of other contenders. These include Microsoft, Sony, and Gemstar, the inventor of VCR Plus. Like so many communications battles, this one is being fought in court by TV Guide and Gemstar.[13]

A lot of money will be spent on lawyers before viewers get unlimited video content over the Internet. Not all of it will be spent in court. Since intellectual property is involved, distributors must work out agreements with the owners. But the process is starting. Broadcast.com licensed a variety of films for Internet broadcast, for example.[14]

Broadcast.com is on the right track. At its Web site, you can find a variety of television shows and other video content that can be viewed on line. It's still funky: you get short clips on a tiny window. Imagine a fast Internet connection and a wired TV, and you can see where this will go. The problem for Broadcast.com is twofold: how do you pay the rent for the next few years while faster networks get built, and how do you attract viewers when they have broadband? TV Guide has solved both problems. The magazine is a cash cow. And its powerful brand and electronic reach will bring the viewers in.

AOL has this kind of brand and reach. AOL dominates consumer access to the Internet—at narrowband speeds, that is. Like AT&T before its cable acquisitions, AOL is dependent on plain old telephone service to reach consumers. By contract, AT&T, now the largest U.S. cable provider, must deliver cable modem connections from At Home, its own cable Internet company.

With limited access to cable, AOL needs broadband alternatives. Unfortunately, they aren't as attractive as cable. AOL has inked agreements with telephone companies for joint marketing of AOL and speedy telephone connections, called DSL. DSL is fast, but probably not fast enough to move real-time video home-to-home. AOL also bought a piece of Hughes Electronics for broadband satellite access to its customers.[15] Satellite is perfect for video delivery, but cannot handle two-way communications at high speeds. Naturally, AOL thinks it should have "equal access" to AT&T's customers over its cable network.

And the story is even more complicated than this. At Home has contracted with its cable partners not to offer full-motion video segments longer than ten minutes. The cable companies have reserved those services for themselves.[16] At Home was free to pay $6.7 billion in stock for Excite, another first-generation portal.[17] But it can't compete with cable.

Others are ready to do so. Internet Ventures Inc. contracts with rural cable operators to provide high-speed Internet service. IVI customers have Internet access to seventy-five international and domestic television stations. AT&T's TCI refused IVI carriage on its cable system. Along with AOL, IVI is in court and before the FCC to force the issue.[18]

A few movies here, a few TV stations there are manageable. But when this all gets sorted out, there will be millions of video Web sites to choose from. This is where portals come in: helping viewers navigate through unlimited choices, and consolidating audiences for advertisers.

Large sums of money will be spent on networks, lawyers, and lobbyists before the dust settles on the collision of TV and the

Internet. The clash between TV and Internet economics occurred when the merger between Lycos and USA Networks went off the rails. Barry Diller wanted to value Lycos using something like traditional media metrics. Lycos investors had their eye on the tickertape. A compromise could not be reached.[19]

We understand that real money is made on the Internet by selling stock, not by advertising or anything else. But eventually this will change. Within five years, we expect the majority of American homes to have broadband access to the Internet for their TVs, PCs, and a variety of other devices. The next generation of Internet portals—and Internet billionaires—will be at their service.

48

Retreat from the Event Horizon: AT&T

In a short time since his arrival at the helm of AT&T, CEO Mike Armstrong has engineered a flurry of acquisitions, buying Teleport, TCI, and MediaOne, among other properties, for over $120 billion.

Now, $120 billion is serious change, no matter how you look at it, and investors need to know why he did what he did and whether or not he will succeed.

In the mid-nineties, AT&T was split up for the third time in four decades, spinning off its hardware division Lucent Technologies in addition to NCR, a failed computer company acquisition of a few years earlier. This was not one company's attempt to maintain forward momentum. Rather, it was one part of a spectacular unraveling of a global information industry torn apart by the spiraling forces of cyberspace.

Since its last breakup in 1984, AT&T's performance had been mixed. We remember having lunch in late 1995 with a well-respected brokerage company research department head who was stunned when we pointed out that AT&T had barely grown in the decade since divestiture. AT&T's stock stepped lively, a nose ahead of the S&P during the decade-long bull market. Profits grew smartly, too, with a few hiccups. But AT&T was a layoff play, as the company squeezed costs out of the bloated structure it salvaged from the Bell System.

As for real growth, AT&T was pretty much of a bust. Total revenues, as reported by the company, grew by an average of 2.4 percent per year between 1984 and 1995. After bumping along during the 1980s, revenues turned up in the early 1990s, and were particularly buoyant in 1994. Yet even between 1991 and 1995, growth averaged only 4 to 5 percent per year. Performance of the core business was even worse. Adjusted for its acquisitions of computer company NCR and McCaw Cellular, growth for that decade dropped to barely 1 percent a year. If you think "dot-com" shares are inflated now, in the mid-nineties AT&T investors were paying twenty-five times earnings for a company that, adjusted for inflation, had been shrinking for a decade.

AT&T was closing in on the Event Horizon.

We published this assessment in late 1995. Three months later, *Fortune* jumped on the bandwagon with a violent attack on the company's ability to generate value,[1] and most of the business press followed like howling wolves. Over the next two years, the drama of AT&T's approach to final disaster began to unfold. Top executives left, including one president chosen from within and one brought in from the outside. Eventually, the CEO himself was forced out.

In 1991, AT&T outlined its financial strategy, the centerpiece of which was long-term revenue growth of 10 percent or more.[2] The idea was to retain market share in the U.S., while building the business internationally. The company fell far short of this goal. By its own reckoning, the global information industry was growing at 8 to 10 percent per year.[3] Even with its acquisitions, AT&T was losing market share rapidly.

By the mid-nineties, sales of equipment had done better than services, increasing by 6 percent a year since the start of the decade. Network Systems, now Lucent Technologies, accounted for the bulk of equipment sales with products it sold to phone companies. Sales to business and consumer markets averaged a relatively strong 11 percent per year. Equipment sales also expanded rapidly outside the U.S., as the company opened new markets. After providing a one-time boost in 1991, however, NCR became a drag on performance.

On the hardware side of the business, AT&T's biggest customers, the phone companies and cellular operators, were becoming less and less able to afford its products. The president of one AT&T customer told us that he no longer had the cash flow to maintain his network, and said he saw little likelihood of being able to raise the capital to replace it. His company soon sold out to another. To hold onto its hardware business, AT&T would have had to invest in a huge new round of research and development, or perhaps make acquisitions, which would have given the Justice Department the willies.

Then there was the issue of competition: AT&T's biggest hardware customers were also its biggest rivals in the phone business. AT&T could not be both supplier and competitor, and at some point was going to have to decide which it would be. The wonder is that during all the years AT&T managed to juggle these two, its customers didn't leave in droves.

Worse for the hardware outlook, the phone companies had thought they could lead the information revolution simply by adding multimedia services to their phone lines. But they forgot the price in price-performance. Bringing two-way TV into every living room over the telephone network would have cost phone companies as much as $10,000 per customer. Why bother when DirecTV can deliver 250 channels over a satellite that cost $8 for each person it reaches? As the phone companies abandoned these over-reaching plans—already in 1995, Bell Atlantic and Pacific Bell (since acquired by SBC) had canceled multibillion dollar network rebuilds—AT&T's future in hardware must have looked pretty dim.

International opportunities had been a bright star for the equipment business for some time. But that was no cakewalk either, with hungry European and Japanese rivals struggling to keep factories running, and pricing their products accordingly. The weak dollar helped exports for a few years. But even so, by mid-decade the company's international sales were just about where they were in 1991, at a quarter of the total.[4]

In 1994, Network Systems launched a new program called Customer Architecture. AT&T's plan was to alleviate the enormous Moore Curve pressures on its phone company customers by delivering networks that it would manage, and for which AT&T would hold the bag. This strategy, which placed Network Systems in the role of general contractor and facilities manager, tested the company's abilities—technically, financially, and managerially. With the Bell Atlantic and Pacific Bell rollbacks unraveling this strategy completely, an unbranded Network Systems had to retreat to big iron by the ton again. But its customers needed lightweight composites by the ounce.

For AT&T, getting out of the telecommunications equipment business looked like unloading a huge headache.

There are probably people who wished it had been the other way around. Long the weak sister with little influence over corporate planning and less over AT&T's stock price, AT&T's hardware business took off like a rocket when it was was finally unleashed as Lucent Technologies. Free from AT&T, able to learn from its lessons, and with an inspired management team, Lucent branded itself, made critical elements of its original Customer Architecture work, and returned huge amounts of value for shareholders.

Left alone, AT&T continued to close on the Event Horizon.

AT&T's long-distance business faced the Black Hole price pressures as everyone else did in telecommunications services. It was designed to sell services at 15¢ a minute (or more) each to a market careening toward distance-insensitive prices of under a cent per minute. AT&T was hard pressed to hold revenues steady as its prices fell by 5 to 10 percent per year. What would happen when they started falling 25 percent and more per year? AT&T had experimented with raising basic rates, but the higher prices just didn't stick. Per-minute revenues continued to fall.[5]

Volume should have made up for the deficiency, but didn't. Since the late 1980s, the volume of calling minutes handled by AT&T had increased by less than 7 percent per year. Volume increases like that would kill most companies in the computer business, where they know what price cuts are all about.

The Internet wasn't helping AT&T either. At about this time, in 1995, we received an offer to sign up with the AT&T Business Network, an on-line service. The price was 4 to 5¢ per minute ($24.95 per month for the first ten hours, plus $2.95 per month for each additional hour).[6] But a competing Internet company offered us well under a cent a minute, about *85 percent* less. If there was a communications revolution going on, AT&T didn't seem to know about it.

AT&T might have been able to wholesale services to low-cost Internet companies, but it would have lost the huge retail markup it enjoyed for long-distance services. These generated gross margins of 40 percent plus in long-distance, numbers any computer company would have killed for.[7]

Caught between a rock and a hard place in its effort to grow wireline revenues, AT&T had sensibly switched to wireless, where two-thirds of new customers came from the acquisition of McCaw Cellular.[8] At the time, you could still charge cellular customers per-minute rates that would make a long-distance operator blush. For years, however, McCaw's revenues per subscriber had been falling gradually. New digital-cellular companies threatened steep price cuts. These newcomers, without AT&T's baggage, looked to have the advantage when this high-stakes game of chicken began. To compound these risks, AT&T paid $2,800[9] for each of McCaw's subscribers, then promptly abandoned McCaw's brand. AT&T would have to crack a market headed for a price collapse with an unbranded service. The Black Hole loomed even closer.

Compounding the structural issues, management entered a deep and highly public crisis of its own. Several senior executives left to form new companies like Teligent, Global Crossing, and Qwest. Presidents came and went. The CEO was dismissed and Mike Armstrong brought in.

Armstrong's strategy was to pull AT&T firmly and completely away from the Event Horizon. Coming from DirecTV, he had a firm grasp of the essentials. He saw clearly that each American home spends an average of $30 a month on local phone service, a similar amount on long-distance, somewhat more on cable TV, and often another $20 a month on Internet service. He wants it all. Period.

He attacked across a broad front, buying cable TV companies left and right as well as At Home. He let Microsoft shore up his debt-laden balance sheet in return for a shot at putting Microsoft software—but never the Microsoft brand—in the set-top boxes AT&T's customers will use to get all the services he plans to sell them. Armstrong was aggressive on price, especially in wireless. Demand exploded.

Armstrong's biggest challenge is in meeting the technical problems of Terminal Velocity, which are acute in every AT&T market, while growing sales, market share, and profitability. Grafting something new that moves in Moore Time onto something old that doesn't is a formula for financial disaster. Growth in demand soon crushes the ability of the underlying infrastructure to take the load. All hope of growth and return evaporates.

To date, Armstrong has proven an adept acquirer, surprising his competitors at every turn. But now he has made it clear how much of their business he really wants, they will respond vigorously. Several have picked up wireless cable licenses, which have the power to deliver cable TV over the air at distances of several miles. With smart antennae placed closer to homes, these same properties can carry two-way traffic at very high speeds—you could send a movie both ways at the same time—at a fraction of the cost Armstrong has incurred buying TCI and MediaOne. This is a serious challenge, and one that many local phone companies may turn to once they free up some of their assets.

What investors must look for now in AT&T is the ever elusive quality of generalship: AT&T must execute.

49

Kid Power!

Among the many consequences of the Big Bang is the transfer of market power to children. Today, kids drive the pace of information-technology improvements. Prices have dropped to a level at which kids can take over.

As we have said before, toys like Nintendo 64 and Sony PlayStation aren't toys: they have more horsepower than the average home PC.[1] The software and communications applications kids want so they can drive these systems are what push technology to the limits.

A three-year-old PC works just fine for routine office work using programs like Microsoft Word, Excel, or Outlook. It's games that take advantage of the fastest new chips and lots of memory. Even the fastest PCs cannot keep up with kids. Before the Big Bang, kids were happy to get out-of-date hand-me-downs from the office. Today they laugh at them. It's Mom and Dad who are driving the clunker now.

Of course, kids are also a big market. This year, some 30 million video-game consoles will be sold, bringing the total in use to over 130 million.[2] That's a lot of kids and a lot of horsepower. All those devices could be connected clear around the globe without encountering another processor as powerful.

These impact of post-PC computers in the hands of kids has not yet reached the Internet. On-line video games have not been a hit. While kids like the idea of taking on all players, they find that the 500 milliseconds latency on the Internet is an eternity when you're playing to blast one of your friends into virtual oblivion.[3] Many Web-based game sites exist, but they require fast Internet links to work well. Limited to standard telephone line connections, most kids still have to meet in the real world to play games together.

Watch how experienced players move through a PlayStation game. They are completely absorbed in it. Despite its limitations, they create a virtual reality, with imagination compensating for missing or slow-to-arrive bits. Add to this another generation or two of computer price-performance improvements and a fast Internet connection, and you've got quite a cocktail. We believe that Internet demand is entering a stall from which it will not escape until faster residential connections are widely available. Only once kids can spend hours on line engaged in virtual adventure with their friends, can serious growth resume. It won't just be video games. History shows that new forms of communications lead in new directions: the telephone is not an improved telegraph.

With lots of bandwidth at their disposal, kids will transform how the Internet is used in ways that are difficult to predict. With toys much more powerful than mainframes ever were running loose in homes around the world, kids will dictate the volume and direction of network traffic, and the large amounts of wealth that will flow with it.

The impact is big for society at large. For the first time in history, kids know more than their parents. They always thought they did, of course, but now it's true. One of us volunteered to help with a computer class for second graders at the local public school. The so-called teacher kept having problems with the newly installed local area network. Meanwhile, a pixie in pigtails whose feet didn't reach the ground was happily showing all the other kids what to do. At home, it's the same story: we rely on twelve-year-old system administrators to keep the network up and running.

For suppliers, the risks are enormous. The twelve-year-olds who make this market happen have no brand loyalty and will gravitate instantly to whatever works fastest and cheapest and doesn't hang them up. Like the Internet, PC demand is also in a stall. But games do not run on Windows, and fast Internet connections may not help Microsoft. As any child will be more than happy to tell you, Windows this isn't. Kids will take into this brave new world products that are cheap, simple, reliable and fun.

Along with on-line games, the intersection of television and the Internet will open the floodgates for something new. Those who "have the con"—most likely the TV remote—will influence the purchase decisions. We expect kids to call the shots. Nintendo's GameBoy Camera was an instant hit. This is a fifty-dollar digital camera you stick on top of a GameBoy to take pictures of your-self and your friends.[4] Add video and a fast Internet connection, and kids will create a whole new form of communications.

In 1999, Kyocera introduced a color video PHS cell phone.[5] PHS, or Personal Handyphone System, is a low-cost alternative to cellular in Japan. While limited in terms of mobility, PHS is cheap to install and operate. What's more, it offers good data connec-tions for applications such as video. PHS is popular with Japan-ese teenagers.[6]

Computer geeks with pointy heads and pocket liners are a popular stereotype for teenage boys who stare into video games for hours at a time. As with many such stereotypes, there is some truth to this one. We're convinced that the average age of tech support staff at our Internet company is about fourteen, and falling. However, the reality is that computers are not just for boys.

Girls like computer games, too. More than half the visitors to Sony's multiplayer game Web site are girls.[7] Games for girls now dominate computer game bestseller lists.[8] Almost half of the top-selling computer games are in Mattel's Barbie series. Barbie Fashion Designer is the best-selling children's software ever.[9] In fact, action (including shoot 'em up) games only account for a quarter of game software sales. The biggest category by far is role-playing games—in other words, the kind that seem to appeal to girls.[10] Girls don't dislike action games, but they like other ones, too. Our daughters appreciate the thrill of Descent, but they are also intrigued by Sim City, and of course they find their Tamagotchis cute.[11]

Already, girls are a force in computers that they were not just a few years ago. And it is human interaction that has opened the Net to half of the population historically underrepesented there. More than boys, girls use the Internet to communicate with family and friends. Right now this means e-mail and chat. While men use e-mail more for work, women use it more for education and communicating with family and friends.[12]

Chat rooms, too, are the domain of computer-savvy girls, a major reason for AOL's success.[13] Indications are that girls will use Internet video the same way.[14] Anyone with a teenage daughter knows the power of the telephone, not as a substitute for face-to-face communication, but as an altogether different form of human interaction. Girls love AOL's Instant Messaging; it now reaches 40 million people. The ability of the Internet to accommodate such interaction indicates its power. This, along with on-line TV, is what will take the Internet into every home—not pages of information at a Web site.

Television will no longer be a strictly passive medium. With two-way video, every home will become a TV station, making today's TV vs. PC wars a sideshow. WebTV brings e-mail and Web surfing to the living room, but we don't see a lot of pent-up demand for "convergence" between TVs and PCs. This is vendor-driven logic. We expect the real solution to be messy: lots of cables, devices, and unread user manuals. At home, we're counting on our kids to sort this out.

The influence of girls on the future of information technology can only go up. Slightly more American males use the Internet than females, but this will change. At school, more girls than boys already use the Internet.[15] More to the point, more girls than boys in the United States are finishing high school, and far more are going to college.[16] This trend is occurring elsewhere as well. This means that intellectual capital is being accumulated at a faster rate by females than males. And girls are not more "artsie" than boys. In England, for example, more girls get top marks on high-school math and science tests.[17] At prestigious Cooper Union in New York, women make up 38 percent of engineering students.[18]

These are the people who will make the Internet happen in the future. Already, they can make the difference between success and failure. Teenage girls made PHS a success in Japan—and sent it off the rails when they moved on to something else. Teenage girls made AOL a success—this is where they rendezvous with their friends. AOL is keeping its appeal fresh. It's ICQ feature, for example, alerts subscribers if their friends are on line so they can chat. Girls love it. One of our daughters asked us to switch to AOL just so she could have this feature.

On one level, low-cost information is driving a shift in market power to children. But before long these better-educated girls will be women. Already, American women are establishing new businesses at twice the rate of men.[19] Half of Amazon.com's customers are female, up from 35 percent two years ago.[20] The CEO of a big wireless carrier told us that his company could double sales without adding a single dollar in new plant if it had the same market penetration among women as among men. They'd better get with the program.

As fathers of daughters, we are delighted with the new opportunities open to them. As investors, we are cautious about the ability of companies to adapt.

50

Building the Virtual Companies: MFS

As we said in our chapter, "The Black Hole in Cyberspace," Jim Crowe took our ideas very seriously. So seriously that he made his company, MFS, Black Hole compliant and sold it to MCI World-Com for a cool $14.4 billion.

Crowe, now CEO of Level 3, succeeded because he recognized the power of the Internet to drive the diseconomies of scale that favor companies as varied as Dell, Cisco, Schwab, and Wal-Mart. To harness these diseconomies, he built a virtual phone company, leaving out the parts he didn't need. Doing this, he built large amounts of value quickly, value that a much larger company realized that it needed to grow and prosper.

At the time Crowe built MFS, there was a mad grab for telephone customers around the world, and the stakes were going sky high. Bell Atlantic paid $1,000 per line for NYNEX. Internationally, the rush for customers pushed valuations even higher than the U.S. and European average of about $2,000 each. Companies like New Zealand Telecom and Hong Kong Telecom pushed Asia/Pacific valuations over $10,000 per line,[1] a lot of money to pay for a mile of copper wire.

Winning bidders in the digital cellular auctions in the U.S. valued their wireless licenses at nearly $40 per person (or "pop") living in the area served.[2] That was a pretty stiff price just for *the right to compete* with a half-dozen other companies. They then had to spend hundreds more to turn up service.

In short, billions of dollars were changing hands in the pursuit of direct electronic access to consumers. These outlays would have to sit on somebody's balance sheet for a long time. Billions more were in the pipeline with major privatizations like those of Deutsche Telekom and France Telecom then coming on stream.

Meanwhile, MFS had a plan afoot that would leave these carriers under water on their obligations. With its acquisition of Internet service provider UUNet, MFS has in a stroke made itself one of the world's preeminent carriers. The company paid only a few dollars per pop, and in a fashion that shifted the riskiest part of the network ownership—old-fashioned wires—onto others.

MFS created the first virtual phone company with logical, rather than physical, access to its customers, and did it on a global scale.

MFS paid $2 billion in stock, not cash, for UUNet, which had 543 locations, 288 of them outside of the U.S. UUNet operated in Canada, most of the European Union, Japan, and Taiwan. By providing wholesale Internet access to retail providers, UUNet's reach extended well beyond its own geographic locations. In total, by acquiring UUNet, MFS reached some 500 million middle-class consumers around the globe.[3] No one else could say the same. The average price per consumer for this: $4.

Remember, that was $4 worth of paper, not cash, and these were middle-class consumers, not Third-World villagers. With this one acquisition, MFS had secured direct links to hundreds of millions of people all over the world, and it hadn't bought a single piece of wire or a wireless licence.

Until then, MFS served a niche market, building fiber rings around major cities in the U.S., Europe, and Asia. The company offered mainly business customers a way to bypass the local phone company for long-distance traffic.

What Crowe saw was the opportunity to lure the vast majority of business and residential customers to the MFS network through a dial-up over the local phone system. For the most part, MFS intended to leave the "last mile" of these connections to somebody else.

This final link to the customer is the riskiest part of the network. While still largely a phone company monopoly, now competitors with better technology, from wireless to cable television, were getting ready to pluck this goose. But the price, as Crowe correctly foresaw, would be staggering: AT&T recently spent over $100 billion on TCI and MediaOne.

Phone companies spend thousands of dollars to install a new line to a customer; so will most of the new competitors. MFS's goal was to sit back and let them duke it out. Like DirecTV, with its customer-owned satellite receivers, MFS shifted much of the cost of network infrastructure to its customers, who bore the cost of reaching MFS via telephone.

Without local connections, MFS had to forego part of the market. But at less than 20 percent of world telecom demand, local service was dwarfed by long-distance and international traffic and was by far the smallest part of the market. And getting smaller; today it is under 12 percent.[4]

Of course, MFS still had direct fiber connections to big customers in major markets, and its strategy called for gradually adding more local connections as technology and regulatory issues were resolved. When the local bandwidth bottleneck finally broke, MFS planned to be ready with big upstream pipes to deliver high-speed services, like TV, over the Internet.

Buying virtual access to customers on the cheap and shifting physical access costs to others makes for strong openers. But MFS also structured its network like the Internet. This method uses transmission capacity far more efficiently than the circuits employed by other carriers, and the Internet was beginning to wreak havoc on long distance pricing.

MFS combined good strategy with good timing. AT&T had just announced unlimited Internet connections for $19.95. Others soon followed. Never mind that they weren't ready to meet the enormous demand for service these offers brought in.[5] Simply posting "all you can eat" menus was enough to set the bum's rush in motion. The market for Internet stocks collapsed. UUNet, for example, plunged from almost $100 per share to the low twenties in four months. This was an incredible opportunity to bottom-fish the world over for Internet companies looking to the exits. MFS pounced, and bought access to half a billion customers at job-lot prices.

The UUNet acquisition leveraged MFS's existing network in major American, European, and Asian cities. MFS built on its UUNet deal with a rapid series of Internet moves in Europe. The company boasted the "world's most extensive international Internet infrastructure."[6] MFS was running big Internet access hubs in Paris and Frankfurt.[7] Combining these with UUNet's existing European presence, MFS made itself an Internet powerhouse in Europe, providing much of the continent's backbone.

Doing this, MFS flew right under the regulatory radar of the Europeans, who never would have let MFS in had they realized that it was a virtual company with the same power to undermine the prices of their government-owned phone monopolies as a company with wires into every home.

The Europeans were faced with the very real threat that by the time Deutsche Telekom and France Telecom were privatized, MFS could be the largest carrier in Europe, capable of outperforming them from any quarter.

Moreover, MFS was designed to grow at Internet rates, not at the much, much slower pace for phone lines. And, as MFS built the video and advanced service capability of its Internet backbone, it would be able to harness European customers to its network with impunity. The monopoly rents enjoyed by the dominant players in these markets were far higher than in the U.S. MFS could offer low prices and still see extremely high margins, something the locals could not.

MFS bet that the best margins flow to the player that traps the most bandwidth, not the one that physically connects the most customers. In a world dominated by bandwidth, the winner is whoever offers the most of it for the least. The number of customers the player connects is, by itself, immaterial. This forced MFS to conclude that its entire network must be designed to be profitable by offering high bandwidth at Internet prices. Crowe reasoned that the market would not long sustain carriers trying to sell for 25¢ (or more) per minute what they could get on the Internet for a cent (or less), no matter how many customers they have.

Perhaps the smartest thing MFS did in all of this was to shore up its balance sheet. Its major competitors the world over faced (and still face) serious threats to their cash flows, were lumbered with old low-capacity plant, and had enough debt to sink the Bismarck. MFS's debt-to-equity ratio was in the 25 percent range, extremely healthy for the industry, as we saw in "The Next Penn

Central." While others were just beginning to realize how big a problem their bloated balance sheets had become, MFS joined a select few positioned to grow. This combination of technological and financial strength was compelling and contributed directly to WorldCom's rich offer for MFS.

Investors reward companies that turn low-cost Internet access to their advantage. The potential for arbitrage between what consumers are used to paying and the cost at which access over the Internet can be provided is big and getting bigger. This gap, growing at the speed of Moore's Law, explains the sky-high valuations of so-called "dot-com" companies. Investors should be edgy about any investment that commands millennia worth of earnings. But if the lumbering Baby Bells, for example, can trade for twenty-five times earnings, the spread starts to make sense.

MFS did everything right. GTE, the largest phone company in the United States and one of the largest in the world (GTE itself is in the middle of a merger of its own with Bell Atlantic), recognized that MFS had a longer reach than itself. It announced that it would use UUNet for its own dial-up and dedicated Internet service nationwide. Since GTE's wired and wireless networks combined reached one-third of the U.S. population in 28 states,[8] the new arrangement would have given GTE a national GTE-branded service that it would otherwise have been unable to sell on national television.[9]

Nevertheless, for MFS success was not assured. It is tougher to execute a strategy than to think it up. More to the point, even if not everyone can execute with the same skill, anyone could replicate the MFS strategy in almost any market. Penetration rates were low. Barriers to entry were almost nonexistent. There were no "brand" leaders like today's AOL or Yahoo! And while this may be telecommunications, capital intensity was low. We heard about one start-up Internet company that blanketed the state of Connecticut for $150,000 (that's 5¢ per pop), a fraction of the cost of a single McDonald's franchise.

We were asked by two venture funds whether MFS's strategy could be duplicated. The answer was not "Yes, it can," but "Yes, it must." There was, and is, no other way to go.

This logic was not lost on MFS, and when the WorldCom offer came in, MFS sold for real money.

MFS redefined what it means to be a phone company. Traditional approaches, which involve spending thousands of dollars per customer cannot continue. Like electric utilities that built huge nuclear reactors just as cheap cogeneration systems were coming on stream, these carriers—or, more accurately, their investors—will be stuck with "stranded" investments they can never recover. That is, unless they persuade the government to socialize these costs, which is possible, and perhaps even likely.

An investment banker advising a phone company in a developing economy asked us about the best way to build the telephone and cable television networks in that country. We advised them to do it right the first time: apply the MFS strategy right out of the gate.

51

Investing in the Moore Curve: Direct Satellite Services

In the first few years after its introduction, DSS, the digital satellite minidish systems offered by Hughes Aerospace, and Echostar, signed up ten million U.S. customers, making it the single most successful product introduction in history. New DSS dishes went in at the rate of over two hundred thousand a month, roughly equal to the number of new cable television subscribers.[1] Receiver prices fell from $700 at introduction to only $200 in 1999, an astonishing improvement in price-performance.

The fact that DSS offers far better quality and variety over CATV does not alone explain this incredible growth. *What makes DSS sell is not that it is a new market; but that it is a shrewd play for consumer dollars already being spent.* The idea is to offer consumers much, much more than they get for what they are already spending, unleashing a consumer surplus for additional spending from *existing* entertainment budgets.

With the mass coverage of satellite, costs are extremely low. At $8 capital cost per person reached in the U.S., DSS offers infinitely cheaper consumer access than competing media, such as coaxial cable or optical fiber. DSS carriers like DirecTV will be able to discount video rental stores into oblivion should a price war start.

DSS offers enormous benefits. Consumers get several times as many channels for the same price as cable, order-of-magnitude improvements in image resolution, and full CD quality-sound in stereo. They can customize their own screen-based TV guide by giving the system a few simple preferences like "PG-13" or "no sports" or "baseball only." This control is a boon to parents of small kids. Overrides are uncomplicated, and consumers can select a couple of on-screen guides, one for daytime and one for after hours, for example. No competitor offered anything nearly as powerful and as simple to use.

DSS receivers are equipped with narrowband and broadband data ports to support home networks of personal computers of almost any capacity. They can take downloads of nearly 30 million bits of information a second[2] and have a storage filling capacity of over one terabyte an hour—a trillion bytes—enough to load even the biggest in-home recording devices very, very quickly.

With e-mail that runs in the background, DSS was perfectly positioned to revolutionize Internet applications. It freed consumers from the stranglehold of the underpowered phone lines. And it was the only consumer communications product sold that was ready to plug into a powerful residential computer.

This is savvy positioning. Moore's Law says that soon, the thousand-dollar home computer will process one billion instructions every second and record dozens of movies.[3] DSS is *already* capable of harnessing that power.

Market potential like this has not been lost on Microsoft. The software giant prepared a DSS plug-in card for personal computers running its Windows and NT operating systems. Microsoft also arranged with Hughes for DSS capacity to reach its Windows customers.

Full home theater connections are provided in the basic DSS kit. The venture capitalists who funded DSS with Hughes told us that by their estimation, an incredible *70 percent of DSS subscribers immediately upgrade their televisions* once they see what DSS can do. Indeed, any television more than a few years old probably can't handle all the features that DSS offers.

DSS sits at the center of four driving forces in consumer electronics: home theater, personal computers, communications, and children. Consequently, DSS is not a simple substitute for cable TV.

DSS broadcast standards are digital, high definition, and proprietary. There is *nothing* standing in the way of DSS suppliers offering their customers proprietary, high-definition, DSS-compatible televisions with full Internet capability. DSS is, like the Internet itself, eliminating television standards.

Despite its benefits, DSS pricing is low enough to capture consumer dollars now flowing to video rental outlets. The drop in driving time alone makes installing a DSS an easy decision. DSS is no more expensive to buy than a VCR. And it is a lot less tedious to program. Indeed, DSS probably took all the growth out of the video rental market.[4]

What is perhaps most remarkable about DSS is that it *shifts almost the entire cost of network infrastructure to the consumer* in the form of a two-hundred-dollar satellite dish. While DSS cost Hughes about $8 a person to cover the North American continent, this cost actually goes *down* in larger markets like China and

Latin America. Information providers rent base stations and transponder time, the cost of which is tiny when spread across all customers. Cable operators and phone companies, by contrast, bear the thousands of dollars it costs to pass each house, subscriber or not. The bigger the territory, the more they must spend.

In the near future it is possible that smart antenna technology will turn DSS into a two-way competitor to cable TV.[5] Technology is being developed using inexpensive ceramic materials that might make inexpensive roof-top devices capable of tracking high-powered low earth orbiting (LEO) satellites. This would, at a stroke, reduce significantly the worth of phone companies and cable companies. Investors need to keep a careful eye on these kinds of developments. A high-powered two-way LEO system with cheap antennae from Radio Shack could all at once eliminate the need for telephones, cable feeds, video rentals, and local TV stations. Moore's Law has a way of making such ideas a reality.

52

Europe: Painful Restructuring Ahead

As economic circumstances shift, the relative competitiveness of Europe, Japan, and the United States constantly changes. But in one area, Europe always stands out: quality of life. American business may have restructured itself to achieve productivity leadership, but in terms of education, life expectancy, infant mortality, crime, and divorce, the United States trails Europe badly. While the social fabric of America seems to unravel dangerously, Europe remains a place where no one is abandoned. "From each according to his ability, to each according to his need," may no longer be the rallying slogan it once was, but in Europe, the least powerful members of society are not forgotten. And while the United States gets strip-malled from one end to the other, and lets its highways crumble and public services fray, Europe nourishes the majesty of its history and invests relentlessly in its unparalleled infrastructure. No American who has visited the beautifully maintained cities of France or experienced the dazzling efficiency of Germany's train system can depart unawed.

And yet, the tough question cannot be ignored: how can the Europeans pay for this marvelous quality of life? After a brief period of economic glow following the decision to forge Europe into a single market, European industry appeared routed across virtually every front by competitors from America and Japan. For a decade or more, unemployment rates have been creeping up, reaching double digits in the 1990s—rates that would have been considered cause for revolution a generation ago. At the same time, government debt expanded to unsustainable levels, even in thrifty Germany—the money for all these high-profile government works had to come from somewhere. The expansion of the public sector has reached its limits in Europe, which is now facing a sobering truth: the European Union has not created a single new private sector job *in thirty years.*

In 1993, then Chancellor Helmut Kohl of Germany put it this way: "It seems as if there is still nothing more important than thinking about how we can expand our recreation time. . . . If we want to secure Germany's future, we cannot organize our country as if it were one big recreation park."[1] No kidding: the continent is turning into a giant Euro Disney, complete with fairy-tale castles, futuristic monorail trains, lots of people on vacation, and a sinkload of red ink.

All of Europe's cultural and social advantages come at a cost, one that Europe may not be able to afford much longer. Government largesse depends on high taxes, which in turn depend on high wages. But high labor costs are driving business out of Europe. In the 1990s, wages in Germany, for example, leapt ahead of those in the U.S. and Japan, driving German manufacturers to shift production abroad, in some cases to the U.S. In Italy and France, labor costs, including benefits, also pulled ahead of costs in the U.S. during this period; even in Britain, once the poor man of Europe, paychecks rose nearly to U.S. levels. Militant unions in Germany and France kept pushing for raises, despite sky-high unemployment rates.

Of course, there is no reason why Europeans should not be paid more than others—as long as they produce more. Unfortunately, they do not. The surplus of wealth needed to maintain the level of services Europeans take for granted depends on productivity growth. Wages can grow, as long as production grows more. BMW and Mercedes-Benz opened factories in America not because workers in Germany are paid too much per hour, but because they produce too little in return for those fat paychecks. German labor productivity fell behind the U.S. and Japan in virtually every type of manufacturing. In services, German workers didn't do much better.[2]

The cause is simple. In the race to substitute information for other resources, including labor, Europe has dropped far off the pace.

In addition to its quality of life, Europe has many other comparative advantages. By forging the continent into one free trade area, Europe could create the richest, largest, and most dynamic market in the world. But interminable fights over currency and political union suggest that it will be business as usual in Europe, as high-paying jobs continue to slip away to other parts of the world. Along with free trade, information-driven productivity improvements could help reverse this trend.

If Europe's experience in information technology is anything to go by, the future does not look good. In information technology, the European market is now the world's largest. Many of the original developments in computers took place in Europe, particularly in Britian—the English produced the first electronic computer at Cambridge University during the war. Many advances in telecommunications originated in France (and Alcatel remains a leading supplier of telecom equipment). Even in semiconductors, European players once vied for leadership. Whatever their contributions in the past, however, European companies do not set the agenda today; their American rivals do. Europe pays for this in jobs.

When the price of information falls far enough, industry can replace mechanical effort with knowledge, a process central to creating productivity gains. But policy makers in Europe try to prop up the cost of information while it falls around the world. Much like the Community Agricultural Policy which keeps food prices in Europe high, restrictions on the flow of information forcibly prevent European industry from fully exploiting its productivity potential.

The challenge for business, government, and labor is to exploit the fall in information costs, not to get slam-dunked by it. This means observing the first Iron Law of Information: cheap information always chases out expensive information. Its corollary states that information always flows to the least regulated economy.

With notable exceptions, such as the United Kingdom, most European governments, however, believe that the good of the state is best preserved if state-owned companies keep the price of information well above costs and extort monopoly rents from their citizens. Far from doing Europeans any good, these policies keep down usage and force companies to move their value-added services to other countries, like the United Kingdom. France actually restricts the use of foreign languages by its citizens and limits their exposure to foreign culture.

In the European Union as a whole, market-unification plans usually mean extending German and French policies of state control to other countries, such as the United Kingdom. This, the Germans and the French seem to think, will level the playing field. It may, but at a very high price.

The United Kingdom sees great advantages in Franco-German

policy. So long as France and Germany keep the price of information high, the United Kingdom can use our Iron Laws to siphon off their information businesses. As a result, the United Kingdom is becoming the information entrepôt of Europe. Britain is the Heathrow Airport of the European information business, the place where all European information streams head like so much raw material to be collected, managed, and then redistributed piecemeal in the form of high-priced finished goods to the other members of the European Union.

The consequences of the United Kingdom's policy for the continentals is incalculable. Riding its low-cost information strategy, Britain is emerging as the dominant force in services in the Union. It could easily wind up controlling EU banking, advertising, accounting, and insurance markets by early in the next century. A new age of British imperialism will have begun. Britain's information costs are lower and its overseas connections are wider and deeper, giving it significant economies. Using the Iron Law, Britain keeps itself less regulated than its neighbors and is thus better adapted to exploiting the markets of the next century.

By keeping the cost of information artificially high, Europe keeps its citizens from riding the information-cost curve. For European companies, the cost of information may *not* be cheaper than natural resources or labor. By contrast, British industry, and competitors from other countries which locate in the U.K., can exploit the low cost of information there.

Continental governments are trying desperately to regain control, trying to offset the high cost of information with lavish subsidies elsewhere. In everything from the Common Agricultural policy to high-tech R&D programs, the European Union is pouring money into a dike that simply cannot be held. All the while, European industry is losing its competitive position; flagship companies are falling by the wayside despite rising government

R&D expenditures. There is something quixotic in Community policies.

Markets eventually force organizations, managers, and workers to change. Companies that don't respond go out of business; workers who lose their jobs find new opportunities at new companies. There has been no greater demonstration of creative destruction than the massive restructuring of American industry which took place over the past decade. Companies with household names like IBM, General Motors, and Sears, Roebuck veered toward collapse. Millions of people—first factory workers and then managers—lost their jobs. Yet millions of other new jobs were created, largely at new companies that rose from the ashes of the old ones. A harsh environment, no doubt, but American industry transformed itself without creating a mass of chronically unemployed workers. As this book shows, organizations need to change to capitalize on information-driven efficiencies.

A climate in which organizations can adapt is key to reaping the benefits of the low cost of information. Wal-Mart revolutionized retail distribution by eliminating all the middlemen (except itself) between factory and consumer. As a result, Wal-Mart has steadily reduced the amount of transportation required for everything it sells.

High severance costs make layoffs expensive in Europe, so productivity increases cannot be quickly translated into labor savings. At the same time, a crushing burden of payroll taxes makes workers expensive to hire, so employers are reluctant to take them on even if conditions improve. And there is far less labor mobility in Europe than in the U.S., even within countries; people simply don't move as much for new jobs or anything else. Between countries, there is essentially no movement of workers, except at the highest and lowest levels of business.

Most European countries have excellent schools. European

workers are well educated, and well trained once on the job. They do indeed have the skills to change cheap information into valuable knowledge. But too many European governments continue to restrict the flow of information between citizens, artificially propping up its cost. This reduces the potential for the cost-effective substitution of information for other resources.

Ironically, Europe has the training and education to revector workers displaced by layoffs, and to do so at good wages. But the high cost of information prevents this adjustment from happening. By contrast, in the United States and the United Kingdom, information flows freely, but the education is not always there to keep people working at jobs that will sustain the middle class. In the U.S., the market clears and people find work, but too frequently at wages that will not support their families.

These pressures have unexpected consequences in Europe. For example, London is awash with highly educated young adults who cannot find work in Germany, France, or elsewhere. In the United Kingdom they settle for "McJobs," working in shops, restaurants, and cafes. Clearly, they find this preferable to the unemployment queues they face at home. However, it is a shocking waste of intellectual capital. It also indicates that the transfer of power to children that we describe elsewhere in this book will be retarded in Europe.

One of the principal purposes of the European Union is to prop up industrial dinosaurs that have lots of employees. As a result, the biggest companies in Europe don't need to adapt to market forces, or to make the organizational changes necessary to benefit fully from the productive potential of information technologies. And we're not just talking about coal mines, steel mills, and post offices here: in 1992, the EU announced a program to save two million jobs in the *computer industry.*[3] If computer companies can be paid to ossify, then no industrial policy is too reactionary. Eventually, economic realities forced many companies to lay off workers in the 1990s, but much damage had already been done by that time.

The worst consequence of Europe's turn-back-the-tide policies are lost opportunities to improve productivity. This improvement is precisely the medicine Europe needs to raise paychecks and pay for the social services its citizens now enjoy. But in addition, the Europeans have created an environment in which old companies, not new ones, are encouraged. The new companies are needed to create the jobs that are inevitably lost in the old ones.

The real advances in information technology come from small, entrepreneurial companies. Over the past decade, small and medium-sized companies, not the largest ones, led America's boom.[4] High-growth start-ups and new high-wage jobs are endangered species in Europe. Despite its current problems, Europe has enjoyed strong productivity growth since the Second World War. But the Europeans have not created a climate in which innovation can thrive. The Europeans, especially the Germans, have demonstrated their ability to improve existing ways of doing business; they have not done well when it comes to inventing new ways of operating.

After decades and hundreds of billions of dollars, America's investment in information technology began to pay off in the 1990s. While American companies had improved manufacturing productivity through automation, services and corporate management—white-collar jobs—had long resisted efforts to raise efficiencies. Then computer networks began to break down the hierarchical structures common to most organizations. With the Internet and other forms of direct communication between those producing information and those needing it, the need for layer upon layer of management to "process" information quickly vanished. Redundant middle managers paid with their jobs, but the productivity of the survivors improved, often dramatically.

In Europe, such shifts will not come easily. Strong unions and backward looking governments slow change, but so do attitudes. Executives in France, graduates of the *grandes ecoles polytechniques,* run their businesses the way Napoleon ran his army. They demand respect from their subordinates, and get it. Informality is not accepted; only fellow graduates of the *polytechniques* address each other by first names or in familiar forms of speech. In Germany, a similar rigidness, a "this is the way we do things" attitude prevails. Of course, this is a generalization, and attitudes are more relaxed in Italy and Britain. Still, there is an inertia in European business that resists the efficiency improvements that can spring from new technology.

53

Japan: The Long Recession

We'd like to end this book where we started: with Japan. We've advised Japanese companies for nearly a quarter of a century, some of them continually during that time. We have made good friends there and probably have about as good an understanding as Westerners get of Japanese business thinking. Indeed, we have been privileged to work with some Japanese companies at the most senior levels, where leaders of industry have allowed us to understand how they see their deepest corporate problems.

Over the years, we have had to balance two things: what we knew Japanese companies had to do to succeed, and what we knew they *could* do under reasonable circumstances. This gap, always large, has grown immeasurably in the last twenty-five years. Where our advice might once have been difficult to implement, today it is often impossible.

They are very good reasons for this.

When we embarked on our first book, we had been in the information industry for about fifteen years. We had been struck by how Japan had given "guidance" to its automobile makers not to export. Honda had been told not even to make cars, let alone export them. Yet all these firms succeeded mightily for a generation, and only recently have suffered setbacks. By contrast, the companies that had been instructed to export furiously and into which the government had pumped massive amounts of aid for forty years—companies dealing in computers, telecommunications, and integrated circuits—were abject failures in almost every market they entered.

We knew that if we could lay one set of companies on top of the other, almost the way you "read" aerial photographs in high-school geography, we would create some sort of three-dimensional sense of where the issues lay. We could, in effect, decode the Japanese business model and determine its strengths and weaknesses.

From this exercise, we developed our Four Keys to Value Creation (though originally the keys started out as four flaws): we noticed that all the failing Japanese companies were integrated both vertically and horizontally, all had highly centralized management, all had far too many layers, and none delivered customer service overseas. Our flaws quickly became what not to do, and hence our Keys.

Time and again, we noticed that Japanese organization, encumbered by so much management baggage, was incapable of responding to market realities.

Our first book, *Beating Japan,* told its readers that if they saw Japanese companies making any serious attempt to eliminate the fatal flaws in their management structures then they could be sure that Japan was on its way back as a competitive power.

In the early stages of writing that book, we were engaged over a two-year period by one of Japan's biggest high tech firms to make recommendations that would help that firm recover a position in a market it had been in since its founding, in the last century. We saw firsthand as our ideas developed how they would work in practice—or not work, as the case would be. That was a decade ago. The company was never able to deal with the issues we presented, and has entered a time of great and easily avoidable turmoil that has cost very many of those we advised in top management their jobs, including the CEO. Only a few months back, one of the senior executives told an internal meeting that he wished they had taken our advice!

In *Beating Japan*, we foresaw the collapse of that nation's entire way of doing business. But writing a book full of predictions, no matter how well founded you think those predictions are, and then seeing it become reality—seeing an entire country literally go down the drain—is a sobering experience. In many ways it was more frightening just because it was so predictable.

The book, and the events that followed over the next decade, drove us to be even more systematic, to gather all the ideas we had put before other clients (such as the Canadian government, as we mentioned in the introductory chapter), and to evolve the complete system of thinking on which this book is based.

But still, we come back to Japan and the reasons for its continued lassitude.

Japan is an isolated, island nation without natural resources, driven since the mid-nineteenth century by its need to secure raw materials for production. With the rapid industrialization that followed Commodore Perry's arrival in 1853, Japan's leaders became obsessed with the country's lines of supply. For the past fifty years, Japan has maintained an aggressive export strategy to cover huge imports of everything from wood to fish, iron ore, and oil.[1]

During this time, the country tried to engineer a power shift into information technology big enough to replace the heavy manufacturing that consumes so much imported energy. This shift failed in key sectors like computers and telecommunications, throwing Japan back onto the business of the past, where it is being chased down—and caught—by a new generation of upstarts from Asia and Latin America. And now even by resurgent Americans.

This is a position of weakness that Japan has to overcome in order to survive. Just when it needs leadership most, however, its political and corporate management have come up empty. Japan today is a country roiled by corporate and political scandal and ineptitude.

Whether Japan can survive and grow in the twenty-first century entirely depends on whether it can rebuild itself like the inside-out organizations we described earlier in this book. If Japan continues to compete on its outside lines, with overweight organizations and endless layers of distribution, it will be destroyed by the Ciscos and Dells of this world.

Small and isolated, crowded and bereft of natural resources, Japan must export or die. Exports give Japan a sense of security and economic self-sufficiency in a hostile and capricious world. And export it does. But while Japan may in many periods sell twice as much to the U.S. as it buys, its balance of trade with the rest of the world is not so favorable.[2] Without exports, Japan will face a threat to its security and prosperity. Sixty years ago, such fear drove Japan to secure its sources of oil and other raw materials by military force.

Many people outside Japan don't appreciate Japan's predicament. Compared with the United States, Canada, and parts of Europe that are richly endowed by nature, Japan has virtually nothing. Japan is a trading nation; it must sell its wares (most of which are luxuries like cars and cameras) to buy necessities (without which it cannot survive). Nobody ever froze to death because he didn't have a cassette tape player.

Along with Japan's success has come an increasing propensity to consume. The postwar generation of savers and workers is being replaced by a new breed of consumers and relaxers—or so it seems to the old guard. In truth, the Japanese remain thrifty and diligent by world standards. Nevertheless, they are enjoying at least some of the rewards of their past efforts. They want to travel, spend more time with their families, drive new cars. As a result, less of the country's output is available for export. This change comes at a time when Japan's long-term growth rate is declining.

Since Japan must export to pay for oil and other natural resources, the Japanese are extremely sensitive to protectionist sentiments in the U.S. and Europe. Pressure to reduce its trade surplus persists, and will only get worse. But no amount of Structural Impediment Initiatives and jawboning at the World Trade Organization will change the facts. Japan cannot abruptly shift production overseas or open its markets to a flood of imports without threatening its security. Admittedly, its trade position leaves quite a bit of room for error, but given what is at stake, Japan needs a healthy buffer.

The only alternative Japan has is to cut raw material imports. The less Japan imports, the less it will need to export. In this way "harmony" with its trading partners can be achieved. Dematerialization of industrial production offers Japan a way out. Japan needs to become a giant Wal-Mart, growing fast and consuming less.

Perhaps more than any of its western competitors, Japan needs to sever oil consumption from growth. The oil *shokku* of 1973 brought the country's industrial juggernaut to a screeching halt. The Japanese saw themselves running on empty, the eventual losers in a *Mad Max*–like scramble for the few remaining drops of oil in the world. That's why the greatest advances in fuel efficiency in the industrialized world during the past two decades have been in Japan.

While many Third World producers of raw materials have suffered from falling commodity prices over the past decade, most countries have benefited from the dematerialization process. None more than Japan, where the effects have been dramatic.

Japan's success in getting the natural resource monkey off its back has been mixed. After the U.S. oil embargo in 1941, Japan attacked Pearl Harbor and grabbed the rich oil fields of Indonesia, a strategy that ultimately proved futile, to say the least. In response to the Arab oil embargoes of the 1970s, Japan truly made energy efficiency the "moral equivalent of war" (in the immortal words of Jimmy Carter). In a tactical sense, Japan's efficiency drive paid significant dividends, wringing more steel and cars out of every barrel of oil. But so far, Japan's grand plan to move up the industrial food chain has not worked well.

Nowhere has failure been more conspicuous than in information technology. Despite decades of government subsidies and dogged determination, Japan's electronic giants, including Fujitsu, Hitachi, NEC, and Toshiba, have a few stunning victories and many expensive losses to show for their efforts in computers and telecommunications.

In the U.S., by far their biggest export market, Japanese companies dominate one large market—cars—and several smaller ones, notably consumer electronics, cameras, and copiers. But these markets are mature and have been disrupted by suppliers from all over Asia.

For a decade, production in Japan of each of the following products has declined or stopped growing: calculators, cameras, motorcycles, stereos, tape players, trucks, TVs, and VCRs. Passenger car production expanded during this period, but exports from Japan fell. Consumer electronics—Japan's first real success— have been particularly hard hit.

In short, Japan is slumping after a home run and a couple of base hits early in the game. To restart growth, Japan needs another big hit like cars. And the Japanese know it better than anyone; they've suffered through a decade-long slump unlike anything experienced in the U.S. since the Great Depression. Unemployment has hit 4.8 percent in the official tally,[3] which means double that in reality (Goldman Sachs estimates the "real" rate is a stunning 15 percent[4]), and the highest numbers since the immediate postwar period. Japanese business and government leaders are under heavy pressure to solve the unemployment issue.

But as we have seen in this book, learning how to substitute information for other resources—which would solve all Japan's trade, oil, and growth problems in a single shot—has powerful social consequences that are not welcome everywhere.

The empowerment of consumers at the expense of producers, for example, places centrifugal forces on organizations which turns them inside out, as in the case of Cisco. Companies must become increasingly integrated with their customers, like Schwab, and much less focused on themselves.

To execute these principles, a Japanese company would have to surrender huge amounts of decision-making power to foreign customers. This would disrupt the delicate balance of relationships among the Japanese, built up over two thousand years of history. There is also inertia to be overcome. Japan was extraordinarily successful until the late eighties. It takes a long time, just as it did for us in the Great Depression, to realize that what is happening isn't a short-term blip.

Inertia in Japan has a peculiarly Japanese quality. While we talked about organization, many Japanese managers would listen patiently and then ask about their products. Few could accept that an information-intensive process could lock in customers, raise the costs to customers of going elsewhere, and build a profitable long-term relationship. This idea would be seen as purely tangential and not the main point—a typical Western fancy demonstrating a profound lack of engineering sophistication.

Taken together, these forces have made change most difficult. Companies that should have been completely rebuilt a decade ago and probably a few times since have done nothing. That decade is an unrecoverable millennium in Moore Time.

Japan's traditional system of relationships hasn't served it well, either. Huge banking scandals have wiped out probably a good trillion dollars of savings. The result is that for small business— the entrepreneurs who might rebuild Japan and reenergize its business sector—there is no capital. None.

What we see today is a country with big business in paralysis, small business driven to the wall, rapidly rising unemployment, a banking system with no money, and a government that literally does not function (and is not intended to, something few people realize).

This is not a happy prospect, and may lead to social unrest: the Japanese are exceptionally tolerant and will do anything to please, but they will not stand by and watch their livelihoods destroyed. An economy without the small business capital it needs to soak up all those middle-aged "salarymen" thrown out of work is a time bomb with no time left.

Worse, unemployment in Japan hasn't been generated by restructuring, in which the flip side of layoffs in one area is rapid growth in another as the economy shifts gears. It is due to an economic slowdown: there simply is no demand for all those laid off people.

Japanese business leaders understand that information will dominate the world economy in the twenty-first century. Unfortunately, thirty years and billions of dollars of government and private investment made Japan the Saudi Arabia of memory chips—and little else. Japan also is strong in a few other commodity hardware markets such as fax machines, laptop computers, printers, and disk drives, but prices for these products go nowhere but down, and competitive pressures from Korea and Taiwan (not to mention the United States and Europe) are relentless.

In more complex systems which account for the bulk of the market, such as communications networks, Japan's role is marginal. At home, a program of rigorous import substitution guaranteed a big and protected information technology market for Japan's electronics giants, but exports pale in comparison. In high-growth areas like services and software, Japan is nowhere.

Poor results in information technology, which is as close to resource-free as you can get, have left Japan chugging along in the same resource-intensive industries it first staked out thirty and forty years ago. Nevertheless, there remains plenty more room to make its manufacturing more efficient, and to increase the "knowledge intensity" of its cameras, rice cookers, and pickup trucks.

In response to pressure from its trading partners, Japan shifted some production overseas. To do so without hurting domestic living standards, Japan shifted low value-added production offshore, and focused on capital- and knowledge-intensive opportunities at home. Information technology was going to make all this happen. But IT, which at the crack of the bat sounded like it might be a grand slam for Japan, has started looking like a single, or a double at best.

Information technology was not the right challenge. While it achieved certain well-defined objectives, the Ministry of International Trade and Industry could not drive all of Japan on a forced march to victory in computers. The reason was simple: Japan wanted to solve problems for foreign customers from afar, without talking to them. As every successful company profiled in this book has shown, however, prosperity can only be assured by using IT to secure the closest possible integration with customers, something the Japanese have never done overseas.

Many of Japan's industrial giants diversified with unrestrained gusto into information technology during the 1970s and 1980s. Most of these investments have been disasters, because they served the needs of Japan Inc., not the needs of customers. Nippon Steel found it much easier to sell clean steel production processes, with which it is intimately familiar, than laptop computers, about which it knew nothing more than did scores of its faceless competitors.

Much of Japan's success in manufacturing has been attributed to *kaizen,* the art of incremental improvements. Focused on quality and efficiency, *kaizen* has produced successive generations of better and cheaper cars, TVs, and cameras. But the major shifts required in corporate organization described in this book are unknown there. Trying to turn generations of *kaizen*-driven management tradition into the coring out of corporate organizations, Cisco-style, is exceptionally difficult. Most Japanese firms to whom we have proposed this immediately grasp why it must be done and then refuse to do it. Why? Fear, pure and simple.

This may be changing, however slowly. The decade-long financial *shokku* of the 1990s is forcing Japan to reconsider its ways.

Japan brings many strengths to the table. Extravagant living is not the Japanese way, and many were uncomfortable with the excesses of the eighties. The Japanese come much more naturally by economy than we do; their country has proven its capacity to reduce waste, to operate efficiently. The Japanese can turn the slogan "less is more" into reality if anyone can.

A uniquely Japanese system of business administration, well adapted to the country's lack of natural resources and concomitant need to be frugal, could do for Japan what thirty years of exports has not achieved: reduce its dependence on an unstable source of oil and other raw materials, improve its antagonistic trade relations, enable production and management to move overseas, and finally allow Japan Inc. to embrace foreign customers.

If it can exploit information costs, for the first time in its history Japan will be secure, able to act with confidence, and free to find a new role commensurate with its economic achievements. Bringing information costs down may be this new role, a part scripted just for Japan to play on the new world stage.

The potential is there for the Japanese to become oil-free barons of the post-industrial era, shifting the center of gravity in the energy world from Riyadh to Tokyo. This way, Japan could have real political clout without threatening anyone. At the moment, Japan finds it difficult to flex its muscles militarily, or even politically, because of its history and fragile position as a trading nation dependent on foreign resources.

Poor productivity in services is a problem in all countries, but in Japan more than most. By substituting information for labor, capital, and raw materials, Japan will further increase in the value of knowledge, and may have a shot at improving its standard of living as its population declines in the next century.

In the 1990s, however, the Japanese export juggernaut ran aground, particularly in high tech, where the high-wage, high-growth opportunities of the future lie. This poor performance has little to do with a high yen or the bursting bubble economy. Rather, structural flaws in their organizations made it difficult for decision makers in Japan to connect with overseas customers.

Can Japan restructure? In Tokyo, they certainly have their doubts. Japan's business leaders have always looked to their American counterparts for inspiration, and they don't like what they see when they study a decade of restructuring in America: layoffs, layoffs, and more layoffs.

By the early 1990s, many thought these painful dislocations were a thing of the past, since productivity was rising rapidly in most sectors. Instead, to maintain their edge, American companies—even the most profitable ones—continued to lay off tens of thousands of employees. For the Japanese, this take-no-prisoners approach to labor relations has always been shocking. What they find even more horrifying is that they might have to take the same bitter medicine in Japan if they are going to turn their companies around.

What the Japanese don't see is the great driver of the U.S. economy, its ability to use ever lower costs of information to soak up unemployment quickly and to create large amounts of wealth in the bargain.

We were struck on a recent visit to Japan by the number of times we heard the phrase "hidden unemployment." This refers to the millions of workers, particularly in white-collar jobs, who are kept on the payroll even though their employers could get along without them. Many companies have allowed their management ranks to balloon. The president of one large electrical manufacturer told us, "When I started working at this company as a young man, there were four layers of management in the factories, from machine operator to plant manager. Today there are nine." In the past, redundant salarymen kept on until retirement were called "window-watchers." Japan has run out of windows.

Without sharp cuts in costs, Japanese products will remain uncompetitive on world markets. Detroit has taken back market share from its Japanese competitors not because of its great quality improvements, but because of sticker shock. One of us recently priced new minivans; the Japanese ones were thousands more than a similarly equipped Dodge Caravan. At some point, as Detroit discovered, buyers walk.

To cope with its cost handicap, Japan Inc. needs to do more than cut golf and take-out sushi budgets. The "restructuring" mantra is repeated everywhere in Japan. For some companies, this means moving production offshore, to Malaysia for TVs or America for cars. Most managers hope that a combination of belt tightening and a heavy dose of technology will carry their companies through to sunnier days. It will not. Japan will not recover until it changes its thinking. And business as usual will lead to further reversals in many markets won through decades of hard work.

Japan must use information to cut costs. But efficiency improvements alone will not help if the wrong products are sold in the wrong way. Which markets to abandon? Which products to cut? Which layers of management to eliminate? Which research projects to abandon? Choices like this cannot be made properly without close contact with customers, and this is where Japan's industrial giants fall down.

Most Japanese companies are not structured to absorb information efficiently from their overseas customers, to filter the kind of noise they get from these chaotic markets. To restructure their corporate bureaucracies—in effect, to improve the productivity of white collar workers—they need to know what it is their overseas customers want. Future success will require a profound change in how these companies are organized and do business. For Japan to exploit the opportunities that lie ahead, the country must go through what we call a second Meiji restoration.

The first Meiji restoration was a period of renewal for Japan after centuries of isolation, but it did not happen overnight. Rather, this process took from 1853 to 1868, with civil war battles far bloodier than those at Gettysburg. What ensued was a period of industrialization and growth unparalleled in history. Many think that the Japanese miracle took place after the Second World War. In fact, it took place in the previous century, when

Japan transformed itself from a feudal society into an industrial superpower.

Japan has many advantages. And Japan's companies have proven their abilities in the past. But Japan's advantage will be wasted if structural barriers to change are not removed. These barriers restrict the flow of information, in effect preventing the substitution of knowledge for natural resources, labor and capital that might otherwise take place. After a decade of spending the national wealth, the country has less to fall back on by the day.

Notes

Preface

1. "Iridium official says Chapter 11 isn't viable option," *Wall Street Journal,* 19 July 1999, p. A4.

PART I

Chapter 1

1. Kennedy, E.C., *SPQR* (London: 1961), p. 55.

Chapter 2

1. "Microsoft Reality Check," *Upside,* August 1999, p. 128; "What Do You Want To Buy Today," *Business Week,* 7 June 1999, p. 32.
2. "Fisher's Photo Finish," *Business Week,* 21 June 1999, p. 34.

Chapter 4

1. "Call It the Net Effect," *Business Week,* 12 July 1999, p. 50.

Chapter 7

1. Matsushita, Konosuke, *The Matsushita Perspective: A Business Philosophy Handbook* (Tokyo: PHP Institute, 1997).
2. Kotter, John P., *Matsushita Leadership* (New York: Free Press, 1997).

Chapter 8

1. "Singapore works hard to keep its competitive edges sharp," *Financial Times,* 8 July 1999, p. 4.
2. "Still lingering in negative territory," *Financial Times,* 30 June 1999, p. II.

Chapter 9

1. "FT 500 Survey," *Financial Times,* 28 January 1999, p. 4.
2. "PC Sales Accelerated During 4th Quarter," *Wall Street Journal,* 29 January 1998, p. B2. During 1997, Dell sold 12,230 machines for each of 365 days. During 1998, it sold 20,167 machines a day, an increase of 65 percent.
3. "FT 500 Survey," *Financial Times* 28 January 1999, p. 4.
4. "In today's economy, there is big money to be made in logistics," *Wall Street Journal,* 6 September 1995, p. A1.
5. "500,000 clients, no branches," *New York Times,* 3 September 1995, section 3, page 1.
6. "Guess who may be your travel agent," *Wall Street Journal,* 7 March 1995, p. A19.
7. "Make it Simple," *Business Week,* 9 September 1996, p. 99.
8. "Call It the Net Effect," *Business Week,* 12 July 1999, p. 50.
9. "Get Big—Or Get Out," *Business Week,* 2 September 1996, p. 60.
10. "Get Big—Or Get Out," p. 60.
11. "Get Big—Or Get Out," p. 60.
12. "Get Big—Or Get Out," p. 60.

Chapter 10

1. "Now AOL Everywhere," *New York Times,* 4 July 1999, Section 3, p. 1.
2. "America Online's fancy accounting methods," *Wall Street Journal,* 3 June 1998, p. C4.
3. "Yahoo!, Inc.," BT Alex. Brown, Wall Street research report, 13 October 1997; "Yahoo! surges in first quarter," *Financial Times,* 9 April 1998, p.

26; "AT&T seeks broad marketing, technology alliance with AOL," *Wall Street Journal*, 18 June 1998, p. B6; "Above the Crowd," newsletter, 20 April 1998.

4. "Online Persuaders," *Wall Street Journal*, 12 July 1999, p. R12.

5. "America On-line," Salomon Smith Barney, 27 February 1998, p. 7.

6. "AOL swings to profit," *Wall Street Journal*, 7 May 1998, p. B6; "AOL," Salomon Smith Barney research report, 27 February 1998, p. 7.

7. 24m shares x $86 = $2b.

8. "Internet Wave Report II," Salomon Smith Barney research report, 20 March 1998, p. 8; "Amazon.com's junk bond raises an issue," *Wall Street Journal*, 4 May 1998, p. B12a; "The perils of artistic growth," *Financial Times*, 26 May 1998, p. 15; "Weaker dollar, dearth of data weigh on bonds," *Wall Street Journal*, 6 May 1998, p. C21.

9. "The Bottom Line," *Wall Street Journal*, 12 July 1999, p. R8.

10. "Reading the Riot Act," *Wall Street Journal*, 12 July 1999, p. R46.

11. "Dell tops $12 billion in annual revenues," Dell corporate press release, 2/18/98; $4m/day Internet sales run rate.

12. Charles Schwab 1Q98 Financial Report; "Top players hold positions," *Wall Street Journal*, Interactive Edition, 29 May 1998.

13. *http://www.census.gov/epcd/www/ecensus.html*

14. "The Route To Asia," *Wall Street Journal*, 12 July 1999, p. R22.

15. "The Economics of e-commerce," Morgan Stanley Dean Witter, *U.S. and the Americas Investment Research Market Watch*, 5/19/98, p. 13.

16. "Making business sense of the Internet," *Harvard Business Review*, March–April 1998, p. 128.

17. "Level 3 sells junk bonds," *Wall Street Journal*, 24 April 1998, p. C1.

18. "Competition chief hits at WorldCom-MCI," *Financial Times*, 26 May 1998, p. 19.

19. Tony Naughtin, CEO of InterNap, 26 May 1998 Blackstone presentation.

20. "Above the Crowd," newsletter, 23 March 1998.

21. Graham Benjamin, *The Intelligent Investor* (New York: Harper Business, 1973) p. xiii.

22. "The power of virtual integration," *Harvard Business Review*, March–April 1998, p. 75.

23. "Reinvesting the dinosaur," *Financial Times*, 8 June 1999, p. 13.

Chapter 11

1. Keynes, John Maynard, *The General Theory of Employment Interest and Money* (London: MacMillan, 1967), p. 249.

PART II

Chapter 12

1. "Will video game machines turn into PC killers," *New York Times,* 8 January 1995, p. B3.
2. "Philips Electronics, Sony Units to Unveil TV Set-Top Box for Access to Internet," *Wall Street Journal,* 10 July 1996, p. B7.
3. "Sega Plans to Launch Hookup to Internet For Its Game Players," *Wall Street Journal,* 18 September 1996, p. B9.
4. "Intel Puts Chips on 'Hybrid Applications,'" *Wall Street Journal,* 6 August 1996, p. B12.
5. "Sony's defence of the living room," *Financial Times,* 26 August 1996, p. 8.

Chapter 13

1. "Fathers of Invention: How Level 3 worked its way to the main floor," *USA Today,* 1 April 1998.
2. Lakeville Internet had a $25 monthly charge for up to sixty hours of 2.4k bps–28.8k bps intermittent dial-up service, which equals $0.0069 per minute.
3. AOL charged $9.95 per month, which included the first five hours; equaling $0.03 per minute.
4. Forty-two pages weigh 8.7 oz; first class/priority mail letter is $3 in U.S.; airmail to Japan is $7.40.
5. Standard rates quoted over the phone for our account.
6. Rates quoted by AT&T over the phone for our "CustomNet" service: in U.S., for 926–5,000 miles, peak $0.1590 for the first thirty seconds, $0.0053 for each additional second; off-peak $0.1110/.0037; to Japan, peak $0.4650/.0155, off-peak $0.4530/.0151.

7. Rates quoted by AT&T over the phone for our "CustomNet" service: in U.S. for 926–5,000 miles, peak $0.1590 for the first thirty seconds, $0.0053 for each additional second; off-peak $0.1110/.0037; to Japan, peak $0.4650/.0155, off-peak $0.4530/0.0151.

8. NYNEX rates quoted over the phone, for local calls 8am–9pm, 8¢ for the first three minutes, 1.3¢ for each additional minute; 9pm–11pm 40 percent off; 11pm–8am 65 percent off.

9. NYNEX rates quoted over the phone, for local calls 8am–9pm 8¢ for the first three minutes, 1.3¢ for each additional minute; 9pm–11pm 40 percent off; 11pm–8am 65 percent off.

10. *Business Week,* 14 November 1994, p. 81.

11. "WorldCom Reaches Pact to Buy MFS in $14.4 Billion Stock Deal," *Wall Street Journal,* 26 August 1996, p. A3.

12. The cost of sending a forty-two-page document by e-mail is less than one two-thousandth the cost of sending it by fax.

13. *Wall Street Journal,* 10 August 1995, p. A1.

Chapter 14

1. "Viacom Offering 31 Million Blockbuster Shares," *New York Times,* 20 July 1999, p. C4.

2. "Detour from the superhighway," *Financial Times,* 28 March 1995, p. 15.

3. "Last Stand," *Business Week,* 3 March 1997, p. 67.

4. "Blockbuster Chairman Out; Viacom to Issue Shares in Unit," *New York Times,* 23 April 1997, p. C1.

5. "Viacom Asks Hollywood Studios to Cut Video Prices to help its Blockbuster Unit," *Wall Street Journal,* 19 June 1997, p. B2.

6. "Fisher's Photo Finish," *Business Week,* 21 June 1999, p. 34.

7. "Can George Fisher Fix Kodak?" *Business Week,* 20 October 1997, p. 116; *Business Week,* 7 July, p. 100.

Chapter 15

1. "Call It the Net Effect," *Business Week,* 12 July 1999, p. 51.
2. Bell Atlantic *Investor's Reference Guide,* April 1994; Bell Atlantic *Annual Report,* 1994, various pages.
3. This calculation assumes that the United States has 160 million access lines.
4. "David Ogilvy, 88, Father of Soft Sell In Advertising, Dies," *New York Times,* 22 July 1999, p. A1.
5. "Delivery via the satellite route," *Financial Times,* 18 July 1996, p. 8.

Chapter 18

1. Letter from the authors to Mel Karmazin, 30 March 1999.
2. "Microsoft to Buy WebTV for $425 Million," *Wall Street Journal,* 7 April 1997, p. A3.
3. "Microsoft Will Describe Chip Project to Upgrade PCs," *Wall Street Journal,* 6 August 1996, p. B4.
4. "BSkyB plans closer ties with BT," *Financial Times,* 9 December 1994, p. 17; "BSkyB and BT to launch digital TV," *Financial Times,* 5 May 1997, p. 19.
5. "News Corp to set up Satellite TV Service in Japan," *Financial Times,* 13 June 1996, p. 13.
6. "Deal By Murdoch For Satellite TV Startles Industry," *New York Times,* 26 February 1997, p. 1.
7. "EchoStar to Buy Satellite-TV Assets of News Corp., MCI," *Wall Street Journal,* 1 December 1998, p. B8.
8. "Rupert Does the Cyperhustle," *Business Week,* 12 July 1999, p. 88.

Chapter 19

1. "Panasonic Deal to Make Digital Records for Replay," *New York Times,* 9 June 1999, p. C9.
2. "Iomega Enters Zip Drive Licensing Deal With Matsushita, Pushing Stock Up 16%," *Wall Street Journal,* 11 September 1996, p. B4.

Chapter 21

1. "Telecommunications Survey," *The Economist,* 23 October 1993, p. 8; "Wireless World," Salomon Brothers research report, April 1996, p. 24.
2. "American Portable Telecom," Salomon Brothers research report, 6 June 1996, p. 16.
3. "U.S. Wireless Demographics," www.ctia.org, 19 September 1996.
4. "Cell-phone prices may decline," *Wall Street Journal,* 11 January 1996, p. B3.
5. "AT&T stock plunges," *Wall Street Journal,* 25 September 1996, p. A13.

Chapter 23

1. "Net view of Clinton tape gets mixed reviews," *Wall Street Journal,* 22 September 1998, p. B10.
2. "Top home-use software ranked," CNET, 11 September 1998.
3. "A new microchip ushers in cheaper digital cameras," *Wall Street Journal,* 21 August 1998, p. B1.
4. "Blockbuster seeks new deal with Hollywood," *Wall Street Journal,* 25 March 1998, p. B1.
5. "Japan Manufacturers Reorganize To Develop Digital Products," Dow Jones News, 10/11.
6. "Digital TV seen as home multimedia server at JES," *EE Times,* 10 October 1998.

Chapter 24

1. "Are Music Companies Blinded By the Fright," *Business Week,* 28 June 1999, p. 67.
2. "The Home War, On Line Banking Has Bankers Fretting PCs May Replaces Branches," *Wall Street Journal,* 25 October 1995, p. 1.
3. "Improved distribution, not better production, is key goal in mergers," *Wall Street Journal,* 29 August 1995, p. A1.

Chapter 25

1. "The Sex Industry," *The Economist,* 14 February 1998, p. 22.
2. "Sex sells, so cable cos. find ways to keep it selling," *Wall Street Journal,* 12 December 1997 (Interactive Edition); "Playboy to acquire Spice, adult entertainment firm," *Wall Street Journal,* 4 February 1998 (Interactive Edition).
3. "Small but perfectly formed," *The Economist,* 3 January 1998, p. 67.
4. "As other Internet ventures fail, sex sites are raking in millions," *Wall Street Journal,* 20 May 1997 (Interactive Edition); "Shoppers start buying gifts from their own computers," *Wall Street Journal,* 9 December 1997 (Interactive Edition).
5. "U.S. may face enforcement hurdles in crackdown on Internet gambling," *Wall Street Journal,* 6 March 1998, p. B18.
6. "Can pay, won't pay," *The Economist,* 14 February 1998, p. 13.
7. "As other Internet ventures fail, sex sites are raking in millions," *Wall Street Journal,* 20 May 1997 (Interactive Edition).
8. "As other Internet ventures fail, sex sites are raking in millions,"; "Adult Sex lures entrepreneurs cashing in on Internet porn," *Wall Street Journal,* 19 November 1997 (Interactive Edition).
9. "Broadcast TV's viewership fell in latest season," *Wall Street Journal,* 22 May 1997, p. B5; "CBS may prevail in sweeps race but loses out with key groups," *Wall Street Journal,* 26 November 1997 (Interactive Edition).

Chapter 26

1. "A greener bank," *The Economist,* 23 May 1992, p. 79.
2. "Cleaning up," *The Economist,* 8 September 1990, survey p. 26.

PART III

Chapter 27

1. "Can George Fisher Fix Kodak?" *Business Week,* 20 October 1997, p. 116. See also *USA Today,* 15 October 1997, p. 2B; and "Fisher's Photo Finish," *Business Week,* 21 June 1999, p. 34.

Chapter 29

1. "Schwab Lands Feet First on Net," *New York Times,* 10 February 1999, p. C1.
2. "Schwab Lands Feet First on Net."
3. "Where No-Frills Net Trades Are Sacred," *Business Week,* 28 June 1999, p. 93.
4. "Where No-Frills Net Trades Are Sacred."
5. "Channel Conflict," *Wall Street Journal,* 14 June 1999, p. R9.

Chapter 30

1. "The Network's Big Problem," *Fortune,* 9 November 1998, p. 44.
2. "Discovery: Beyond Bloody Gazelles," *Business Week,* 21 June 1999, p. 80.
3. "Following a Tough Act," *New York Times,* 17 June 1999, p. C1.
4. "Where Have Television's Big Stars Gone?" *New York Times,* 14 June 1999, p. C1.
5. "TV Networks are Scrambling to Deal with Era of New Media," *New York Times,* 28 May 1999.
6. "Shrinking Network TV Audiences Set Off Alarm and Reassessment," *New York Times,* 22 November 1998, p. A1.
7. "Technology and Entertainment Survey," *The Economist,* 21 November 1998, p. 12.
8. "Where Have Television's Big Stars Gone?" *New York Times,* 14 June 1999, p. C1.
9. "Fewer Viewers More Commercials," *New York Times,* 8 June 1999, p. C1.
10. "The Network's Big Problem," *Fortune,* 9 November 1998, p. 44.
11. "TV Networks Win More Concessions From the Studios," *Wall Street Journal,* 24 May 1999, p. B10.
12. "Basketball brainwave nets fortune," *Financial Times,* 19 April 1999, p. 14.

Notes

Chapter 31

1. During the 1990s, retail sales have grown at 4 to 5 percent per year (nominal). Statistical Abstract of the United States, Table 1267.
2. "Amazon.com gets real at distribution site," *Wall Street Journal,* 16 November 1998, p. B7C.

Chapter 32

1. "FT 500 Surveys" *Financial Times,* 28 January 1999, p. 4.
2. "Internet a 'booster rocket for sales,'" *Financial Times,* 3 September 1997, FT-IT p. 2.
3. "Compaq Stumbles as PCs Weather New Blow," *Wall Street Journal,* 9 March 1998, p. B1.
4. "Michael Dell Turns the PC World Inside Out" *Fortune,* 8 September 1997, p. 79.

Chapter 33

1. "Sony's defence of the living room," *Financial Times,* 26 August 1996, p. 8.
2. "Microsoft," Salomon Smith Barney research report, September 1997, p. 53.
3. "Wireless world guerrillas," *Financial Times,* 19 January 1999, p. 12.
4. "Sun Microsystems," Salomon Smith Barney research report, 11 August 1998, p. 8.
5. "TCI in pacts with Microsft, Sun," *Wall Street Journal,* 12 January 1998, p. A6.
6. "Microsoft," Salomon Smith Barney research report, September 1997, p. 53.
7. "Jini out of the bottle," *The Economist,* 23 January 1999, p. 58; "The perils of home networking," *The Economist,* 23 January 1999, p. 72.
8. "Windows 2000 portends product convergence," *Wall Street Journal,* 28 October 1998, p. B8.

9. "A dud at its birth, Windows NT is back," *Wall Street Journal*, 29 July 1996, p. A1.

10. "Linus operating system gets big boost," *Wall Street Journal*, 27 January 1999, p. B6.

11. "How the competition got ahead of Intel in making cheap chips," *Wall Street Journal*, 12 February 1998, p. A1.

12. "Intel lags behind in cheap chips," *Wall Street Journal*, 12 February 1998, p. A11.

13. N64: 64 bit processor, 94MHz; PlayStation: 32 bit processor, 34MHz, 30 MIPS (from Web sites).

Chapter 34

1. Corporate press releases: 1997 (4/21/97), 1996 (2/4/97); www.ryder.com/message.

2. "IBM to let firms lease, replace PCs for a flat fee," *Wall Street Journal*, 14 April 1997, p. B5.

3. Bell Atlantic Annual Report, 1994, p. 25.

4. www.ge.com/capital/aviation/as1

5. "Muni market faces turmoil from megadeal," *Wall Street Journal*, 22 April 1997, p. C1.

6. "A wealth of facts on America's richest," *USA Today*, 14 April 1997, p. 10B.

7. "A brief history of the Penn Central Railroad," Penn Central Railroad Home Page [http://prozac.cwru.edu/jer/pc/docs/history.html], 24 April 1997.

8. "Bell Atlantic and NYNEX Stocks Drop," *New York Times*, 24 April 1996, p. D1. Bell Atlantic valued NYNEX at $22.1 billion.

9. Debt to total capitalization is reported as 0.77 in the 1995 annual report on the company's Web site.

10. "WorldCom Reaches Pact to Buy MFS in $14.4 Billion Stock Deal," *Wall Street Journal*, 26 August 1996, p. A3.

11. FCC Statistics of Common Carriers, Forms 952–7/9; YE95 grown one year.

12. "RBOCs," Salomon Brothers research report, January, 1996, p. 1.

Chapter 35

1. "Cisco@speed" *The Economist,* Survey of Business and the Internet, 26 June 1999, p. 12

2. "Cisco: Crunch Time for a High Tech Wiz," *Business Week,* 28 April 1997, p. 80.

3. "Cisco: Crunch Time for a High Tech Wiz"; and "Cisco's Skid," *Business Week,* 3 March 1997, p. 64.

4. "Big shift in corporate attitudes on electronic commerce," *Financial Times,* Information Technology Review, 2 July 1997, p. 2.

5. "Big shift in corporate attitudes on electronic commerce."

6. "The Corporation of the Future," *Business Week,* 31 August 1998, p. 104.

7. "For Cisco, Focus on Small Companies Pays Off," *Wall Street Journal,* 27 May 1999, p. B8.

8. "Mind the money tracker," *Financial Times,* 12 April 1999, p. 12.

Chapter 36

1. U.S. Department of Commerce.

2. "Intel's Net Handily Beats Expectations," *Wall Street Journal,* 14 January 1998, p. A3.

3. "Intel, AMD prepare to Square Off in New Chip Battle," *Wall Street Journal,* 17 February 1999, p. B4.

4. "Intel Corp.," BT Alex. Brown, Wall Street research report, 21 August 1998.

5. "Intel lags behind in cheap chips," *Wall Street Journal,* 12 February 1998, p. A11.

6. "Intel: Can Andy Grove keep profits up in an era of cheap PCs?" *Business Week,* 22 December 1997, p. 70.

7. "Intel Puts Chips on 'Hybrid Applications,'" *Wall Street Journal,* 6 August 1996, p. B12.

8. "Intel Shifts Its Focus to Long-Term, Original Research," *Wall Street Journal,* 26 August 1996, p. B4.

9. "Intel's Quick Web Technology Aims To Cut Down on 'World Wide Wait,'" *Wall Street Journal,* 19 January 1998.

10. "Intel Proposal Is Angering Web Publishers," *Wall Street Journal,* 16 January 1998.

11. "Intel Agrees to Buy Dialogic for $780 Million," *Wall Street Journal,* 2 June 1999, p. B10.

12. "Intel Invests $200 Million in Williams Communications," *New York Times,* 26 May 1999, p. C4.

13. "Intel and Microsoft Split Over Internet-TV Gear," *Wall Street Journal,* 3 October 1997, p. A3.

14. "Intel and Microsoft Split Over Internet-TV Gear," p. A3.

15. "Intel Agreement Indicates a Rift With Microsoft," *New York Times,* 16 September 1998, p. C1.

16. "Intel, AMD Prepare to Square Off in New Chip Battle," *Wall Street Journal,* 17 February 1999, p. B4.

17. "Intel: Can Andy Grove keep profits up in an era of cheap PCs?" *Business Week,* 22 December 1997, p. 77.

18. "Andy Grove: The PC Industry Won't Be the PC Industry," *Fortune,* 24 May 1999, p. 160.

Chapter 37

1. *Wall Street Journal,* 23 April 1999, p. B2; p A11.

2. *Wall Street Journal,* 1 June 1999, p. A20.

3. "US West Inc.'s Trujillo is thinking big again," *Wall Street Journal,* 30 June 1999, p. B6.

4. US West press release, 22 January 1999.

5. "MCI purchase of SkyTel," *Wall Street Journal,* 1 June 1999, p. B6; "AT&T prepares massive bond offering," *Wall Street Journal,* 18 March 1999, p. A3; "AT&T puts cable agreements on hold," *Wall Street Journal,* 20 May 1999, p. B9.

6. "DSL Providers," BT Alex. Brown, Wall Street research report, 1 June 1999, p. 10.

7. "AT&T makes big investment," *USA Today,* 6 May 1999, p. 3B.

8. "AT&T grabs powerful position," *Wall Street Journal,* 6 May 1999 (electronic edition).

9. "AT&T makes big investment," *USA Today,* 6 May 1999, p. 3B.

10. "Money for nothing," *Wall Street Journal,* 12 May 1999, p. A3.

11. International Settlement Rates, FCC Report 97–280, 7 August 1997; "Iridium shares fall," *Wall Street Journal,* 17 May 1999, p. B6; "Credit Markets," and "Iridium to cut prices," *Wall Street Journal,* 23 June 1999, p. C24, B9; Iridium Form 10Q, 31 March 1999: "Because an amendment has not been agreed to and Iridium has not received a waiver, the entire outstanding balance of approximately $800 million, along with the entire outstanding balances on the guaranteed bank facility, senior subordinated notes and notes payable, all of which have cross-default and/or cross-acceleration provisions, are classified as current in the condensed consolidated financial statements of Iridium. Iridium had approximately $480 million outstanding under the guaranteed bank facilities, $337 million of senior subordinated notes and $1.4 billion of notes payable."

12. "AT&T Wireless," *Forbes,* 19 April 1999, p. 190.

13. "U.S. carrier capex update," BT Alex. Brown, Wall Street research report, 14 May 1999, p. 6.

14. "Olivetti plans big bond issue," *Wall Street Journal,* 11 May 1999, P. A17; Olivetti 1H98 sales were $3b lire, TI's 1998 sales were $44b lire; Chase ad in the *Wall Street Journal,* 9 July 1999, p. A8.

15. "Cable barons," *National Post,* 18 May 1999, p. C7.

16. Debt equity ratio was 88 percent at YE96; "TCI Group," Salomon Brothers research report, 30 September 1997, p. 2.

17. "Telecom Services," Goldman Sachs research report, 2 October 1998, p. 127.

18. "Choosing the right mixture," *The Economist,* 27 February 1999, p. 71; *The Economist,* 12 June 1999, p. 58.

19. "Telecom offerings," *Wall Street Journal,* 10 May 1999, p. C20.

20. "Microsoft may buy interest in U.K. firm," *Wall Street Journal,* 12 May 1999, p. A3.

21. "And for his next trick," *Wall Street Journal,* 5 May 1999, p. A23; "AOL bets big," *Wall Street Journal,* 22 June 1999, p. B1.

22. BCE 1999 First Quarter Report.

23. "Productivity gains from technology may reach limit," *Wall Street Journal*, 15 June 1999 (Interactive Edition); "Keep the tax man off line," *Wall Street Journal*, 29 June 1999, p. A14.

24. "Survey finds PC usage in homes has dropped," *Wall Street Journal*, 21 June 1999, p. B7.

Chapter 38

1. "Fight of the (next) Century," *New York Times*, 7 March 1999, p. C1.

2. "How Sony beat digital-camera rivals," *Wall Street Journal*, 25 January 1999, p. B1.

3. "Fight of the (next) Century," *New York Times*, 7 March 1999, p. C1.

4. McLuhan, Marshall, *Understanding Media: the Extensions of Man* (New York: Signet Books, 1964) p. 268.

5. "Sony Introduces Playstation II, on Which a Big Bet Is Riding," *New York Times*, 3 March 1999, p. C4.

6. "Sony's Shakeup," *Business Week*, 22 March 1999, p. 52.

Chapter 39

1. "What BMW sees in South Carolina," *New York Times*, 11 April 1993, p. 5.

2. McInerney, Francis and White, Sean, *Beating Japan* (New York: Truman Talley Books/Dutton, 1993), p. 141.

3. "Driven back to basics," *Financial Times*, 16 July 1992, p. 10.

4. McInerney and White, *Beating Japan*, p. 141.

5. *The State of the Environment*, Organization for Economic Co-operation and Development, Paris, 1991, p. 146.

6. "Nissan receives environmental excellence award," Nissan press release, 13 November 1992.

7. "Nissan receives environmental excellence award."

8. "Nissan receives environmental excellence award."

9. "Vehicle sales jumped during late May, reflecting a shift in production to U.S.," *Wall Street Journal*, 4 June 1993, p. 2; "Will Nissan get it right this time?" *Business Week*, 20 April 1992, p. 83.

Chapter 40

1. *http://www.census.gov/epcd/www/ecensus.html*
2. Table 867, *Statistical Abstract of the United States,* 1998 edition.
3. Charles Schwab 1998 Financial Report; "Top players hold positions," *Wall Street Journal,* Interactive Edition, 29 May 1998.
4. "Asia's culture hampers Internet commerce," *USA Today,* 16 February 1999; "For frazzled online brokers," *Wall Street Journal,* 4 March 1999, p. B6.
5. "Wal-Mart Stores, Inc.," Harvard Business School pamphlet, 6 August 1996, p. 5.
6. "Wal-Mart posts a 27% profit increase," *Wall Street Journal,* 11 November 1998, p. B9A.
7. "New technology calls the tunes," *Wall Street Journal,* 8 March 1999, p. A18.
8. "Car dealers warned to get Net savvy," CNET News.com, 8 February 1999.
9. "Asia's culture hampers Internet commerce," *USA Today,* 16 February 1999, p. 6B. E-commerce reaches $268.8b in 2002, up from $11b in 1997; retail + wholesale trade = $4 trillion in 1994, *Statistical Abstract of the United States,* 1998 Edition.
10. "Telecommuting on the rise," CNET News.com, 8 October 1997.
11. "Managers find ways to narrow distance gap," *Wall Street Journal,* 6 April 1999, Interactive edition.
12. "More firms embrace 'virtual office,'" CNET News.com, 8 June 1998.
13. "Will the boom in Internet commerce lead shopping centers to extinction?" *Wall Street Journal,* 17 February 1999, Internet edition.

Chapter 41

1. "Play with the big boys," *The Economist,* 15 May 1999, p. 65.
2. "Sega Is Giving New Product Special Push," *New York Times,* 12 July 1999, p. C4.
3. "Sega Plans to Launch Hookup to Internet For Its Game Players," *Wall Street Journal,* 18 September 1996, p. B9.

Chapter 42

1. North River Ventures *Client Letter,* August 1995.

2. "Sales surge for wireless-phone makers," *Wall Street Journal,* 8 February 1999, p. B5.

3. "Next Stage on the Cellular Tour," *New York Times,* 27 July 1999, p. C1.

4. "The National Operators-Europe," Salomon Smith Barney research report, 5 May 1998, p. 20.

5. "Wireless Quarterly-Europe," Salomon Smith Barney research report, 2 September 1998, p. 53.

6. "AT&T Wireless," *Forbes,* 19 April 1999, p. 190.

7. "As worlds collide, AT&T grabs a power seat," *Wall Street Journal,* 6 May 1999, p. B1.

Chapter 43

1. Smith, Adam, *The Wealth of Nations* (New York: The Modern Library, 1937), p. 639.

2. White, Sean, *The Profitability of Land ownership, 1570–1640.* Cambridge University postgraduate thesis.

3. "Buena Vista winery recognized as a leader in organic farming," Buena Vista Winery press release, 31 August 1992.

4. Cable Network News, 29 September 1992.

5. "Organic wine hits the mainstream," *New York Times,* 19 November 1991, p. D1.

6. "Wine is bottled in more shapes and sizes," *Wall Street Journal,* 9 December 1993, p. B1.

7. "Passing the jug," *New York Times Magazine,* 15 November 1992, p. 48.

8. "California's double whammy," *Financial Times,* 16 January 1993, p. VIII.

9. "Certifiably Carneros," *California Farmer,* 21 September 1991, p. 10.

10. "Bugs, weeds, and fine wine," *Business Week,* 10 August 1992, p. lx.

11. "Certifiably Carneros," *California Farmer,* 21 September 1991, p. 10.

12. "Buena Vista winery recognized as a leader in organic farming," Buena Vista Winery press release, 31 August 1992.

13. "Certifiably Carneros," *California Farmer,* 21 September 1991, p. 10.
14. "Certifiably Carneros," p. 11.
15. "U.S. is steadily losing share of world trade in grains and soybeans," *Wall Street Journal,* 3 December 1992, p. A1.
16. "U.S. is steadily losing share of world trade in grains and soybeans," p. A1.
17. "Le déclin de l'agriculture allemande," *Le Monde,* 10 December 1992, p. 18.
18. The State of the Environment, OECD, 1991, p. 185.
19. "Future of big vegetable growing area in California threatened by salt water," *Wall Street Journal,* 1 July 1993, p. A2.
20. "Environmental truce clears smoke in rice fields," *New York Times,* 12 December 1992, p. 8.
21. "U.S. and Florida lean on sugar producers to restore polluted everglades," *New York Times,* 16 January 1994, p. 20.
22. "Organic profits go against the grain," *Financial Times,* 30 April 1993, p. 32.
23. "Soil quality and financial performance of biodynamic and conventional farms in New Zealand," *Science,* 16 April 1993, p. 344.
24. "Where Riesling is king, experiments and trouble reign," *New York Times,* 25 November 1992, p. C1.

Chapter 44

1. "Net's backbone begins to flex," *Financial Times,* 16 September 1996, p. 11.
2. Brock, Gerald W., "The Economics of Interconnection," Teleport Communications Group consultant's report, April, 1995.
3. "Sprint Offers a Plan to Retool An Overloaded Phone System," *Wall Street Journal,* 2 June 1998, p. A1.
4. "AT&T to Acquire TCI for $37.3 Billion," *Wall Street Journal,* 25 June 198, p. A3; "Drop in AT&T Stock Price Raises Concern on TCI Deal," *New York Times,* 6 July 1998, p. D2.
5. "Sprint Pieces Together Wireless Cable for Homes," *Wall Street Journal,* 6 May 1994, p. B4.

Chapter 45

1. "Losing their way," *The Economist,* 12 June 1993, p. S4.

2. "Lufthansa managers buoyed by second-quarter results," *Aviation Week & Space Technology,* 12 July 1993, p. 1.

3. "Aviation and the environment," speech by Hans-Peter Reichow of Lufthansa, in Sydney, on 30 October 1992.

4. "Losing their way," *The Economist,* 12 June 1993, p. S9.

5. "Lufthansa says deficit narrowed in first six months," *Wall Street Journal,* 13 August 1993, p. B5D. Note: In 1992, Lufthansa lengthened its depreciation schedule for aircraft from ten to twelve years, boosting profits, but its write off of equipment remains extremely conservative by industry standards; CEO Weber maintains that the company would be profitable if it wrote off its planes over twenty years or more, as does British Airways. See "Lufthansa chief plots turnaround strategy," *Aviation Week & Space Technology,* 8 March 1993; "Lufthansa AG loss narrows for the year," *Wall Street Journal,* 18 March 1994, p. A7.

6. "Lufthansa managers buoyed by second-quarter results," *Aviation Week & Space Technology,* 12 July 1993, p. 2; "Lufthansa chief plots turnaround strategy," *Aviation Week & Space Technology,* 8 March 1993, p. 2.

7. Lufthansa annual report, 1992.

8. "Losing their way," *The Economist,* 12 June 1993, p. S5.

9. "Losing their way," p. S18.

10. Press conference presentation by Dr. Klaus Schlende, deputy chairman, Lufthansa, 13 May 1993, p. 4.

11. "Aviation and the environment," speech by Hans-Peter Reichow of Lufthansa, in Sydney, 30 October 1992, p. 5.

12. Lufthansa annual report, 1992.

13. "Aviation and the environment," speech by Hans-Peter Reichow of Lufthansa, in Sydney, 30 October 1992, p. 5.

14. "The Lufthansa Integrated Environment Concept," company brochure, August 1992.

15. "Hush kits for Boeing 737-200s," Lufthansa press release, 6 August 1993.

16. "Getting competitive at Lufthansa," *Aviation Week & Space Technology,* 8 March 1993, p. 2.

17. Lufthansa annual report, 1992.

18. "Managing the future," *The Economist,* 19 December 1992, p. 68.

19. *Conde Naste Traveler* and *Check-in* magazine surveys.

Chapter 46

1. "How to bust the Wintel monopoly," Spectral Shifts, 10 March 1998.

2. "Long Distance Industry," BancAmerica research report by Robertson Stephens, 5 January 1998, p. 3.

3. "Long Distance Industry," p. 15.

4. "Higher costs in line for Internet users," *Financial Times,* 13 February 1998, p. 6; "Qwest Communications," Salomon Brothers, September 19 1997, p. 11.

5. "True competition in the long-distance market," MCI press release, 27 January 1997, Figure 9.

6. "Qwest Communications," Salomon Bros., 19 September 1997, p. 7.

7. "There's life after AT&T—and how," *Business Week,* 26 March 1998, p. 7.

8. We guestimate data traffic is growing 50 to 60 percent per annum 1990–2000; see "Optical Networks," BT Alex. Brown research report, 23 September 1997, p. 5.

9. "AT&T prepares campaign to battle MCI's '10–321' plan," *Wall Street Journal,* 7 April 1998, p. B7.

10. AT&T account executive, 4 July 1998.

11. "Long Distance Industry," BancAmerica report by Robertson Stephens, 5 January 1998, p. 15.

12. Telephone Conversation with AT&T account executive, 7 April 1998.

13. "1996 Section 43.82 Circuit Status Data," FCC, December 1997.

14. "Is Europe about to become the most liberalised telecoms market in the world?" *The Economist,* 3 January 1998.

15. "Transatlantic Internet cable goes into service," *Financial Times,* 5 March 1998, p. 8; "There's life after AT&T—and how."

16. "Transatlantic Internet cable goes into service," *Financial Times,* 5 March 1998, p. 8.

17. FCC Order 97–280, "In the Matter of International Settlements," p. 10, 76.

18. "Internet Phones Are Catching on as Global Experiment," *Wall Street Journal,* 24 November, 1997, p. B6.

19. "Internet telephony may cut costs of calls, executives say," *Wall Street Journal,* 2 February 1998, Interactive Edition.

20. "Japanese Phone Giant Buys a U.S. Stake," *New York Times,* 1 October 1997, p. D2.

Chapter 47

1. ".com everywhere," BT Alex. Brown research report, 1 June 1999, p. 51.

2. "Advertising industry," Salomon Smith Barney research report, 15 May 1998, p. 30.

3. ".com everywhere," p. 77.

4. "Yahoo! Inc.," BT Alex. Brown research report, 13 January 1999, p. 11.

5. "Broadcast News," Salomon Smith Barney research report, 31 March 1998, p. 39.

6. "Broadcast News," p. 15.

7. GM spent $2.2 billion on advertising in 1997, $3.2 if dealer expenditures are included; "Broadcast News," Salomon Smith Barney research report, 7 September 1998, p. 15.

8. "Disney to buy Infoseek stake for web help," *Wall Street Journal,* 19 June 1998, p. A3.

9. "Disney agrees to acquire majority stake in Infoseek," *Wall Street Journal,* 13 July 1999.

10. "Disney agrees to acquire majority stake in Infoseek."

11. Corporate press release, 26 April 1999.

12. "Internet Wave Report II," Salomon Smith Barney research report, 20 March 1998, p. 23; ".com everywhere," p. 25.

13. "Battle over digital TV heats up," *Wall Street Journal,* 27 May 1999, p. B1.

14. Internet Ventures, Inc., 2 June 1999 petition to the FCC for Declaratory Ruling that Internet Service Providers are Entitled to Leased Access to Cable Facilities.

15. "And for his next trick," *Wall Street Journal,* 5 May 1999, p. A23; "AOL bets big," *Wall Street Journal,* 22 June 1999, p. B1.

16. *Wall Street Journal,* 25 June 1998, Interactive edition.

17. "For At Home, now comes the real excitement," *Wall Street Journal,* 28 May 1999, p. B1.

18. Internet Ventures, Inc., 2 June 1999 petition to the FCC For Declaratory Ruling that Internet Service Providers are Entitled to Leased Access to Cable Facilities.

19. "A TV titan and a webmaster clash over Lycos," *Wall Street Journal,* 12 March 1999, p. B1.

Chapter 48

1. "AT&T Has No Clothes," *Fortune,* 5 February 1996, p.

2. "AT&T outlines corporate strategy," *Investor Relations Bulletin,* 12 December 1991, p. 2

3. 1994 Annual Report, p. 4.

4. 1994 Annual Report, p. 41; 1991 Annual Report, p. 37.

5. 1994 Annual Report, p. 24; executive presentation.

6. AT&T mail offer.

7. 1994 Annual Report, p. 24.

8. 1994 Annual Report, p. 11.

9. 11.5 billion transaction divided by 4.030 million subscribers at year end equals $2,853 per subscriber; 11-4 Investor Relations Bulletin, p. 2; 1994 Annual Report, p. 11.

Chapter 49

1. Nintendo 64 has a 64 bit processor, 94MHz; PlayStation has a 32 bit processor, 34 MHz, 30 MIPS processor (from Web sites).

2. "PC software and interactive entertainment," BT Alex. Brown research report, 25 November 1998.

3. "Wanna Play," *Wall Street Journal,* 28 March 1996, p. R8.

4. "Interactive entertainment overview," BT Alex. Brown research report, 29 May 1998, p. 7.

5. "Visual phone VP-210," *Asia 21,* July 1999, p. 41.

6. "Enter, son of Walkman," *The Economist,* 22 June 1996, p. 64; "Fall and rise," *Wall Street Journal,* 16 September 1996, p. R22.

7. "The players," *Wall Street Journal,* 22 March 1999, p. R14.

8. "It takes a child to raze a village," *New York Times,* 5 March 1998, p. G1.

9. "Girls just want to have fun," *New York Times,* 14 February 1999; "Girl games: plenty and pink," *New York Times,* 10 September 1998.

10. "Game machine trends," Solomon Smith Barney research report, 9 October 1998, p. 4.

11. "Girls just want to have fun," *New York Times,* 14 February 1999.

12. "Falling through the net," U.S. Dept. of Commerce, July 1999, Chart II-56.

13. "Media Navigators," Alex. Brown research report, 2 June 1997, p. 9.

14. "Girl Games," www.hotwired.com/wired/5.04.

15. 34 percent v. 31 percent, "Falling through the net," U.S. Dept. of Commerce, July 1999, Charts II-14, II-22.

16. "American colleges begin to ask, where have all the men gone?" *New York Times,* 6 December 1998; Census Bureau data.

17. Clever girls," *The Economist,* 15 April 1995.

18. "Bringing feminine mystique to engineering," *New York Times,* 22 June 1999, p. F3.

19. "Women and work," *The Economist,* 18 July 1998, p. 12.

20. "The view from the top," *Wall Street Journal,* 12 July 1999, p. R52.

Chapter 50

1. "Latin American Telecommunications Services," Salomon Brothers research report, November 1995, p. 19.

2. "In the Loop," Salomon Brothers research report, June 1996, p. 16.

3. "MFS opens ISP interconnect facility in Frankfurt," Corporate Press Release, 9 July 1996.

4. MFS, "Bandwidth and Bottlenecks," corporate presentation, 7 May 1996.

5. "AT&T is facing delays on its plan for Internet access," *Wall Street Journal,* 1 March 1996, p. B2.

6. "UUnet Technologies adds new international services," corporate press release, 20 May 1996.
7. MFS, "Bandwidth and Bottlenecks," corporate presentation, 7 May 1996.
8. Information from GTE's home page, 22 July 1996.
9. GTE/UUNet joint press release, 10 July 1996.

Chapter 51

1. "Even a Sky Can Have Limits," 4 August 1999, p. 4C.
2. "Direct Broadcast: The New Gateway," *Inter@ctive Week,* 22 April 1996, p. 18.
3. *Wall Street Journal,* 19 June 1995, p. R6.
4. "Major Entertainment Companies to Show Mixed Results," Dow Jones News Service, 12 June 1996; "Entertainment Industry Outlook Is a Tear Jerker," *Wall Street Journal,* 9 July 1996, p. B1.
5. "Creating a Long Shot," *TECHcapital,* July/August 1999, p. 53

Chapter 52

1. "The United States economy, back in the driver's seat," *New York Times,* 27 February 1994, Section 3, p. 6.
2. "America the super-fit," *The Economist,* 13 February 1993, p. 67.
3. "Delor's rescue plan to save two million computer jobs," *The European,* 5 November 1992, p. 38.
4. "America's little fellows surge ahead," *The Economist,* 3 July 1993, p. 59.

Chapter 53

1. See also from the authors: *Beating Japan: How Hundreds of American Companies Are Beating Japan Now—and What Your Company Can Learn From Their Strategies and Successes* (New York: Truman Talley Books/Dutton, 1993).

Notes

2. In 1989, for example, Japan had a trade surplus of $45 billion with the U.S.; its total fuel imports in the same year were $43 billion; *Japan Economic Almanac 1990.* [Japan statistics].
3. "Japan's jobless rate falls for the first time in 10 months," *Financial Times,* 30 June 1999, p. 1.
4. "Down and out in Japan," *Financial Times,* 8 July 1999, p. 15.

Glossary

After Market Sales Sales of products and services you can make after you sell a product for the first time. Sell a computer and follow up with lots of software and accessories.

Annuity Stream An annuity pays out money at regular intervals. Companies that move from one-time product sales to long-term contracts turn those one-time sales into virtual annuities.

The Big Bang This happens when microprocessors get so powerful and so cheap that there is an explosion in demand for computer-powered consumer electronics. So, a business market that might be in the millions of computers turns into a home market for billions—a huge leap forward.

Black Hole in Cyberspace This is a point of price-performance so powerful that it sucks in whole companies. Internet retailers, for example, can be so cheap that they swallow whole chains of retail stores.

Brand Envelope Brand is managing how your customers experience your products. A brand envelope defines the limits of that experience.

Channel Management This is the management of channels companies use to sell their products. If a company sells through retailers, managing these retailers is known as channel management.

Days of Sales This is the number of days it would take a company to sell goods just to catch up with a competitor. One company may turn a sale into cash in five days; another in ten. The difference is five days of sales.

The Dead Zone This is the backwater businesses find themselves in when they are unable to keep up with the Moore Curve. A company may run on a system, for example, that has remained unchanged for a decade. Its competitors may use computing systems to run faster, leaving the company in a Dead Zone that grows in size exponentially as the computer price-performance increases.

Debt Ratio The ratio of debt to shareholder equity on a company's balance sheet.

Deleverage Businesses often borrow in order to raise the money to grow. This is called leverage. Some companies have huge debts to finance a large number of fixed assets, like machines. They need to monetize these assets, by selling them or leasing them, in order to get the capital they need to become more competitive.

Diseconomy of Scale In the days of Henry Ford, businesses benefited from economies of scale: the bigger the production runs of identical cars, the better. The Internet by contrast benefits those who can customize all their products and services for each individual. Thus: diseconomies of scale.

Disintermediation When transportation was expensive, businesses frequently used intermediaries like wholesalers and retailers to take their products to market and carry the risks of getting them there. The Internet encourages companies to sell directly to their customers, in effect, disintermediating the market and driving out all the intermediaries.

DSL A Digital Subscriber Line. It's what phone companies hope to use to connect powerful consumer electronics systems from TV's and personal computers to their networks.

DSS Direct Satellite System: this brings television service into your home or office over a satellite. DirecTV, EchoStar, StarTV, and BskyB are examples of companies that offer this service.

Event Horizon The Event Horizon is the circumference of a Black Hole. In physics it is a point of no return; once things slip over the Event Horizon into a Black Hole, they are never seen again. For us, this is a point where a company can no longer resist the gravitational pull of price performance and slips into oblivion, never to be seen again.

First Mover The company that makes the first move in a brand-new market. You might say that Apple had the first mover advantage in personal computers or that Sony had the first mover advantage with Walkman.

The Four Keys These are our four essentials to building a company capable of withstanding the pressures of the falling cost of information. They are that a company bust be decentralized, vertically and horizontally disintegrated, have no more than four layers of management, and deliver customer service.

Horizontal Integration   A business with several loosely related businesses. For example, a company that has a portfolio of electrical or electronics businesses.

The Hubble Effect   Edwin Hubble observed that the farther away from each other that galaxies in the universe are, the faster away from each other they move. Our observation is that the more distance a company puts between itself and its customers—either through intermediaries or old technology—the faster their customers will move away from them.

Hybrid Applications   Putting more than one thing on the same system. A personal computer, for example, is a hybrid; there are lots of things you can do with it.

Import Substitution   What a lot of emerging economies (like the U.S. in its early days) do to get themselves going. They create barriers to imports and try to substitute homegrown products for their consumers. They hope by doing this to keep their trade deficit down and lower their need for foreign currency to buy imports.

Information Cost Curve   This is the rate at which information costs are falling. Today this is the Moore Curve.

Information Singularity   The Information Singularity is a point where all forms of information are undifferentiated. The Internet is such an event: it doesn't differentiate between a phone call and video from your camcorder, let alone between network television and your camcorder.

Interior Lines   A military term meaning that your forces are arrayed in a convex curve, allowing you to move troops from one part to the other over much shorter distances than your opponent who must go all the way round the outside to get to the same point.

Inventory   Parts, work-in-progress, finished goods.

ION   Sprint's Integrated Optical Network.

IP   The Internet Protocol: how communications are packaged to travel over the Internet.

IPO   Initial Public Offering: the first offering of shares in a new company to the public.

Iron Laws of Information   Our four rules about how cheap information operates on an organization.

ISP   Internet Service Provider: the company you go to get Internet service for your home or office.

IT   Information technology: a broad term covering all the different elements of the information business from computers and communications to software and microchips.

Kaizen   The Japanese term for continual improvements.

Layoff Play   Where a company makes its target rate of return by firing people instead of growing its markets.

LEO System   Low Earth Orbit satellites: these are close enough to the Earth that there is little delay in sending communications up and back to the satellite, making conversation possible. These satellites have short lives, however, and soon fall back into the Earth's atmosphere where they burn up.

Market Cap   The value of a company that is the price of its shares multiplied by the number of shares.

Market Entropy   The tendency of ever cheaper information to create disorder, or entropy, in markets.

MIPS   Millions of Instructions per Second: a measure of computing power. One MIPS used to cost millions of dollars. Today it costs a few cents.

Monopoly Rent   The extra profit a company makes because it has a monopoly.

Moore's Law   Dr. Gordon Moore's prediction that microchip price-performance will double every 18 months.

Moore Time   This is time on the Moore Curve where microchip price-performance doubles every eighteen months, cutting the time you get to make decisions to fractions of what it was.

Near-Debt Instrument   This is an equity that acts like a bond.

OEM   This stands for Original Equipment Manufacturer. This is not what the item means, however. In a confusing twist, it means a company that buys the original equipment and resells it.

Order of Magnitude   When something increases by a power, it is said to grow by an order of magnitude. Thus 10^3 is an order of magnitude larger than 10^2.

Orphans and Widows   This usually refers to a class of investor requiring steady dividend and interest income and less interested in more risky capital appreciation.

PCS   Personal Communications System, another term for digital cellular service.

Plays   A company may be said to be a "layoff play," for example, when it makes its earnings numbers by laying people off rather than by growing the business.

Points of Presence   Companies that carry communications services have facilities from which they manage the network. These are their "points of presence." A PoP may be as small as a small underground vault located on a suburban street.

Portal   These are the "doors" to the Internet, as it were; the place that allows you to select where you want to go on the Internet. Yahoo! is an example.

post-PC   This is a device with as much processing power as a PC, such as a video-game console or a cell phone.

Price-Performance   The bang you get for your buck when you buy something. Twenty years ago you got very little computer bang for the buck, for example, while today you get lots more. Typically, computer price-performance doubles every 18 months whereas automobile price-performance can actually get worse.

Product Cycle   This is the time period between product introductions. A manufacturer may replace a product after a year, making the product cycle one year.

R&D   Research and development.

Securitize   To securitize is to turn an asset, like a factory, into cash by hiving it off into a security and selling that security. Whoever owns the security owns the factory.

S&P   Standard and Poors.

Shokku   Japanese for "shock."

Structural Impediment Initiatives   An initiative by the U.S. government to overcome barriers to free trade built into a trading partner's way of doing business. For example, a country may allow in goods free of duties, but industry in that country may allow only local companies to bid, creating a structural impediment to trade.

Supply-Chain Management   Companies have realized that with the Internet they can become much more efficient than before by subcontracting large parts of their operations and then using the Internet to manage the flow of goods and services from the subcontractors to the company's customers, thus managing the chain of supplies.

Upsells   This refers to when a customer is persuaded to buy a better version of the same product and/or to buy lots of additional things with the product. Buying a fully loaded car gives your dealer a profitable "upsell" of the basic model.

Velocity of Capital   Operating income over total capital.

Vertical Integration   A form of corporate organization in which many of the activities required for a business are undertaken internally. Henry Ford built Ford Motor around company control of everything that went into its cars, integrating "vertically" from sheep to wool to fabrics to car seats to cars.

The virtual economy   An economy that exists in cyberspace rather than in factories or stories it said to be "virtual" rather than real.

Write-down   When assets, for example, are no longer worth what they should be given what you paid for them and how much they have depriciated, they are posted to the books as a lost and "written-down" on the balance sheet.

Index

Index

Index

Index

Index

Index

Index

Acknowledgment

We would like to acknowledge the support of the two people without whom this book would never have been possible. Our publisher, Truman "Mac" Talley, has edited all our books and saw the potential for this one long before we did. He doggedly pushed us for three years to get down to the job of putting it all together and guided us every step of the way. Unlike our previous books, which had much narrower focuses, this one covers a lot of ground. He showed us right from the beginning the shape it must take to succeed. Equally, we would be nowhere without our agent Kathi Paton. Kathi, too, saw value in our ideas and has steadfastly supported us through three books, offering the kind of constant support no author can be without.